The
Conscious
Body

The Conscious Body

A Psychoanalytic Exploration of the Body in Therapy

PERRIN ELISHA

American Psychological Association • Washington, DC

Published by
American Psychological Association
750 First Street, NE
Washington, DC 20002
www.apa.org

To order
APA Order Department
P.O. Box 92984
Washington, DC 20090-2984
Tel: (800) 374-2721; Direct: (202) 336-5510
Fax: (202) 336-5502; TDD/TTY: (202) 336-6123
Online: www.apa.org/books/
E-mail: order@apa.org

In the U.K., Europe, Africa, and the Middle East, copies may be ordered from
American Psychological Association
3 Henrietta Street
Covent Garden, London
WC2E 8LU England

Typeset in Goudy by Circle Graphics, Inc., Columbia, MD

Printer: The Maple-Vail Book Manufacturing Group, York, PA
Cover Designer: Mercury Publishing Services, Rockville, MD

The opinions and statements published are the responsibility of the authors, and such opinions and statements do not necessarily represent the policies of the American Psychological Association.

Library of Congress Cataloging-in-Publication Data

Elisha, Perrin.
The conscious body : a psychoanalytic exploration of the body in therapy / Perrin Elisha. — 1st ed.
    p. cm.
 Includes bibliographical references and index.
 ISBN-13: 978-1-4338-0909-5
 ISBN-10: 1-4338-0909-5
1. Consciousness. 2. Mind and body. I. Title.

 BF311.E4825 2011
 150—dc22
                                    2010020484

British Library Cataloguing-in-Publication Data

A CIP record is available from the British Library.

Printed in the United States of America
First Edition

doi: 10.1037/12306-00

CONTENTS

Acknowledgments .... *vii*

Chapter 1. Introduction: The Mind–Body Problem
            in Psychoanalytic Theory and Practice 3

Chapter 2. Philosophy and the Mind–Body Problem:
            Influences on Psychoanalysis 29

Chapter 3. Psyche and Soma in the Work of Sigmund Freud:
            Theoretical Foundations 65

Chapter 4. Klein and Object Relations:
            Contemporary Developments 99

Chapter 5. Kohutian, Intersubjective,
            and Relational Theories 129

Chapter 6.   Attachment Theory and Neuropsychoanalysis............ 155

Chapter 7.   Conclusions 177

References 195

Index 207

About the Author 219

ACKNOWLEDGMENTS

I would like to thank Dr. Lionel Corbett, Dr. Margaret Sperry, Dr. Christine Lewis, and Dr. Josh Hoffs for their commentary and guidance in this endeavor. Each provided encouragement and refinement that kept the process going. Dr. Erik Craig also provided invaluable attention to detail in the early stages of this work. It's not often that one receives this kind of attentiveness, and it is appreciated. Pacifica Graduate Institute provided the education necessary to undertake such an endeavor and to formulate the questions I most wanted to ask. Thank you to those with the proposal committee of Division 39 of the American Psychological Association, who had faith in this work—including Dr. Johanna Tabin, Dr. Nancy McWilliams, and Dr. Frank Summers. Thanks also to Ed Meidenbauer, who helped enormously in the important final evolutions.

I would also like to express my deepest gratitude to Dr. Anna Lisa Cohen and Dr. James Gooch for the space to explore the embodied dimensions of these ideas in the form of actual experience. I am deeply indebted to my Iyengar yoga teachers: Kofi, Stephen, and Paul—your knowledge is everywhere in these pages, although words have not done it justice. Your dedication helped grow my body and mind strong enough and flexible enough to sustain and enjoy this endeavor. Most important, thank you, Rich Ryan, for containing and supporting the minutia of the daily work and for challenging and stimulating my mind with patient, thoughtful conversation every step of this long journey. The breadth, depth, and sensitivity of your mind made for a fertile pot in which my ideas could grow.

The Conscious Body

1

INTRODUCTION: THE MIND–BODY PROBLEM IN PSYCHOANALYTIC THEORY AND PRACTICE

The shadow of the *mind–body problem* has compromised the integrity of Western thought since at least the time of Plato. The lack of a consistent model of the relationship between qualities of mind and qualities of body has resulted in ever-evolving theories of philosophy, medicine, religion, and psychology. How is consciousness or thought related to sense data that humans perceive and to the physical world of matter? Does one create or control the other, or are they coordinated—and if so, how? Or, as more recent theories suggest, are these two dimensions more adequately described as manifestations of an underlying, unifying field? If so, what exactly is this underlying field, and what can one know about it? And how do humans know about it? Given that consciousness is either a manifestation of mind or part and parcel of the underlying field, how accurately can human consciousness ever reflect on itself? These questions and their answers also imply beliefs as to a relationship between spirit and matter, aiding in the complications and historical convolutions.

As psychologists, we are primarily interested in the practical application of these questions. When you have a stomachache, is it primarily a quality of mind, brain, body, or a complicated mixture of each? The answer to this question interests medical professionals chiefly as it guides treatment intervention methods. Consider a psychotherapy patient seeking help with chronic headaches, or chronic hunger (the compulsive overeater). The patient has had a complete medical workup and there is no known physical cause for the symptom; the symptoms have been labeled *psychosomatic*. How, then, do psychotherapists go about understanding the phenomenon, the meaning, and the method of treatment? What are the goals of successful treatment? Do we simply negate the symptom, or is there something else to be gained or learned in the treatment? If there is something "else" to be gained in the treatment, as experience shows me there is, then we are supposing an intricate and meaningful link between the world of psychological experience and the world of physical bodies. Phenomenologically, this may seem obvious and simplistic. People experience the meaningful matrix of body–mind–brain every day. Surprisingly, psychoanalytic metapsychology has struggled to articulate a model of the mind that adequately accounts for this phenomenological reality in a manner that aids treating symptoms on that frontier, engaging both somatic and psychic experience.

In fact, Freud's initial encounter with the hysteric in Charcot's laboratory—which marked the shift in his studies from anatomy to psychology and the dawn of depth psychology—brought him face to face with the mind–body problem. A decade later, it was Freud's inability to satisfactorily explain the transformation of somatic energy into psychic libido that led to his abandonment of the *Project for a Scientific Psychology* (S. Freud, 1895/1966d). Psychoanalytic metapsychology was designed at first as an attempt to navigate the mystery of the mind–body frontier in the service of both science and clinical work with patients suffering in body and mind.

In the following pages, I investigate the theoretical framework of psychoanalysis in an effort to elucidate the unconscious assumptions about the body, which are largely drawn from historical contexts in which theory was developed or altered. The primary aim of this work is not for the sake of theory but to answer the practical question of whether or how psychoanalysis can engage a *somatically linked consciousness*. This is a term borrowed from the disciplines of somatic psychology and ecopsychology and is elaborated on below. The term captures a sensibility which I argue has been split off from the psychoanalytic endeavor, risking a psychoanalytic collusion with states of disembodiment, meaninglessness, alexethymia, and isolation. I present here an argument for a model of development of the mind, which is less linear and more circular, and for developing a theoretical language that can speak to the experience that the mind is properly rooted in the body, never fully abstracted or differentiated.

The more I have read the works of Freud and of those who interpret Freud, the more convinced I am that researchers' interpretations of theory and of history are hermeneutic by nature: That which we observe is primarily and irrevocably influenced by the observer. In the literature, one can find reference not to one Sigmund Freud but to many; likewise with each major contributor to metapsychology. In that light, and in light of the fact that this work is hermeneutic both in method and organization, it is worth noting the perspective from which I come to this topic.

I find truth in Ian Grand's statement that

> it is the body itself that is often reviled, and along with it, life and its vicissitudes. To be in this body is to be in life, to be with the immediacy of the possibilities of ecstasy and suffering and meaning that we make in our human living. It is to deal with pain and suffering from disease, from war, from natural disaster, from work, from the vicissitudes of daily social living. It is also to live with the praises and hallelujahs of the religious ecstatic, the feelings of wonder and curiosity and awe and love, the immediate sense of connection with the surround, our fear, our pride, our hate. (Johnson & Grand, 1998, p. 181)

Likewise, the vision of myself as clinician that I bring to the therapy room includes an intimate embodiment of the flesh.

Theoretically, I align myself with the more tightly held circle of psychoanalytic psychology and dynamic talk therapy that reaches toward the depths and wonders of the human psyche with the vehicle of the mind and the verbal articulation of emotional and somatic realities. I find these models of psychic structure and therapeutic interaction to be indispensable. At the same time, I am cognizant of the potential relative absence of a deep connection to and embodiment of somatic reality in the analytic therapy room. I find the psyche's experience and expression through the body to be underutilized and ambiguously referred to in academic and clinical settings. The intent of this book is to examine the historical context out of which the profession emerges in order to better view the context in which psychologists practice and the unconscious references that are present in the therapy room.

The most useful framework I have found for making sense of the physical body in relation to psychological well-being can be stated in two parts. Although the first is well represented in the literature of psychoanalysis, I have not found the second to have a voice within psychoanalytic theory. The first includes the general notion that psychological content can be expressed via the body when it is repressed from conscious awareness, processing, or expression. This is the concept of somatization as a defense mechanism in which "emotions are communicated only through physical complaints . . . . This defense, typical of hypochondriacal patients, involves the transfer of painful feelings to body parts" (Gabbard, 2000, p. 31) and occurs when feelings are intolerable or unacceptable relative to an individual's overall affective capacity. This concept is a notion of pathology and is fundamental to the definition of *somatoform disorders*. The presence of somatization as a defense mechanism is a generally accepted tenet in the field of clinical psychology as a whole.

The second piece of my personal framework, as opposed to the pathology-based notion of somatization explained earlier, includes the ways in which somatic experience is not only a component of healthy psychological functioning but one that I find essential in my own integration. I find echoes of this experience in the writings of somatic psychologists, poets, ecopsychologists, and colleagues whose analytic journey is paralleled by explorations in body work, yoga, or close involvement with the natural world. For example, a colleague wrote to me about her experience in body work concurrent with psychoanalysis:

> I was unconsciously being systematically taught to override, to deny this bodily realm of existence. This was the "mortal" realm, inherently inferior, and also suspect, "the Way of all Flesh" that the Bible eschewed as corrupting. Of course I also grew up in an environment where emotional life was disavowed. Ten years ago I began to wake up to emotional life, which proved so shocking as to end up reconfiguring my entire sense of myself as a person. This decade, I am beginning to have faith, I will add in the miracle of my own physicality. . . . The alive/sensate feelings continue to expand in me . . . . The alive, energetic feelings have been expanding regularly over the past weeks. . . . This is all quite shocking new territory for me, all the more awesome for its being a previously unimagined world. (Anonymous, personal communication, July 22, 2003)

My personal journey has involved learning to discriminate between the ways in which psychological meanings become expressed defensively through the body when they are psychologically disavowed from the ways in which body states, sense perceptions, and an authentic, dynamic state of embodied awareness can become integrated as an expressive and psychologically deepening dimension of experience. These personal experiences have shaped my life direction and interests.

My own model of mental health has incorporated a sense of physical aliveness in which I feel most human. This sense of being enlivened in the psychic *and* somatic realm is central to my own well-being and has come to include what has been called a *somatically linked consciousness*. In other words, it is through the acuity of my physical senses in relationship to the capacity of my psychological mind that I feel most connected to a sense of the world's aliveness, my own feeling states, my own creative process and productivity, and the ability to be meaningfully interpersonally related. My professional work has impressed upon me the absence of this capacity in depressed, substance-dependent, and eating-disordered patients in particular and impressed upon me the great need to not only interpret psychosomatic meanings but also model an attitude and capacity for embodied being in relationship. I have also found that a somatically linked consciousness is an invaluable vehicle for listening to the transference–countertransference field and for "tuning in" to the subtleties of the psychotherapeutic attunement process. It appears to me that I must listen with my somatic as well as my psychic consciousness to work most effectively.

The format of this study has grown out of my continual efforts to reconcile this personal sense of well-being and therapeutic intervention with psychoanalytic theories. Extensive thought and exploration into the history, theories, and practice of depth psychology has left me with the distinct impression that psychologists as a profession are still working to distinguish and integrate the realms of psychic and somatic experience and their prospective meanings. The repeated assumption that the somatic dimension of experience is somehow equated with what is unconscious or prepsychological (e.g., Freud, 1915/1961b, 1923/1961d; McDougall, 1989; Ogden, 1989) simply does not reconcile with my own experiences. I also propose that the influence of attachment theory and neuropsychology has ushered in a new way of thinking about and approaching the physical body but that this new paradigm must reckon with historical precursors that limit its integration into psychoanalytic metapsychology.

Research into the history of analytic thought reveals inconsistencies, unreconciled differences, and chasms between the founding belief systems of the field (Ellenberger, 1970). It is my experience that such theoretical conflicts bear direct influence on our work as clinicians; theoretical conflicts potentially manifest as a discontinuity between analytic theory and lived experience of human beings, including those who enter psychotherapy as patients. This hermeneutic exploration of psychoanalytic text attempts to discover if or how the experiential meaning of the body has been or might be integrated within the theoretical framework of psychoanalytically oriented psychotherapists.

It is recognized that the impetus for this writing grows out of personal experience and out of my own impression that psychoanalytic theories tend to make assumptions regarding the nature of somatic experience. On the one hand, this perspective might offer a fresh look at psychoanalytic theories and assist in elucidating new possibilities of organizing conceptualizations as to the meaning of the somatic pole of experience. On the other hand, the author recognizes the necessity to bracket one's own experience in order to maintain intellectual flexibility.

HISTORY OF THE MIND–BODY PROBLEM

The difficulty within psychoanalytic metapsychology to articulate a model of the mind–body relationship is related to the history of the philosophical mind–body problem and its many twists and turns through history. Chapter 2 of this book begins to explore the historical variations of the mind–body questions and proposed solutions in depth, especially as they impact psychological theorizing in modern history.

A brief look at the history of this dilemma introduces the reader to the nature of the questions explored in these pages. In pre-Socratic times, spirit and matter (gods and earth) were assumed and experienced to be one and the same. The gods spoke and "emoted" through thunderstorms and floods; spiritual malaise manifested itself in maladies of the body and was treated as such. With the dawn of Western civilization the properties of mind and matter began to be considered as separable. Empiricism, fully alive by the 17th century, is the ultimate manifestation of the separate study of the material world. Romanticism represents an opposing sensibility: That human life and the physical world are not reducible to observable facts but, rather, influenced by the abstract and unknowable. We know the evolving tension between matter and mind as *dualism*. We know the ongoing realization that these two qualities can never be entirely separated or one explained without the other as the mind–body problem, which is composed of many questions: What is mind, where is it, what laws does it follow, does it depend on or evolve from matter or does matter evolve from it? And what is "it," exactly—namely, is mind the property of conscious thought and reflection, or do humans consider mind to be inextricably bound up with spirit in the religious sense?

The mind–body problem contains within itself the separate problem of "mind" and "spirit," or the "spirit–matter split." The political, philosophical, and religious history of the mind–body problem is so interwoven with the "spirit–matter problem" that it deserves brief acknowledgement here, to be explored in depth in Chapter 2. Wolfgang Geigerich (1985), in his lecture "The Nuclear Bomb and the Fate of God," traced the dissociation of that which humans hold sacred from the material and natural world to the birth of the concept of "nuclear ash," the despiritualized matter of the modern world that has no intrinsic value in and of itself. He called this act the culmination of "God's exodus from sensuous reality into absolute spiritualization . . . [this is] the first nuclear fission and made possible the nuclear explosion of physics." It was this shift in consciousness, which Geigerich called the "dissociation of being," which made the natural world accessible to modern empiricism and scientific research. Thus, the material aspects of the world were isolated from consciousness in order to facilitate their being known; consciousness gained enough distance from the physical world to view it objectively. In doing so, however, the matter of the physical world, now separate from consciousness, became devalued in a spiritual sense—that sense that tells us what is sacred to life.

Along a similar line, authors such as Robert Romanyshyn (1989) have illustrated how the historical development of linear perspective corresponds to the isolation of consciousness from the physical and interpersonal world. Linear perspective vision establishes the conditions for transforming one's experience of the world which would "objectify, dominate, purify, and ultimately deaden matter. Linear perspective space nourishes a scientific vision of the world, but also allows a pornographic vision of it" (Romanyshyn, 1989,

p. 210). The evolution of linear perspective is another way to illustrate the historical separation of spirit and psyche from matter.

The historical theme is that knowledge, reflective capacities, and technical advances are gained over the course of Western civilization as mind and body, spirit and matter, are differentiated. However, their absolute differentiation is impossible and dangerous. The quest to understand how these dimensions are related or unified is broadly referred to as the mind–body problem, and the proposed solutions can be broadly categorized by philosophical movements such as empiricism, romanticism, materialism, dualism, idealism, and their variations explored in Chapter 2. Freud began his studies as the tides of romanticism and empiricism were colliding. Modernism and postmodernism would soon collide. As the paradigms of the "modern" and "postmodern" worlds were meeting, the 20th century ushered in a new paradigm of quantum physics, which both portends and gives face to a rising tide in the Western sensibility that the mind–body division is—like the division between observer and observed—not an absolute one. It was within this shifting cultural context that Freud and his followers modified their thinking and theories in an attempt to find a satisfactory model for the psyche/soma relationship in health and pathology. Throughout this course of history, if one moves away from a monistic biological reductionist stance, the mind–body problem invariably confronts theorists with the spirit–matter question: How to explain the orchestration of the mind–body correlation or relationship, and how to describe the motivating force of humanity within any system? This book investigates unconscious biases and limitations built into psychoanalytic metapsychology via the nature of the mind–body problem and efforts to find a language suitable to the lived phenomenon of the mind–body matrix.

WHY THIS BOOK? THE GUIDING QUESTION

The primary question guiding this work is: What is unconscious within the text of psychoanalytic metapsychological organizing principles in regard to the relationship between mind and matter or psyche and soma? Or, how has the mind–body split unconsciously informed psychoanalysis? Again, the goal of answering this question is to speak to the ability of psychoanalysis to engage a somatically linked consciousness. Put another way, I explore how psychoanalysis has colluded with unconscious, dualistic notions about the relationship between psyche and soma, and how this collusion may manifest as treatment attitudes that collude with dissociation, alexethymia, and isolation. Such a collusion is particularly dangerous in the treatment of pathologies that themselves include dissociation, such as depressions, eating disorders, and schizoid disorders.

I believe it is imperative that depth psychology begin to address what is unconscious within its own theories regarding this fundamental duality of mind or spirit and matter. This work seeks to illuminate, in clinically relevant ways, the portrayal of the relationship between psyche and soma in psychoanalytic thought. It is recognized that a host of mind–body therapies have arisen in recent years; however, I am interested in the tradition of psychoanalysis itself and how psychoanalysis itself can address the nature of the mind–body relationship.

At this point in my argument for a study of the psyche/soma relationship in psychoanalytic theory, many readers may assume that contemporary theories have moved beyond the dualisms and limitations that may have restricted Freud and his early followers. In fact, psychoanalytic theory itself has evolved within these shifting metaphysical grounds over the past century; certainly the subject of the mind–body relationship has been addressed and debated by psychoanalytic writers.

I believe there are several unexplored and relevant questions in the psychoanalytic literature. Despite new evolutions of theory, new visions themselves "often incorporate many of the features of existing ideology, and so are bound within the same epistemological, moral, and experiential universe as the structures they attempt to challenge" (Kidner, 2001, p. 2). It is my assertion that while contemporary thinkers, particularly in the interpersonal and intersubjective schools, have taken up the ramifications of postmodern views of self and other, observer and observed, a reconciliation of early views of the mind–body problem in psychoanalysis has not been adequately undertaken. New theories always evolve from and draw on previous ones; often these evolutions have not examined whether previous implicit assumptions have been carried forward.

This investigation is, then, an attempt to make conscious the embedded assumptions that restrict contemporary psychoanalytic thinking about the body. No such study has been done that explores the implicit philosophical or epistemological assumptions that informed Freud's metatheoretical propositions and then systematically examines the evolution of metatheory in light of whether or to what extent these assumptions have been either retained or replaced.

Some readers may begin to wonder as to the clinical necessity of such an abstract endeavor into the philosophical and metapsychological principles of our intellectual history. Modern schools of psychoanalytic thought tend away from the abstractions of metapsychology and toward a clinical theory of process and technique. I argue that as therapists our collective theories do deeply inform our thinking and implicitly direct our clinical interventions. Our attitudes, values, and unconscious biases are embedded in theory and conversely implied in our therapeutic interactions.

The impetus for this research was born out of my own trouble reconciling my love of psychoanalysis with hesitancy about the potentiality of disembodiment that may be subtly valued by psychologists' theoretical reference points. I sought to understand: What did Freud do with the contradictions and mysteries he discovered in the psyche/soma relationship, and how did his thinking evolve over his lifetime; what are the unconscious assumptions built into his theoretical framework that he drew from his own history and from the philosophical and scientific biases of his time; and how have subsequent theorists either altered, done away with, or carried forth these implicit assumptions? What do humans really believe about the physical body and its place in psychological well-being and, consequently, how do humans understand and respond to symptamotology that involves the body?

To perpetuate the illusion that body and mind or observer and observed are actually separable invites particular dangers. Namely, states of intellectualized dissociation that I see in my consulting room underlying symptoms of eating disorders, extreme depressions, and relational difficulties. To take a differentiation of the mental from the physical to a static extreme rather than a fluid, dynamic matrix invites psychological maladies underlying many common disorders. I call on the reflections of nonanalytic authors to illustrate my point. David Kidner (2001), in his book *Nature and Psyche: Radical Environmentalism and the Politics of Subjectivity*, articulated the connections among objectivism, reductive positivism, the separation of mind and body, industrialism, and the alienation, depression, and anxiety afflicting the modern personality. Kidner's argument is that although these problems are generally seen as unconnected, it is in fact unconscious assumptions that obscure their interconnectedness. Numerous ecopsychologists and depth psychologists have articulated these connections from differing theoretical vantage points.

In Freud's day, the face of individual suffering was characterized largely by hysteria. "Hysterical" symptoms included a broad range of what one might now call psychosomatic symptoms, affective disorders, and dissociative states. In his early days, Freud sought to clearly distinguish organic disease from psychic disturbances and to develop a psychological theory that was based in the neurological sciences; *The Project for a Scientific Psychology* (S. Freud, 1895/1966d) is a work with which Freud struggled immensely and ultimately abandoned.

A century later, phenomena such as eating disorders, depression, and schizoid personality tend to dominate the psychological scene. Elizabeth Wurtzel's *Prozac Nation: Young and Depressed in America* (1995) is a modern-day fable capturing the mind–body dilemma of psychological suffering. Her personal description of depression speaks to the way that depression lives in and reveals its nature through the body:

> My dreams are polluted with paralysis. I regularly have night visions where my legs, though attached to my body, don't move much. I try to walk somewhere—to the grocery store or the pharmacy . . . and I just can't do it. Can't climb stairs, can't walk on level ground. I am exhausted

in the dream and I become more exhausted in my sleep, if that's possible. I wake up tired, amazed that I can even get out of bed. And often I can't . . . I am trapped in my body . . . I am perpetually zonked. (Wurtzel, 1995, p. 2)

This is an apt description of the *unenlivened body*. It is a physical appendage that has ceased to be filled with the breath of feeling. This and other passages speak to a situation in which there is a deep experiential rift between the "material" and "immaterial" aspects of the person. Wurtzel experiences her mind or spirit as "dead" and her body inflicted with a disease but still living.

Eating disorders, like depressions, are another current psychological, cultural epidemic that, like hysteria, defies an immediate understanding in terms of either a physical or psychological problem. Likewise, their cure defies attempts at categorization and bends the mind of the treatment provider to explore the mind–body, psychosexual matrix of meaning and experience.

A host of extraanalytic authors explicitly link common modern maladies including qualities of depersonalization, identity disturbances, and unenlivened depression to a loss of a somatically linked consciousness and the corresponding compensation by means of intellectualization and dissociation (Berman, 1998; Goldenberg, 1990, 1993; Lowen, 1967, 1990). Later I outline some of these contributions to illustrate both the texture and usefulness of this body of work.

I have wondered why and explored how this sensibility exists in tension to the psychoanalytic appreciation for words. The "talking cure" rests on the essential idea that expression of affect and meaning via words is "healthier" than anything more concrete. "Anything more concrete" may include acting out and somatization; it may also include bodily experience, bodily expression, and embodiment. Stromsted (2005) relayed how this tension was experienced by Marion Woodman in her own training analysis:

> My dream told me to take the images from my dreams and put them in my body . . . Yes, I was in analysis, but my analyst was outraged at the thought of body movement. So he didn't want to know anything about what was going on. His attitude was, "If you can't transform through your dreams there's something wrong with the way you're handling your dreams." I knew that I could have a wonderful time with my dreams because I had been through two years of that, but it didn't change my body. In fact, I got higher and higher into spirit, so my body became more and more exhausted. (p. 13)

Marion Woodman is a Jungian analyst whose life has largely been devoted to the body and body issues. Woodman's life work is born out of her personal experience, retold in a special volume of *Spring* titled "Body and Soul: Honoring Marion Woodman" (Stromsted, 2005). During a severe bout with dysentery in India, Woodman had fallen to the floor and described the following out-of-body experience:

> She wondered why her body wouldn't stop breathing, why her spirit was not taking advantage of this opportunity to finally free itself: "I've been wanting to get out all my life. And here I'm out. All I have to do is take off," she thought . . . I saw it take another breath. I was overcome with compassion for this dear creature lying on the floor faithfully waiting for me to return, faithfully taking in one breath after another, confident that I would not forsake it, more faithful to me than I to it. (Stromsted, 2005, p. 9)

This experience speaks to Woodman's dawning awareness of the sacredness of her own somatic being and began her lifelong exploration of the body and bodily matters within the context of depth psychology. The sensibility embodied in Woodman's work informs and mirrors my own vision of the role of the body for clinical and depth psychology. This vision addresses the tension between the "symbolic" world and the "somatic" world and, for myself, answers the apprehension that bodily experience is a concretization and therefore somehow out of place in an analytic framework.

This work is then a dialogue between my awareness of a somatically linked consciousness and psychoanalytic metapsychology. I have structured the dialogue to represent the issue at hand and the inheritance of its historical complexity. I am primarily concerned with the unconscious organizing principles within psychoanalytic metapsychology, which may exclude such a sensibility from informing psychoanalytic practice. Given the earlier-mentioned orienting principles regarding the psyche/soma dilemma, duality, splitting, consciousness, and the unconscious, I investigate the role of the body in metatheory and its implications for clinical practice. The major metatheoretical developments of the previous century are explored in light of several core concepts in psychoanalytic theory, including the role of words and verbalization, developmental theories, the nature of the unconscious, and the symbolic function.

My main point is not to propose or endorse a particular metapsychology but to elucidate unconscious assumptions about the body over the history of psychoanalysis. In a sense it is placing the body of psychoanalysis "on the couch" and exploring its history and development within psychoanalysis. The value of this, in my mind, is likened to the value of psychoanalytic inquiry into the development of an individual. By making unconscious elements conscious, questioning assumptions, and comparing assumptions with experience, therapists evolve more creative approaches to the world—in this case, the world of treating patients.

It is my hope that these investigations lead to further attention to the language of evolving theories. I believe that making unconscious assumptions conscious may be useful in the development of emerging theories that support the development of embodied, reflective minds in clinical practice.

SOMATIC PSYCHOLOGY AND BODY-ORIENTED
PSYCHOTHERAPIES

An undertaking related to the place of the somatic in psychoanalysis deserves some reflection on the role of so-called somatic psychology. Somatic psychology was born out of the work of Wilhelm Reich (1972, 1973a, 1973b), who was an analyst close to Freud but who split from Freud in the 1930s. Reichian therapists work to dissolve "body armor" by working with tension and energy in the body through directive breathing techniques and muscle manipulation. Reich's work directly opposed notions of duality between bodily life and emotional or mental life, and in fact he saw a primary connection between human bodies and the natural world in his postulation that "orgone energy" was fundamental to all living things. Orgone energy is a term Reich used to describe his concept of biological energy, something roughly analogous to Freud's concept of libido as a motivating or animating force in living beings.

The groups of somatic psychology that have developed from Reich's original ideas include bioenergetics, the Alexander technique, the Feldenkrais method, and structural integration, also called rolfing. Additionally, a variety of sensory awareness exercises that draw on the principles of somatic psychology have been incorporated into other practices to varying degrees (Fadiman & Frager, 2002). In the previous century, it has been the field of somatic psychology that has struggled and experimented with the relationship between the body and mental health, practical methods for achieving mental health via bodily awareness and manipulation, and the sense of spiritual meaning and fulfillment that might become available as consciousness becomes grounded and integrated within the physical self and the natural world (Alexander & Maisel, 1986; Boadella, 1973; Brooks, 1974; Feldenkrais, 1977, 1990; Keleman, 1975, 1979; Lowen, 1967, 1990, 1994, 2003; Reich, 1960, 1972, 1973a, 1973b; Rolf, 1977; Schutz & Turner, 1976).

Works such as Stanley Keleman's *Somatic Reality* (1979) and other works on so-called body-centered therapies include rich descriptions of the value of somatic reality. Keleman (1979) described his personal pursuit of

> the experience that could help me know myself, my world, the nature of living, and to arrive at a path that was satisfying and purposeful. . . . I was led to a deeper and surprising knowledge of my body . . . I began to have a whole range of experiences, which encompassed past and present, ideas and needs, thinking and feeling, urges to act and urges to wait, archetypal pictures and emotions, inner and outer space and time . . . I thought at the time that the strangeness I experienced was due to the releasing of old conflicts and energies that I had to resolve. This was in line with then contemporary psychological thought. It was not until much later that I knew that I had stepped outside the realm of our society's knowledge. We had no tradition of living a bodily life. (p. 11)

Keleman's work suggests that the gap between this kind of somatically linked consciousness in self-experience and models of the self in psychoanalytic discourse needs to be examined to further clarify the need for integration of body-based experiences within analytic theories. Likewise, the very fact that this kind of thinking displaced Keleman from the field of psychoanalysis raises the question of if and how psychoanalysis itself might engage a somatically linked consciousness.

Works such as *The Body in Psychotherapy* (Johnson & Grand, 1998) include the contributions of body-based psychotherapists, some of whom have an analytic background, who perceive a need to both integrate the meaning of and a consciousness about somatic reality into the field of psychotherapy and to envision ways in which this might occur. These writers address the fundamental question of how people actually change in psychotherapy and acknowledge the importance of *felt experience* (i.e., a sensory awareness located in the physical body that corresponds to insight or the capacity for affective experience) in psychotherapeutic growth. Interestingly, this sensibility may be most echoed within psychoanalytic literature by the increasing emphasis on empathy, attunement, and attachment emerging from a neuropsychosocial model. The neuropsychosocial influence may be an opportunity for a reconvergence of the sensibility that split off from Freud with Reich and now exists within the ensuing body-centered therapies.

Barbara Holifield (in Johnson & Grand, 1998), for example, spoke to a sensibility split off from psychoanalysis when she wrote about her personal journey through psychotherapy and explained the shift that occurred when integrating body awareness practices into psychotherapy:

> Now something was different. The body awareness practices had simultaneously facilitated a heightened sensory perception of the outer living world and helped open a gate to my inner landscape: my rivers of grief, angry storms, recognition of interdependency, and a sense of my own strength and delicateness. (p. 60)

Richard Grossinger (in Johnson & Grand, 1998) described his work with body-based psychotherapies as one in which he "learned to inhabit and contain emotions . . . During times of panic I could feel more texture" (p. 88). These contributors each seem to speak toward an actual value or meaning to the world of sensation that was discovered and which led to a sense of embodiment in their own physical selves. This embodiment is consistently described as a feeling of increased awareness, meaningfulness, effectiveness, relatedness, capacity to feel, and a sense of connectedness to both the social and natural world.

Likewise, Maxine Sheets-Johnstone (1992) edited a collection of essays, *Giving the Body Its Due,* that speak to the sensibility of the living body and its meaning-making function in learning, the creative arts, and interpersonal relationships. This work approaches the subject from an interdisciplinary point of view but includes authors such as Eugene Gendlin, who is a phenomenological philosopher and experiential psychologist. Gendlin's work, which includes *focusing*—a method for developing and utilizing bodily awareness for psychological change (Gendlin, 1978), approaches the relatedness of bodily awareness, logic, language, and dreams. This orientation produces a clinical approach which says that

> we need to pay attention *through* the body . . . your own inner phenomenological sense of your own body is not only your sense of your muscles, your legs, the back of your head . . . The bodily sense is also your sense of your situations, your life. (Sheets-Johnstone, 1992, p. 206)

I acknowledge the contributions of these thinkers and the field of somatic psychology as an important field in its own right. I also draw on these writers' explication of why and how the body is important to clinical psychology and psychoanalysis. What has been done in the literature is the above exploration of the practical and technical divide between somatic psychology and psychoanalysis. What has not been done is to investigate the development of psychoanalytic theory to discover how psychoanalytic theory *itself* might collude with unconscious, dualistic notions about the relationship between psyche and soma in ways that predispose analytic thinkers and practitioners to marginalizing or excluding a consciousness of somatic experience. Ian Grand (in Johnson & Grand, 1998) spoke directly to this problem:

> Unfortunately, there has been little dialogue . . . between analysts and somatic theorists who are each advancing theories about the psyche and how it is organized . . . . It seems to me that we need to rethink the whole of psychodynamics from a somatic point of view. (p. 191)

This book speaks directly to that need. It is an attempt to rethink psychodynamics, especially the founding *drive theory* and its relationship to the unconscious, with consideration of the somatic point of view that has been articulated by writers in the field of somatic psychology. Drive theory is Freud's initial motivational hypothesis to describe the biophysiological drives that propel action in service of meeting physiological survival needs. The trick seems to be that drive theory is so interwoven with the historical sense of "discovering" the unconscious—and with the beliefs about working with that which is unknown, not yet disclosed—that it is unclear how therapists evolve from it without discarding what they as a profession most value about it. It was via Freud's drive theory that as a profession and culture therapists first glimpsed with awe and wonder the power of that which goes on largely unknown. I believe that therapists can evolve from the implicit assumptions about the nature of the body built into classical theory without losing sight of the quest to glimpse at the hidden motivations, meanings, and organizations of human experience.

PSYCHOANALYTIC METAPSYCHOLOGY

This book is an investigation of what is unconscious within psychoanalytic metapsychology regarding the body or the mind–body relationship. *Metapsychology* is the philosophical theory that underlies psychology. Metapsychology describes aspects of the mind that cannot be evaluated or measured empirically and are therefore described metaphorically. It is a set of laws or principles that describe how the mind operates, much like the laws of physics describe how matter behaves under certain circumstances. The term is believed to have been derived by Freud from the term *metaphysics,* which refers to the laws, hypotheses, and principles of the science of physics. As in metaphysics, metapsychology is adapted and altered in response to new evidence and observations, so that the metapsychology always strives to describe lived phenomenon. Metapsychology also strives to be a coherent and intelligible whole, so that if one principle is altered, it must be questioned whether other principles remain compatible.

Metapsychology is taken to be the reference point that gives this study structure and form. Metapsychology represents the basic principles that therapists assume to govern the understanding of clinical phenomenon and therefore the method of treatment; it is also the psychologist's shared reference point or language system. It therefore is also the closest representation of the shared unconscious biases and an excellent starting point in which to investigate implicit assumptions about the body.

For the purposes of this study, I have delimited psychoanalytic metapsychology to the works of classical psychoanalysts, object relations, self psychology, relational systems theory, intersubjective systems theory, and the emerging body of neuropsychoanalysis informed by attachment theory. Although this list is far from exhaustive, it is taken to be broad enough for the purposes of the study. Further studies may consider Lacanian theory and Jungian theory and look more specifically into ego psychology.

A definition of the choice of works in the body of psychoanalytic texts to be investigated is also relevant. In selecting theorists, I attempted to broadly represent the historical progression from Sigmund Freud's writings to those of contemporary neo-Freudians. It is recognized that the list cannot be exhaustive or complete but is rather an attempted signifier for general trends in the field. *Classical psychoanalysis* is taken to mean the works of Sigmund Freud and his closest adherents. Freud's own writings over the course of his career as well as broadly known interpretations of these texts serve as the basis of the research on classical psychoanalytic theory.

Object relations is understood to be a vast field with no single or generally accepted school or theory, but it is represented in this work primarily by the work of Melanie Klein (1957, 1961; Klein & Mitchell, 1987; Klein & Riviere, 1937), Donald Winnicott (1958b, 1962, 1965, 1971, 1992), Wilfred

Bion (1961, 1963, 1967), and W. R. D. Fairbairn (1952, 1954). I am concerned singularly with the point of how the shift in emphasis from Freud's thought to that of object relations shifted thoughts about drives and the meaning of the physical body in regard to psyche. The works chosen can be used for this purpose. Besides having chosen authors who represent major metatheoretical shifts, I have also included authors who have addressed evolving roles for the soma in metatheory. The work of Marion Milner (1936, 1950, 1987; Milner & Institute of Psycho-analysis, 1969), Thomas Ogden (1982, 1986, 1989, 1994, 2001), and Joyce McDougall (1985, 1989, 1995) falls into this latter category.

Self-psychology refers to the theories based on the work of Heinz Kohut (1959, 1971, 1977, 1979; Kohut & Wolf, 1978). I have included self-psychologists such as David Krueger (1989, 2002) who have addressed the body in regard to the concept of the self in particular.

Intersubjective systems theory is represented by the writings of George Atwood, Robert D. Stolorow, and Donna Orange (Atwood, Orange, & Stolorow, 2002; Stolorow & Atwood, 1992; Stolorow, Atwood, and Orange, 1999; Stolorow, Brandchaft, & Atwood, 1987; Stolorow, Orange, & Atwood, 2001a, 2001b). *Intersubjectivity* is, generally speaking, the sharing of subjective states. Within psychoanalysis, intersubjective systems theory refers to ideas of the mind and psychotherapy, which emphasize intrapsychic and interpersonal experiences from the vantage point of two or more subjectivities. As in each group of theories, writings of other theorists who have reflected on the works of the above authors in ways that are relevant to the study are included.

The preceding is one of many ways that the field of psychoanalytic theory can be divided. This is simply a framework within which conceptualizations regarding somatic aspects of the psyche can be explored over the historical development of psychoanalytic organizing principles.

EXPLORING THE TERMS

Ambiguity in regard to the varying uses of the terms *mind, body, psyche,* and *soma* is inherent to the mind–body problem itself. Wright and Potter (2000), in their introduction to the collection of essays titled *Psyche and Soma: Physicians and Metaphysicians on the Mind–Body Problem From Antiquity to Enlightenment,* noted that the use of the terms *psyche* and *soma* almost "seems so divergent in basic assumptions and goals that the question arises whether any central core of shared meaning is represented by the pair of terms at all" (p. 1). A study of the mind–body problem must begin by noting that the nature of the problem, the proposed solutions, and the meaning of the terms themselves are inseparable. In this vein, a central aim of this work is to investigate how these terms have in fact been used in psychoanalytic literature. We begin this venture with some general statements. John Ayto's (1991) *Dictionary of Word Origins* entry for *body* states:

> For a word so central to people's perception of themselves, *body* is remarkably isolated linguistically. Old High German had *potah* "body," traces of which survived dialectally into modern times, but otherwise it is without known relatives in any other Indo-European language. Attempts have been made, not altogether convincingly, to link it with words for "container" or "barrel," such as medieval Latin *butica*. The use of *body* to mean "person in general," as in *somebody, nobody,* got fully under way in the 14th century. (p. 70)

The New World Dictionary (Guralnik, 1970) contains a variety of thoughts regarding the definition of *body*. The definition implied in this work begins with the following: "The whole physical structure and substance of man . . . the material frame of a human being . . . the flesh or material substance, as opposed to the spirit" (p. 157).

The terms *soma* and *somatic* tend to be used interchangeably with *body* and *bodily* in psychological literature. I use the terms *soma* and *somatic* as implied in the definition given in *The New World Dictionary*: "Of or pertaining to the body" (Guralnik, 1970, p. 1356).

When therapists speak about the body in psychological contexts, it becomes questionable whether we are speaking about the literal body or the *body image*. Meissner (2003b) defined the body image as "a mental construct through and in terms of which the self experiences its own body" (p. 12). This research has taken a firm stand in that "precarious position" that straddles both the "body as such" and the "body in terms of its meanings" (Gill, 1994), out of the Kantian assumption that humans only know any reality through the mind and therefore the mental representation of it. The two cannot be meaningfully delineated, but the research acknowledges that the discussion of the body is always discussing the interplay between the actual body and the psychological experience of it.

The word *mind* belongs to a family of words coming from the Indo-European base *men-* "think," which has English, German, Latin, and Greek descendents pertaining to memory or the mental faculty (Ayto, 1991). *The New World Dictionary* (Guralnik, 1970) references the multiplicity of qualities at times grouped under the term, including memory, spirit, disposition, thinking, feeling, willing, the soul, the intellect, or a "conscious or intelligent agency or being . . . as opposed to matter" (p. 1063). I employ this definition of the nonmaterial faculties of consciousness, including feeling and thinking, but I address the philosophical complications and scientific debate regarding such a definition.

Psyche is generally used to describe aspects of the human experience that bridge mind and body, defying the more dualistic notion of *mind*, as described earlier, as something that can be opposed to body or soma. The terms *body* and *mind* are often defined precisely by their opposition or not pertaining to the other. A benefit of the term *psyche* is that dualism is not embedded in its definition.

> *Psyche*, from the Greek *psukhe*, like Latin animus, started out meaning "breath" and developed semantically to "soul, spirit." English adopted it via Latin psyche in the mid-17th century, but it did not really begin to come into its own until the middle of the 19th century, when the development of the sciences of the mind saw it pressed into service in such compound forms as psychology (first recorded in 1693, but not widely used until the 1830s) and psychiatry (first recorded in 1846), which etymologically means "healing of the mind." (Ayto, 1991, p. 418)

Both terms *psyche* and *mind* have evolved in the historical context of philosophy and the most fundamental beliefs held by a culture in regard to the human condition and the nature of reality. The nature of this evolution is a primary focus of investigation, and the use of the terms must therefore be redefined throughout the work in the context in which they are being discussed.

ON HERMENEUTICS AS A METHOD OF ANALYSIS

Hermeneutics is broadly defined as the art and science of interpretation. This study is in essence an interpretation of the texts that embody the theory through which depth psychologists make meaning of human experience. We may first recognize that the term *hermeneutics* refers both to a historical concept of philosophy and a methodology of the social sciences. The philosophical position defines the methodology used in this study; this philosophical position is intrinsically related to an epistemological turn from objective scientism toward a relativistic mode of intersubjective interpretation.

Hermeneutics as a method was extended in the time of Aristotle to the art of textual interpretation (Lee, 1988; Palmer, 1969). Palmer (1969) articulated the spirit of Ast's work in relationship to the fundamental principles of hermeneutics. Hermeneutics is interested not in the grammatical meaning of the text but rather in the spirit (*geist*) of the author in relationship to the cultural or historical context of his or her time: Hermeneutics is less interested in facts as ends to themselves but more as a part of the whole. This relationship of the parts to the whole makes up the concept of the *hermeneutical circle:* "The circle as a whole defines the individual part, and the parts together form the circle.... By dialectical interaction between the whole and the part, each gives the other meaning; understanding is circular, then" (Palmer, 1969, p. 87).

Psychoanalysis in practice is exactly this—a constant exploration of the relation of the details to the gestalt to disclose multiple meanings. Likewise, this study is then a hermeneutic dialogue that takes place within the parts and the whole of philosophical and psychoanalytic history; it is likewise much like a psychoanalysis of the "body on the couch." I investigate the history of the mind–body problem in philosophy as well as the placement of the body in relationship to psyche in the history of psychoanalytic theory. Each of these elements is a part of the whole. The whole of the psyche/soma relationship in the theory of psychoanalysis is then perhaps understood in new and insightful ways.

Psychoanalysis is in itself a hermeneutic means of understanding human experience; psychologists may say that psychoanalysis is essentially hermeneutic and that hermeneutics is profoundly depth psychological. Both disciplines are concerned with human meanings and with disclosure of the depths.

Eugen Bleuler coined the term *depth psychology* (*Tiefenpsychologie*) to refer to a psychology of the unconscious (Ellenberger, 1970). The term *unconscious* implies that which is hidden or not directly visible; in *Psychoanalytic Terms and Concepts* (Moore & Fine, 1990) the term is defined as

> mental content not available to conscious awareness at a given time, as demonstrated by parapraxes, dreams, and disconnected thoughts and conclusions . . . . What is excluded from awareness . . . belongs to what has been designated the *descriptive unconscious*. (p. 201)

This descriptive unconscious belongs to the shared topography of hermeneutics and depth psychology. Paul Ricoeur's "hermeneutics of suspicion" examines self-knowledge; Ricoeur, like Freud, argued that self-knowledge includes the need to "find what is presumably unexpected, underlying various surface manifestations. . . . The implication . . . is that more is meant than is intended in each expression, and thus a hermeneutic process is needed to explicate the unsaid" (Idhe, 1983, pp. 150–151).

Depth psychology in its broadest definition acts through insight into that which has been out of sight: making unconscious conscious or disclosing that which is hidden. This is the activity of insight and interpretation, making hermeneutics as an interpretive science fundamental to depth psychotherapy. The hermeneutic stance maintains that interpretation is fundamental to being human, in that being itself is essentially an interpretive act.

On the other hand, there are different kinds of hermeneutics, and there remain differing aims within the field of depth psychology in regard to the kind of interpretation or understanding that is sought. Gill (1994) pointed out a long-standing dilemma in the field of psychology and psychoanalysis: Freud's metapsychology is built upon a natural science framework in that it speaks in terms of force, energy, and substance, whereas his clinical theory is a hermeneutic psychology in that it deals with human meanings. Metatheory and clinical theory are confusingly intertwined, especially in Freudian drive theory, which contains both natural-science and hermeneutic-science terms. This paradox highlights what remains hidden within psychoanalytic assumptions regarding the nature of the body and the physical world; this dilemma is embedded in a confusion regarding the kind of understanding the field of psychology is to engage in.

This confusion stems from the competing ideologies and worldviews that influenced Freud at the end of the 19th century and that underlie a depth psychology. Early psychoanalysis was influenced by the need for an objective hermeneutics, which is defined by the belief that the object is autonomous or, corresponding, that there is an absolute truth. Such a belief is encapsulated in notions of "reality" in early psychoanalysis (Moore & Fine, 1990), which tend to be equated with the external world:

> In this context, reality could be considered as the preexisting, natural world of concrete objects functioning in ways that can be objectively verified by scientific observations. From this viewpoint, *external reality* would correspond to the related terms *factual (material) reality* and *objective reality*. (p. 161)

This study, however, takes a firm stand in the particular form of hermeneutic interpretation that seeks to reveal what is not yet disclosed through an investigation of what is meant and implied by the statements made in theoretical text. This type of hermeneutic inquiry is described by Robert Steele, as cited in Packer and Addison (1989), as an exploration of the textual unconscious:

> As one moves from the invisibility of the scientific prose, which always points past itself to an object, to the recognition that the text, itself, is a place where objects are created and shared when words become worthy of the same scrutiny and analysis as another phenomena. The fact that many objects of science are known to us not from observation but from reading about them or seeing them illustrated in a text makes it plain that the "thing itself" for many scientists is actually a textual representative, a signifier . . . our concern here is to make visible what training and custom has rendered invisible. (p. 223)

Robert Steele (Packer & Addison, 1989) spoke to the method by which a textual hermeneutics seeks to disclose the textual unconscious just as the psychoanalytic method aims to disclose the hidden aspects of clinical phenomena.

I seek to disclose what has remained unconscious within the texts of psychoanalytic theory in regard to the relationship between psyche and soma. The goal is to uncover what is not immediately apparent and to disclose meanings that have been rendered invisible in psychoanalytic theoretical assumptions.

I acknowledge the historical divisions regarding the kind of inquiry psychology is presumed to be responsible to and the effects that this division has on the way that text and experience are interpreted and signified within the literature. However, the writing itself is clearly an inquiry grounded in the human sciences—a relative, historical hermeneutics that seeks to understand the way that the lived experience of mind and body has been interpreted within psychoanalytic literature. It is not assumed that there is an absolute truth that can be found; instead, an exploration into the ways that psychology has attempted to make meaning and interpretation of experience through its text is intended to reveal what may be unconscious in the designing of psychoanalytic theory.

This intersubjective nature of hermeneutic textual interpretation speaks directly to the nature of this work, including the nature of the relationship between the author and the study. It is my "being here in the world" that I bring to the writing, which is in part an attempt to reconcile the text of psychoanalytic theorizing with my own experience of being here in the world. As mentioned earlier, my experience of being here, in the world, is highlighted by and inseparable from the reality and subtleties of my physical existence and the somatic manifestation of psyche. In the language of hermeneutics, one can say that my reconstruction of psychoanalytic text is performed in the subjective context of my own experience and the meaning that I have made of this experience. To this end, my personal experience is necessarily inseparable to the inquiry at hand; my experiences and the potential disparities between this experience and my reading of the texts creates a fresh dialogue and reflective space within which to examine the theories.

On the other hand, I am able to bracket the conscious aspects of meaning that I have ascribed to my experience by placing worldviews regarding the nature of the mind–body relationship in a philosophical–historical context. In this way I can contextualize my own subjective context in order to broaden the scope of thought inherent to the research beyond that of my own biases.

The hermeneutic methodology is also relevant and applicable to the subject matter itself. The hermeneutic circle is engaged not only between myself, the author, and the text of psychoanalysis in its respective sociocultural contexts, but also between aspects of the subject itself. I am engaging the mind–body problem itself as subject to hermeneutic inquiry. By this I mean that I seek to explore the ways in which mind and body or psyche and soma may cocreate the experiential basis of lived human meanings. Put another way, I am pursuing the furthering of the examination of the subject–object division to the psychic–somatic matrix. The research asks: How is the meaning that is made of the body structured by the cultural and philosophical context within which humans think and experience? When as humans we dialogue across time and philosophical assumptions about the nature of reality, can we gain some flexibility in our conceptualizations about the body? If so, how might this flexibility inform psychoanalytic thinking?

The modern world is colored by competing sensibilities that are interwoven in potentially perplexing ways: Positivistic science based on the theories of Descartes and Newton underlies empirical science and much of the technological knowledge to which we credit the modern world, yet the 20th century discoveries of Albert Einstein and Werner Heisenberg seem to undermine the separation of subject and object, "I" and world inherent to the Cartesian-Newtonian worldview. Capra (1975) stated that Einstein's theory of relativity redefined matter not as a fixed object that can be definitively located outside of the subject but as energy and activity. Heisenberg's uncertainty principle drew out the nature of the interconnections between observer and observed, subject and object: "The properties of any atomic object can only be understood in terms of the object's interaction with the observer" (Capra, 1975, p. 68). The way in which these paradigm shifts altered the understanding of the nature of reality is relevant both to the subject matter and the methodology of this research.

This philosophical background is particularly relevant to a study of psychoanalytic metapsychology because of the inherent tension between Freudian use of natural science and hermeneutic science (Gill, 1994). This complication was present in Freud's mind and still necessitates an attempted clarification here, at the outset of this endeavor. Because psychoanalysis is primarily a hermeneutic method and science, this study is also presumed to be a hermeneutic one.

Just as Einstein's theory of relativity redefined matter and Heisenberg's uncertainty principle redefined the relationship between subject and object, hermeneutics defines the nature of psychoanalytic inquiry as inherently different from that of the empirical sciences. Psychoanalysis itself exists in a precarious position between both paradigms (Chessick, 1980; Ellenberger, 1970; Gill, 1994; Hughes, 1994; Ricoeur, 1970). I have suggested that this lack of clarity is related to the birth of psychoanalysis at a time when the competing worldviews of romanticism and empiricism were at great odds. Furthermore, I suggest that this dilemma has consequences in regard to the interpretive meaning of the corporeal dimension of reality. This research has taken a firm stand in that precarious position that straddles both the "body as such" and the "body in terms of its meanings" (Gill, 1994), out of my own assumption that the two are inextricably woven.

I have engaged the mind–body problem itself as subject of hermeneutic inquiry in that I have explicitly wondered how Heidegger's (1962) quest to deconstruct the subject–object divide might be applied to the psyche/soma divide. I have asked how or in what ways mind and body or psyche and soma cocreate the experiential basis of lived human meanings, and to what extent metapsychology speaks to this phenomenon.

SUMMARY OF THE GOALS AND ORGANIZATION OF THE STUDY

Given that the nature of this topic is complex and defies a certain linearity, each observation inviting a new level of questioning, allow me to summarize the earlier foray through broad territory to clarify the central goals of the forthcoming journey. The end goal is to find, discover, or create pathways toward a psychoanalytic language, which does not collude with disembodiment or dissociation from the somatic dimension of life but rather aids and encourages a fully embodied psychological experience. The method toward this goal is to examine the unconscious assumptions built into theory; in other words, to find or discover how original psychoanalytic theory or language has colluded with a disembodied or dissociated psychology. Then, I examine whether these unconscious biases that do fit this category have been either retained or overcome as theory has evolved over the last century. Finally, I summarize the journey to condense themes and suggest pathways for further evolution of theoretical language and clinical practice.

A study of the history of the mind–body problem in philosophy and culture is undertaken first, in order to understand the context out of which psychological theory evolved. It is presumed that this philosophical, cultural, and historical context is an unconscious influence of the constructs of metapsychology. Thus, to analyze psychoanalysis, one must start with its history, its origins, and associations. Chapter 2 is devoted to the history of the mind–body problem, with emphasis on intersections between philosophy and psychology.

The book then moves on to a reflective journey through the evolution of major metapsychological organizing principles, beginning with Freud's contributions of instinct and drive theories and moving to current expansions on or revisions of these theories. Chapter 3 reviews the portrayal of the relationship between psyche and soma within Freud's theory and traces the development of and alterations to his theory through his own lifetime. The goal is not to find the "real Freud," but to explore the "many Freuds" that exist in the minds of his followers and historians who have sought to understand his position on the mind–body problem. In my review of the highly varied literature, I present the reader with what I find to be convincing evidence that Freud himself was unclear as he struggled to integrate his varied influences and the clashing tides of his time, and that this phenomenon lends Freud too many interpretations. This chapter explores the evolution from the *Project*, to the topographic model, psychosexuality, and the structural model. Viewing the evolution of concepts historically provides a systematic means of extrapolating implicit assumptions about the somatic dimension embedded in the building blocks of psychoanalytic metapsychology.

Chapter 4 continues this exploration by following the evolution or modification of these assumptions through the Kleinian and object relations schools. The contributions of Donald Winnicott, Wilfred Bion, Thomas Ogden, and Joyce McDougal are likewise explored in this chapter. Contemporary thinkers have strayed from the drive model to varying degrees. Specifically, the contemporary move away from energy and conflict models toward deficit and field theory models represents an important departure from the notion of a physiologically based libidinal force. What has not been sufficiently explored in the literature is how this theoretical shift represents a shift in the way psychoanalysis imagines the actual body, physiological processes, and its relationship to the unconscious and psychic reality. I assert that and illustrate how the earlier mentioned theoretical models seem to carry forward from classical theories an implicit assumption that the life of the body can be likened to the unconscious or preconscious processes of the mind.

For instance, Kleinian school tends to correlate qualities of infantile states of mind with that which is primitive, psychotic, chaotic, presymbolic, prepsychological, and somatic. In object-driven models, the soma is not the "Id beast" of classical drive theory, but it is overwhelmingly grouped with that which is primitive and prepsychological. I link this notion to what has been called the *ascension myth* in theology and philosophy: The notion that material and somatic reality is inferior to abstract or spiritual reality and that human spiritual development is an ascension out of body and toward spirit. I show how an ascension myth informs psychoanalytic developmental models in that somatically informed states are often assumed to be outgrown or built over by more mature and thus more abstract modes of being or organizing experience. These models emphasize differentiation, and I argue for further attention to writers such as Winnicott and Milner who emphasize reintegration following differentiation. Throughout my critical analysis of implicit assumptions about the body, I attempt to highlight and offer creative leaps beyond an essential hierarchical dichotomy.

Chapter 5 explores the role of the body for those schools of thought that venture further into notions of intersubjectivity and thus carry psychoanalysis further from its positivistic influences. In Chapter 5, contemporary theoretical developments, including postmodern explorations by researchers like Atwood, Orange, Stolorow, Schwartz-Salant, Stern, Kohut, and David Krueger, are explored in light of implicit assumptions articulated in the previous chapters.

Intersubjective systems theory and relational theory represent continually evolving trends of thinking within psychoanalysis. Although neither of these schools of thought claims to contain a comprehensive metapsychology, they do assert that they operate within a paradigm that challenges essential assumptions of classical theory. Thinkers associated with these systems of thought challenge the Cartesian paradigm in general and the conceptualization of an "isolated mind" in particular. These challenges bring about new ways of conceptualizing the nature of dualities such as self and other, subject and object. Consequently, the nature of and developmental path toward reflexive consciousness are altered. As well, these models reconfigure notions about the dynamic unconscious, motivation, and the reality principle. The aim of this chapter is to articulate the implied position of the physical body in these evolving models and to find out whether this new position retains or modifies assumptions about the body built into earlier psychoanalytic models. These questions are highlighted by the fact that these evolutions are not contained within a comprehensive metapsychology, meaning that either old metapsychological assumptions are implied or that one portends to abandon the need for or use of metapsychology in general. I argue that because contemporary theorists themselves evolve out of classical metapsychology, they cannot refute the ongoing existence of this metapsychology and the values and assumptions implied therein.

Chapter 6 investigates the ways in which emerging neurosciences contribute to and inform psychoanalytic ideas. Of interest to this dialogue are the works of researchers who have explored the neurobiology of psychological constructs such as attachment, attunement, relationship, and affect regulation (Cozolino, 2002; Schore, 1994; Siegel, 1999a, 1999b). These researchers hold that there is a convergence occurring between neurobiology and psychology: Previously "psychological" concepts such as attunement are found to have a neurobiological parallel in the developing brain. These developments in psychology's understanding of the physical brain compel us to understand the nature of the relationship between so-called physical and psychological processes in new ways. This chapter likewise investigates the resurgence of interest in attachment research within psychoanalysis. Attachment and neuroscientific research have become associated not only by their concurrent emergence into the psychoanalytic domain but also because neuroscientific research continually emphasizes the ways in which the neurology of the brain is structured and modified within attachment relationship, including the psychotherapeutic one.

Finally, Chapter 7 engages the perspective gained in the first six chapters to gain an integrated understanding of the place of the body in the range of psychoanalytic metapsychologies. With an articulation of the contradictions or tensions therein, one is capable of imagining what a reintegration of the somatic dimension of humanity might look like in psychoanalytic theory and practice and equip to identify which metapsychological principles available fit together and with the emerging knowledge of the neurology of consciousness. The preceding excavation of unconscious assumptions within the theory of psychoanalysis in regard to somatic reality and consciousness is used as a jumping-off point toward ways in which psychoanalytic theory can speak more fully and meaningfully to the experience of being human.

2

PHILOSOPHY AND THE MIND–BODY PROBLEM: INFLUENCES ON PSYCHOANALYSIS

The goals of this chapter are to define the mind–body problem and its relationship to psychoanalysis, to define modern solutions to the mind–body problem, and to begin to draw connections between these solutions and metatheoretical suppositions in psychoanalysis. I also undertake an investigation of the shifts inherent in postmodern thought and link these shifts to developments in contemporary psychoanalysis. This work constructs a foundation for proceeding chapters to engage an informed discussion of the place of the body in evolutions of psychoanalytic thought.

I begin with classical thought because of its huge influence on modern thought and the basic assumptions and problems of modern psychology. It is impossible to understand the mind–body problem in modern psychology without understanding the historical origins of the "problem" and the evolution of "solutions." As Richard Chessick (1980) stated, "certain crucial philosophical concepts form the basic postulates of all major psychotherapeutic systems. These concepts are not consistent with each other" (p. 508).[1] Here I attempt to first name the philosophical postulates within metapsychological concepts,

---

[1]From *Passions of the Western Mind*, by R. Tarnas, 1991, New York, NY: Harmony Books, a division of Random House, Inc. Copyright by R. Tarnas. Selected quotes reprinted with permission.

so that implicit assumptions about the body or mind–body relationship can be made explicit.

ANCIENT GREECE AND THE ORIGINS
OF THE MIND–BODY PROBLEM

The issue of the relationship of mind to body or spirit to matter has been approached in a multitude of ways by philosophers, physicians, and psychologists. Wright and Potter (2000), in their introduction to the collection of essays titled *Psyche and Soma: Physicians and Metaphysicians on the Mind–Body Problem from Antiquity to Enlightenment*, noted that an account of the use of the terms *psyche* and *soma* almost

> seems so divergent in basic assumptions and goals that the question arises whether any central core of shared meaning is represented by the pair of terms at all. On closer examination, however, we find a series of basic problems which recur in different contexts, and a series of core meanings which change through time under the pressure of specific influences. The following studies reveal that the soul is distinguished from the body for a variety of purposes, and that the nature of their subsequent relationship varies accordingly. (pp. 1–2)

This chapter references the works of philosophical scholars who have attempted to summarize the nature of the mind–body problem over the course of Western philosophical thought (Crane & Patterson, 2000; Tarnas, 1991; Wright & Potter, 2000) in order to understand the context in which psychological theorists have lived and worked.

A basic account of the Platonic tradition is reviewed to establish what Richard Tarnas (1991) referred to as "that pivotal position within the Greek mind" from which "we can then move backward and forward—retrospectively to the early mythological and pre-Socratic traditions, and then onward to Aristotle" (p. 5).[2] This historic fulcrum of thought is emphasized as the birth of a "problem" in regard to psyche and soma, before which such a dilemma had simply not existed.

It is widely noted that whereas Descartes is either credited with or blamed for with the conceptualization of a dualism between mental and physical things, this way of dividing the world and human experience had been in the making for centuries (Grigsby & Stevens, 2000). For instance, Berman (1998) explained that in the last millennium before Christ, mystery

---

[2]From "Some Philosophical Assumptions of Intensive Psychotherapy," by R. Chessick, 1980, *American Journal of Psychotherapy, 34*, pp. 496–509. Copyright 1980 by the *American Journal of Psychotherapy*. Selected quotes reprinted with permission.

cults in Greece institutionalized the opposition between mind and body and self and other:

> This emerging consciousness was one in which psyche is imprisoned in the body as in a tomb. It becomes a wide-eyed controversy. Where is it? . . . and so on, as the science of it all begins in a morass of pseudoquestions. So dualism, that central difficulty in this problem of consciousness, begins its huge haunted career through history, to be firmly set in the firmament of thought by Plato, moving . . . into the great religions, up through . . . Descartes to become one of the great spurious quandaries of modern psychology. (pp. 156–157)

The division between body and mind is historically intertwined with the division between body and soul; Berman placed the division of soul and body at the time of Plato and called this the oppositional structure of combative dualism between the two. This particular form of dualism became an integral part of the Western Christian psyche, embedded in the need for salvation and a religion that could bridge the divide between heaven and earth.

If the human being had a detachable soul or Self that could, via certain

> psychophysical exercises, be withdrawn from the body at will, it began to seem likely that this occult entity would outlast the physical body after death. Thus the line from Plato most frequently quoted by the Church . . . in *Theaetetus*: "we should make all speed to take flight from this world to the other, and that means becoming like the divine so far as we can." The destiny of the soul, in other words, is to ascend, to leave the body and merge into the Godhead. (Berman, 1998, p. 158)

This Platonic sensibility, referred to in this research as the *ascension myth*, is inextricably intertwined with the Western consciousness of mind–body dualism and, I believe, underlies a value system that implicitly supports a dissociation from the body, the physical world, and the phenomenological experience of one's life.

David Abram (1996) discussed the effect of this sensibility on modern consciousness:

> Plato, or rather the association between the literate Plato and his mostly non-literate teacher Socrates . . . as the hinge on which the sensuous, mimetic, profoundly embodied style of consciousness proper to orality gave way to the more detached, abstract mode of thinking engendered by alphabetic literacy. (pp. 108–109)

Abram (1996) made the connection between the movement from oral to written expression and the abstraction of consciousness which served to disembody it from the natural world: "The indebtedness of human language to the more-than-human perceptual field . . . could now be entirely forgotten" (p. 102).

Abram (1996) took careful note of that which humans take for granted in the world of written word by imagining himself into early Semitic *aleph-beth* and its transformation into the Greek "alphabet"; the earliest systems of written text by their very nature required that the reader imagine and speak him or herself into the world that was spoken. For example, the absence of vowels in early Semitic writing meant that reading itself was an active, embodied process in which the sound of the breath brought the vowels and therefore the words into conscious life. Abram argued that this ancient engagement with the written word differs in a crucial way from modern experience of the alphabet. The modern alphabet has taken on a new autonomy and permanence that allows for a sense of distance, separation, and independence from that which is written or read.

Abram (1996) explicated the relationship between language and the perceptual field, as it relates to the human experience of distance from or participation with the natural world, and drew the reader into an experiential account of the shift between the ancient and modern world in this regard. Such an effort is required to comprehend the nature of both pre-Socratic experience and Western thought and the origins of the mind–body, psyche–matter divide. In other words, by gaining a broader perspective on the place of Western traditions of thought and the Western experience of the world, humans can begin to visualize that which we tend to take for granted as the nature of the reality of the material world and the psyche's relationship to it.

Socrates and Plato demarcate the origins of Western traditions in thought. I believe it is difficult for the modern person to imagine the nature of pre-Socratic thought and experience. So it is first relevant to comprehend the nature of the change that took place during this time period from 600 to 300 BC and what Tarnas (1991) called the *birth of philosophy*:

> The decisive step had been taken. The Greek mind now strove to discover a natural explanation for the cosmos by means of observation and reasoning, and these explanations soon began to shed their residual mythological components. Ultimate, universal questions were being asked, and answers were being sought from a new quarter—the human mind's critical analysis of material phenomena. Nature was to be explained in terms of nature itself, not of something fundamentally beyond nature, and in impersonal terms rather than by means of personal gods and goddesses. The primitive universe ruled by anthropomorphic deities began to give way to a world in whose source and substance was a primary element such as water, air, or fire. In time, these primary substances would cease to be endowed with divinity or intelligence, and would instead be understood as purely material entities mechanically moved by chance or by blind necessity. . . . And as man's independent intelligence grew stronger, the sovereign power of the old gods grew weak. (p. 20)

This shift has its roots in the early 6th century BC, when Thales and his successors, the "prototypical scientists," made "the remarkable assumption that an underlying rational unity and order existed within the flux and variety of the world" (Tarnas, 1991, p. 19). During this time there was an overlap between the mythic and the scientific explanations of the world; a self-animated substance was still presumed to be at the heart of all matter. Thus, as the new principle of rationality began to take root, it did so gradually and in the presence of an alive and divine natural and physical world. However, as the philosophical revolution progressed, so did the removal of the divine from the physical world. Parmenides of Elea approached a pure abstract rational logic and for the first time explored the difference between the real and the apparent. Sensory perception became, for the first time, a questionable basis for truth. The new truth was a rational, abstract one. Atomism is the radical culmination of this viewpoint in which any notion of a self-animated substance is completely removed from physical matter.

Abram (1996) noted the qualitative difference between pre-Socratic and Platonic ways of thinking and being in his observation that in the Homeric epics,

> human events and emotions are not yet distinct from the shifting moods of the animate earth—an army's sense of relief is made palpable in a description of thick clouds dispersing from the land; Nestor's anguish is likened to the darkening of the sea before a gale; the inward release of Penelope's feelings on listening to news of her husband is described as the thawing of the high mountain snows by the warm spring winds, melting the frozen water into streams that cascade down the slopes—as though the natural landscape was the proper home of those emotions, or as though a common psyche moved between humans and clouds and trees. . . . Here, then, is a land that is everywhere alive and awake, animated by a multitude of capricious but willful forces, at times vengeful and at other times tender, yet always in some sense responsive to human situations . . . This participatory and animate earth contrasts vividly with the dismissive view of nature espoused by Socrates in the *Phaedrus*. (p. 103)

What one sees emerging in the dawn of Western philosophy is a newfound sense of abstraction, rationality, order, and reasoning inherent to a world ruled by order rather than divinity. These elements were progressively separated from what Abram called the *embedded-in-the-world consciousness*: A perceptual basis of thinking and reason that was rooted in direct experience of the natural world through the sense perceptions and the assumption that matter is imbibed with divinity. Although these new qualities of thought and reason are to develop and refine over the course of Western philosophical history, the qualitative reorientation already visible in Platonic doctrines sets the stage for these future developments. The fundamentally new quality present in Platonic thought is the essential division between the material world and the spiritual or divine world.

It is worth briefly mentioning two main motivational factors that heavily influence this turn of events. The first is the Greek search, personified largely by Socrates, for moral standards that could be counted on in an absolute sense. This need largely underlies the Greek notion of archetypal forms or ideas, a notion that profoundly altered Western thought. Socrates sought a method for knowing which acts were virtuous in an absolute sense, independent of specific circumstances, so that a moral guide for living could be ascertained. Such transcendent, changeless, objective, and universal constants were assumed to be the foundation for a genuine ethics, and the archetypal ideas became the basis of the moral dimension. Although the existence of the archetypal ideas and forms does not equate with a split between matter and spirit, it becomes apparent that the absolutism and objectivism present in this conceptualization prefaces a consciousness in which knowledge based on the senses is placed in doubt—precisely because it is subjective in nature. What is now different is that true knowledge, knowledge of the essential nature of things, is found through an abstraction, a reasonable deduction to the archetypal nature of a thing that transcends the physical plane. What is valuable and most important to the fundamental nature of mankind is now beyond the physical world, not inherent to it.

The second motivating factor arises naturally from the first and gains in importance and influence in medieval times. This is the interest in ascension and the immortality of the soul. M. W. F. Stone's paper (in Crane & Patterson, 2000) discusses a central question for medieval philosophers: How can the ancient Greek soul, the form of the body, be consistent with the Christian doctrine of the immortality of the soul? To comprehend the scope of the influence of the Christian doctrine of immortality, one must first look to Aristotle.

Crane and Patterson (2000) cited Aristotle as the starting point in their investigation of the history of the mind–body problem. Aristotle's *De Anima*, the soul that animates every living thing, evokes a sense of an ensouled, animated physical world. Indeed, Aristotle's view of substantial forms, a "rational soul [which] is also an 'immaterial form,' which has its own kind of 'substinence'" (Crane & Patterson, 2000, p. 4), and his reliance on knowledge based on sense perception belie the complexity of the historical march toward abstract knowledge and a dissociation of the mind from the material world.

In a fundamental sense, Aristotle can be considered an empiricist (Crane & Patterson, 2000; Tarnas, 1991) and a functionalist (Crane & Patterson, 2000). Where Plato was interested in the transcendent and in direct intuition of absolutes, Aristotle was interested in the physical world and the particulars. Aristotle was a biologist, and his valuation of knowledge gained directly through sense perception as the basis of science and of the discriminating intellect marks the founding of one of the modern world's favorite "isms": empiricism.

In many ways Aristotle's views challenged some of Plato's most fundamental doctrines. Ethics and morality were to Aristotle defined by the particulars of a situation; Aristotle valued the subjective over the objective. Aristotle deemphasized the existence of absolute Ideas and Forms, which might be abstractly known via the philosopher's intellect, and emphasized that the mind was

> not only . . . that which is activated by sensory experience, but also as something that is eternally active, and indeed divine and immortal. This aspect of mind, the active intellect (*nous*), alone gave humans the intuitive capacity to grasp final and universal truths." (Tarnas, 1991, p. 60)

The active intellect alone has the ability to derive rational knowledge from sensory evidence. What becomes complex is the relationship between this active intellect (*nous*) and the soul. The *nous* is what

> illuminates the processes of human cognition while it yet remains beyond them, eternal and complete. Only because man shares in the divine *nous* can he apprehend infallible truth. . . . In Aristotle's view, the individual human soul might cease to exist with death, since the soul is vitally joined to the physical body it animates. The soul is the form of the body, just as the body is the matter of the soul. But the divine intellect, of which each man has a potential share and which distinguishes man from other animals, is immortal and transcendent. (Tarnas, 1991, pp. 60–61)

In Aristotle, human potential becomes the association between the intellect and the divine. However, a new complication arises regarding the nature of the relationship between the intellect and the soul of the physical body and natural world. Although Aristotle is Plato's student, he has introduced his own complications. Aristotle's soul is the form of the physical body, but it is a separate entity from the active intellect, which is associated with the immortal and divine and serves to maintain a balance and relationship between the mortal and the divine.

Two landmark moves have now been made that will continue to play out over the course of Western thought: With Plato there is dissociation between the physical world and the spiritual world, and with Aristotle there is a separation between the intellect, which has a potentiality to realize its relationship to the divine, and the physical world. Both share a degree of separation between mind and matter; however, for Plato mind seeks to transcend matter into the realm of absolutes, whereas for Aristotle mind is the link between the physical world and the divine realm of the active intellect and does not seek to transcend sensual knowledge. In this way Aristotle attempted to solve the problem of the immortality of the soul. What Aristotle did not challenge is the movement away from mythological explanations for the physical world and an identification between human emotion and the physical world, which is evident in the Homeric epics. Similarly, the experiential emphasis on engagement with or participation in the natural world is deemphasized by both Platonic and Aristotelian traditions in the emphasis on disengagement from the material plane to achieve union with that which is Divine; in both Plato and Aristotle one sees a dissociation of the divine from the material world, even though Aristotle makes this move by way of an intellect that can still derive knowledge from the senses.

In sum, although the subtleties of Ancient Greek thought are complex and largely subject to debate regarding inconsistencies within Plato or Aristotle's works themselves as well as the historical accuracy of interpretations of available written works, what is generally accepted to be remarkably new at this time is that both human intellect and the divine realm have begun to be considered as separate from the physical and natural world. Tarnas (1991) referred to this as an "increased confidence in the power of human thought to comprehend the world rationally, a confidence that begun with Thales, now found in Aristotle its fullest expression and climax" (p. 62).

The dual legacy of classical Greek thought can be described as a balanced tension between empirical analysis and spiritual intuition. Tarnas (1991) cited Raphael's *The School of Athens* as the pictorial representation of this balance in which "Plato points upward towards the heavens, to the invisible and transcendent, while Aristotle motions his hand outward and down to the earth, to the visible and immanent" (p. 68). This picture evidences the difficulties encountered over the entire course of Western philosophy to reconcile the nature of the relationship between that which is absolute, transcendent, spiritual, or mind to that which is physical and material.

REFLEXIVE CONSCIOUSNESS AND DUALISM

To comprehend the nature of the mind–body problem in modern history, one must attempt to understand the nature of the historical consciousness that did not assume this fundamental duality between matter and mind or matter and spirit. Although it may be difficult or impossible for the modern mind to know fully the pre-Socratic mind, an attempt leads us to comprehend the relationship between dualism and self-reflective consciousness as they arose in the Western mind. The hallmark of the Western mind relative to that of the pre-Socratics may well be the capacity for reflection: first, reflection about the world and the state of being in the world, and then self-reflection on the processes of the mind itself. The quality of consciousness prior to the ancient Greeks has been described as "embedded-in-the-world" by Abram (1996): In a comparative analysis, he stated that "a new power of reflexivity was thus coming into existence, borne by the relation between the scribe and his scripted text" (p. 107). Abram explicated this shift in consciousness as related to the introduction of the scripted word; the space between the word on the page and the mind of the writer creates the necessary chiasm for reflexive consciousness. By "chiasm," I am referring to a separation between subject and object, which precludes direct participation but ushers in a sense of knowledge via observation.

To grasp the nature of this shift is to grasp the most fundamental nature of the psyche/soma split inherent to modern consciousness. By looking beyond what humans are, we can understand what we are not and as well appreciate the gains of modern consciousness in the areas of scientific empiricism and a reflective consciousness capable of knowing itself and its object in entirely new ways. This newfound sense of objective knowledge and observation is precisely what distinguishes the Western mind from its pre-Socratic origins.

The importance of this shift for the purposes of this research cannot be underestimated. First, to understand the nature of the Western mind, one must understand what it is not. What it is not is also what has been lost or given up. In other words, for the gain of a distanced observation of the world, which gives rise to the natural sciences, empiricism, and the technological advances of the modern world, what is necessarily lost in exchange is the sense of direct participation with the natural world and a consciousness that is meaningfully linked with the workings of the natural world. Simply put, human intellectual confidence and mastery of the physical world have been gained along with a deepening sense of meaninglessness and alienation from this world (Berman, 1998; Romanyshyn, 1989; Tarnas, 1991). This concept is central to the aim of this research, which seeks to visualize the broad gains in modern consciousness as is relevant to psychoanalysis, a central science of human self knowledge. Because the differentiation or chiasm of mind and body is related to reflective and symbolic capacities, the rest of this book necessarily grapples with the nature of this chiasm and the nature of reflective capacities in the search for an embodied psychology.

To undertake such an investigation, a framework of reference must be established. The mind–body, or psyche/soma, problem has a long history embedded in the Western notion of duality. Duality is closely related to the psychological concept of splitting and the possibility of discriminating consciousness. The splitting of consciousness—although often employed as a defense—is arguably a psychological and physiological necessity. As humans, we continuously split off parts of our awareness to focus effectively on another. Cells and plants divide to propagate. Duality, in the most basic sense, is the nature of the world: light–dark, male–female, and conscious–unconscious. It is through this contrast that people become human, become individuals, and thrive on the ability to differentiate, focus, integrate, and assimilate.

One might also say that the process of differentiation and integration is the basis by which psychological consciousness is gleamed. Opposites are isolated in order to be known as an act of psychological growth. It is then possible that opposites—which may have previously been unconsciously merged—can now consciously forge together in an entirely new creation. This notion that psychological consciousness is born out of differentiation, or splitting, and subsequent reflection, or bridging, is a central idea in the forthcoming exploration of mind and body in psychoanalysis.

Discrimination and integration are a natural, growth-promoting pair of functions inherent to duality. On the other hand, "a dualism [italics added] . . . is a distinction that has become reified, a frozen-fragment of a prior symbolic diversity" (Kidner, 2001, p. 3) This distinction is vital. While I am challenging whether psychoanalysis has reified its conceptualizations of the somatic in a way that precludes "symbolic diversity," creativity, and enlivenedness, I am not advocating for a retreat from discrimination and differentiation, which I believe are necessary precursors to healthy collaboration and integration.

Before moving on, it is worth reiterating the philosophical picture in ancient Greece prior to its decline, for the values and inclinations along with the problems and tensions of Western philosophy had been laid out and an understanding of this situation provides a framework within which to comprehend future philosophical and eventually psychoanalytic endeavors. What is most striking to me is that the tension held between the Platonic and the Aristotelian doctrines fundamentally portrays the tension between the material and nonmaterial, mental and nonmental properties of being human, which, with the birth of Western philosophy, had become for the first time an object of investigation.

This new, *Western mind* is characterized primarily by the tenet that "the world is an ordered cosmos, whose order is akin to an order within the human mind. A rational analysis of the empirical world is therefore possible" (Tarnas, 1991, p. 69). But this new situation of the rational human in an empirical world comes with a new and central complication: How is the observing mind related to the physical world it inhabits and observes? The problem is multifaceted and varies greatly in its conceptualization and even definitions of *mind* itself. However, at heart, the problems revolve around the newfound complications that arose from the birth of the Western philosophical, reflective, empirical mind. Robinson's discussion (in Wright & Potter, 2000) of mind–body dualism in Plato ends with a reference to Plato's own ambiguities and varying solutions: "To the end he is wrestling with the problem that lies at the heart of all psycho–physical dualism, the problem of relating a physical substance to an immaterial one, and to the end he openly admits his bafflement" (p. 55).

The ways in which future theologians, philosophers, metaphysicians, and psychologists have dealt with this new problem of relating a physical substance to an immaterial one can be loosely tied to either the approach taken by Plato or that of Aristotle. "In the end, Plato's loyalty lay with the transcendent archetype," whereas "the overall thrust of Aristotle's philosophy was decidedly naturalistic and empiricist . . . life was the preferred, more real realm of existence" (Tarnas, 1991, p. 66). Platonic solutions lean toward an affinity between God and reason, world-defying desires for ascension and unity with God via reason, notions of pure reason, and idealistic forms and archetypes. Aristotelian solutions, on the other hand, tend to incorporate knowledge based on sensory information and notions of nature as part and principle of a divine order. Aristotelian philosophies are oriented toward the concrete world and the inescapability of the human situation within the tangible world.

Although an in-depth discussion of medieval philosophers is beyond the scope of this project, it is helpful to make the theoretical links between thinkers and across time, as one moves forward toward 17th- and 18th-century solutions to the mind–body problem that most dramatically shaped the underlying assumptions of early psychoanalytic theory. For now, it is sufficient to establish as a framework the basic worldview and philosophical approaches of Plato and Aristotle as a representation of the original problem of dualism, its complications, and the temperamental styles of overcoming them.

MODERN SOLUTIONS TO THE MIND–BODY PROBLEM

Garth Kremerling (2001) defined the mind–body problem as "the difficulty of explaining how the mental activities of human beings relate to their living physical organisms" ("Mind–Body Problem," para. 1). A summary of the most commonly accepted solutions to the problem includes Descartes' dualism, Hobbes's reductive materialism, Berkeley's idealism, and Spinoza's double-aspect theory. A brief review of these solutions provides a frame of reference with which one can then begin to analyze the way that the mind–body relationship was held at the time Freud began his study of the unconscious and began the tradition of depth psychology.

Dualism

Dualism essentially holds that reality is composed of two kinds of entities, mental and physical, and that these things are fundamentally different and separate (Grigsby & Stevens, 2000; Kremerling, 2001). The typical problem that arises from dualism is then how these two entities are related. Interactionism, parallelism, and epiphenomenalism are variations on dualism, which explain the interaction and coordination of physical and mental things in different ways. *Interactionism* holds that a causal relationship exists between mental and physical things. Descartes' dualism was an interactionist theory that supposed a gland in the brain, the pineal gland, was ostensibly responsible for communication and collaboration between the body and the mind. *Parallelism,* on the other hand, assumes a noncausal relationship between minds and bodies. Gottfried Leibniz's theory is one of parallelism; he holds that there is a preestablished harmony that accounts for the truth that the physical and mental "development, features, and actions coordinate perfectly" (Kremerling, 2001, "The Best of All Possible Worlds," para. 3). *Epiphenomenalism* is the "belief that consciousness is an incidental side-effect or by-product of physical or mechanical reality . . . although mental events are in some sense real they have no causal efficacy on the material realm" (Kremerling, 2001, "Epiphenomenalism," para. 1). Epiphenomenalism is close to *emergent materialism*, a common stance of modern neurobiologists to explain consciousness that is not reducible to its biological components but is nonetheless a by-product of these biological components (Armstrong, 1999; Kim, 1998).

Descartes and Leibniz are both rationalists, which places them in the tradition of Plato. Rationalism relies on reason as the only reliable source of human knowledge. In contrast to empiricism, which relies on sense data from the physical world, rationalism is an epistemological theory that believes in *a priori* means and categories for the acquisition of true knowledge. Dualist solutions to the mind–body problem are therefore Platonic in nature, distrusting the senses and relying on abstraction, a priori forms, and reason to reach their final conclusions.

Materialism

Materialism is the "belief that only physical things truly exist" and that "every apparent instance of a mental phenomenon [is] a feature of some physical object" (Kremerling, 2001, "Materialism," para. 1). Western materialists can be historically linked to the atomists of ancient Greece and include Thomas Hobbes in the 17th century. Hobbes relied heavily on the theories of the Aristotelian camp of knowledge based in the tangible, sensible world. Materialistic views are deterministic by nature, insighting the notion of a world governed entirely by physical and natural laws. It is an entirely impersonal world that can be finally reduced to its mechanical laws.

Materialistic philosophies are empirical in nature; they rely on experience as the source of ideas and knowledge. "More specifically, empiricism is the epistemological theory that genuine information about the world must be acquired by a posteriori means, so that nothing can be thought without first being sensed" (Kremerling, 2001, "Empiricism," para. 1). A variation on this theme is emergent materialism, discussed earlier. This view has gained a wider audience in the wake of advances in neurobiology (Grigsby & Stevens, 2000; Hasker, 1999; Kim, 1998; Pinkel, 1992). These thinkers hold that "consciousness and its associated properties are the manifestation of certain processes characteristic of a particular kind of self-organizing system" (Grigsby & Stevens,

2000, p. 16). An *emergent property* is "an irreducible feature (now commonly called supervenient) of a complex whole that cannot be inferred directly from the features of its simpler parts" (Kremerling, 2001, "Emergent Property," para. 1). Empiricism and the materialistic philosophers again hold the Aristotelian perspective in the historical tension between material and mental phenomena and how to account for their compatibility.

Idealism

Idealism, on the opposite spectrum, is the belief that only mental entities are real and that physical things exist only in the sense that they are perceived. Influential idealists include Berkeley, who defended his "immaterialism" on empiricist grounds, whereas Kant and Fichte arrived at theirs by transcendental arguments. Much of German, English, and American philosophy during the 19th century was dominated by the monistic absolute idealism of Hegel, Bradley, and Royce (Kremerling, 2001).

Idealism tends toward the Platonic side of the mind–body problem, in that the emphasis of what is real and true, and therefore most valued, is that which is beyond the physical. The physical is a mere shadow reflection of an abstract reality. However, the picture begins to become more complex as Platonic ideals are shifted in the hands of Berkeley, Locke, and Hume: The empiricist stress on sense perceptions, developed from Aristotle and Aquinas to Ockham, Bacon, and Locke, was brought to the ultimate extreme with Hume. For Hume, only sensory perceptions existed; the organization of those perceptions was the activity of the human mind, without objective evidence or empirical grounding.

> Where Plato had held sensory impressions to be faint copies of Ideas, Hume held ideas to be faint copies of sensory impressions. In the long evolution of the Western mind from the ancient idealist to the modern empiricist, the basis of reality had been entirely reversed: Sensory experience, not ideal apprehension, was the standard of truth—and that truth was utterly problematic. Perceptions alone were real for the mind, and one could never know what stood beyond them. (Tarnas, 1991, p. 340)

In other words, Berkeley's empirical means of arriving at an idealist stance draws on an Aristotelian knowledge via the senses to arrive at a Platonic abstraction of a primary reality based in the mind and its structures.

Immanuel Kant retains a hallmark position in the idealist tradition, in that he sought to reconcile two major advances in thought in the 17th and 18th centuries: that of Isaac Newton and David Hume. Kant's intellectual challenge was enormous:

> On the one hand, to reconcile the claims of science to certain and genuine knowledge of the world with the claim of philosophy that experience could

never give rise to such knowledge; on the other hand, to reconcile the claim of religion that man was morally free with the claim of science that nature was entirely determined by necessary laws. (Tarnas, 1991, p. 340)

Kant's solution drastically altered the conceptualization of the mind–world correspondence:

> In Kant's view . . . the mind is such that it does not passively receive sense data. Rather, it actively digests and structures them, and man therefore knows objective reality precisely to the extent that that reality conforms to the fundamental structures of the mind. (Tarnas, 1991, p. 343)

This is the first subjective, relativistic notion of a world structured by the mind that perceives it. What is a priori are the structures of the mind, thus accounting for the appearance and experience of a world that acts according to mathematical propositions such as Newton's laws but maintaining Hume's stance that what can be known is only an experience of the world, which cannot be assumed to be representative of the world itself. The world as it actually is Kant referred to as the *noumenal*, whereas the *phenomenal* world is the world as humans perceive it with our senses. Tarnas (1991) referred to Kant's theory as the "rejoining of the knower to the known," but which finds humankind in a solipsistic prison: a human who has no firm connection to objective reality outside of the human mind.

This "recombination" of sensory knowledge versus a priori forms has inverted the questions of philosophy and pointed them toward an introspective self-reflection about the nature of the mind itself:

> The task of the philosopher was therefore radically redefined. His goal could no longer be that of determining a metaphysical world conception in the traditional sense, but should instead be that of analyzing the nature and limits of human reason. . . . Thus philosophy's true task was to investigate the formal structures of the mind, for only there would it find the true origin and foundation for certain knowledge of the world. (Tarnas, 1991, p. 347)

The course of idealism then has played a determinant role in the modern and postmodern handling of the relationship between the material and nonmaterial. The idea that experience of the physical world is a subjective activity dominated by a priori categories of the mind seems to further isolate the human *I* from the physical world in which it finds itself. Tarnas (1991) referred to this as the increasing sense of alienation and isolation of the modern position—"the Cartesian schism between the human mind and the material cosmos continued in a new and deepened form" (p. 350).

Idealism and the tensions between scientific determinism, radical skepticism, and religion present in the 19th century are important in the social climate in which Freud lived, studied, and worked. But before I move on to a discussion of the philosophical and cultural influences in Freud's work, I consider the fourth major solution to the mind–body problem.

Double-Aspect Theory

Double-aspect theory is the belief that mental and physical properties are irreducibly distinct features of one thing. This one thing, which Spinoza (Spinoza, Boyle, & Parkinson, 1989) considered to be "god or nature," is present in both mental and physical properties, manifest in different forms. Kremerling (2001) urged one to consider what all of this implies for each living human being:

> We are not substances, according to Spinoza, for only god or Nature is truly substantial; we can exist only as modes, depending for our existence upon the reality of the one real being. Since the one infinite substance is the cause of everything, each of us can only be regarded as a tiny cross-section of the whole. ("Mind and Body," para. 1)

These ideas include implications for a particular kind of relationship between mind and body and the limitations of mental knowledge of the body. The human existence is "cross-sections" of the unitary field, including the organic body composed of physical events and the human mind, both of which are considered to be extensions of "god," either as mental or physical extensions. It is emphasized that there is not a causal relationship between the mental and physical events, but that there is an underlying correlation and order to their harmony.

> Thus, in principle, the human mind contains ideas that perfectly represent the parts of the human body. But since many of these ideas are inadequate in the sense that they do not carry with them internal signs of their accuracy, we do not necessarily know our own bodies. (II Prop. xxviii) If, for example, there must be in my mind an idea that corresponds to each particular organic state of my spleen; but since I am unaware of its bodily correlate, it provides me with no clear awareness of that representational object. (Kremerling, 2001, "Mind and Body," para. 3)

Spinoza drew heavily on Descartes' dualism, and, like Descartes, Spinoza was a rationalist. However, Spinoza envisioned a unitary whole that underlay the nature of the universe, thereby accounting for a synchronized relationship between the physical extension and thought extension of that whole.

> A related stance is that of neutral monism. Neutral monism is the belief that both mental and physical properties are the features of substances of a single sort, which are themselves ultimately neither mental nor physical. In distinct varieties, neutral monism was defended by James and Russell. (Kremerling, 2001, "Neutral Monism," para. 1)

Double-aspect theory differs from dualism in the underlying assumptions regarding causality. Double-aspect theories imply a level of organization, meaning, or order that underlies manifest reality and accounts for the relationship between mind and body. This issue of causality and meaning are discussed in detail below.

Causality and the Mind–Body Problem

Each of the above general approaches to the mind–body problem carries implications as to notions of causality. The historical development of the concept of causality is interwoven with the history of the mind–body problem and was of particular importance at the dawn of psychoanalysis at the end of the 19th century; "since the Enlightenment and the growth of science, exponents of the two most important concepts, determinism and teleology, have been in conflict" (Horne, Sowa, & Isenman, 2000, p. 109). Horne traced the development of rational speculations about causality from the pre-Socratics, through Plato's forms, and Aristotle's fourfold explanation of causality. The presence of a divine order or universal intelligence proper to early mythological explanations of the universe remained present in the Greek idea of *telos*, the final expression of original cause. "Teleology was Aristotle's reworking of Plato's idea of the forms" (Horne et al., 2000, p. 110) and implies an intentionality to the order of the universe that is not completely determined as in the mechanical universe of the Enlightenment.

> In the 17th century, with the beginning of the Enlightenment, there was a shift in the understanding of reason . . . a change in the interpretation of sense data occurred whereby it was shorn of its teleological associations. This empirical method led to the successes of Newton and Galileo and the rise of deterministic science. (Horne et al., 2000, p. 111)

Materialism is the most obvious and extreme form of causality and implication of reductionism espoused by logical positivism and the biological determinism of modern science. Dualism implies causality on the physical level but leaves a separate realm, that of the soul or mind, to theology, teleology, or both. The most far-reaching consequence of the Enlightenment mind is to strip sense data of its teleological associations. In other words, the physical world was made bereft of its own intrinsic meaning. This is the culmination of the spirit–matter split that began with the birth of the Western mind.

The idealist solution to the mind–body problem also retains the division between teleology and the physical world, which presumably is a secondary effect but not inherently meaningful. Idealism implies teleology above mechanical, deterministic causality but denies a theological origination of meaning. The idealist stance is decidedly modern in the sense that "God" is no longer a subject of philosophical propositions.

Double-aspect theory most directly implies a teleological level of organization for the mind–body problem. Double-aspect theory assumes that tangible and intangible realms are both manifestations of something else, that something else being the primary level of reality. Whether this primary level of organization is called "God" or not, it implies an order of intelligence inherent to the underlying organization of the manifest world. It is this intelligence or order of the unitary level of reality that is responsible for the synchronization of the physical and mental realms. This belief system can take on religious overtones by calling the underlying level of reality God, or it can take on a more general spiritual overtone by prescribing meaning and purpose to this level of organization.

What is relevant regarding the implications of causality inherent in a philosophical approach to the world is that notions of causality directly imply a primary cause and order to the world; such allegiances indirectly imply a position regarding the mind–body problem. What is often most evident in a particular psychoanalytic theory is a position on causality. It is from the direct statements regarding causality that one can deduce the relationship between the body and the psyche in that theory, even if these implications remain unconscious in the theorist's writings. In fact, because many theorists do not address the meaning of the body in their theory directly, the assumptions do often appear to remain unconscious. It is for this reason in particular that investigating these assumptions is necessary to confront potentially contradictory themes in the body of psychoanalytic theory. Chapter 3 of this volume explores Freud's varying notions of causality and motivation as they reflect his varying or ambiguous perspectives on the mind–body problem.

Summary

The whole of Western philosophy is dominated by the experience that there are two basic properties belonging to human experience: the material or physical, and the immaterial or mental. Tarnas (1991) placed the varying conceptualizations of how these two properties are related to each other in regard to the nature of reality and the human place in the cosmos, and in regard to the development of the modern mind:

> For the modern world view was, like its predecessors, not a stable entity but a continually evolving way of experiencing existence, and, what is especially relevant to us here, the views of Newton, Galileo, Descartes, Bacon, and the rest were essentially a Renaissance synthesis of modern and medieval: i.e., a compromise between a medieval Christian Creator God and a modern mechanistic cosmos, between the human mind as a

spiritual principle and the world as objective materiality, and so forth. During the two centuries following the Cartesian-Newtonian formulation, the modern mind continued to disengage itself from its medieval matrix. The writers and scholars of the Enlightenment—Locke, Leibniz, Spinoza, Bayle . . . Berkeley, Hume . . . Kant—philosophically elaborated, broadly disseminated, and culturally established the new world view. By its end, the autonomous human reason had fully displaced traditional sources of knowledge about the universe, and in turn had defined its own limits as those constituted by the boundaries and methods of empirical science. (p. 284)

Tarnas (1991) was referring to the character of the modern Western mind at its climax and the complexities inherent to the general character of autonomous human reason. It is within this general character that the earlier mentioned four major approaches to the mind–body problem exist. The previous attempt to organize the plethora of thought patterns regarding the mind–body problem leaves me with the sense of attempting to untangle and separate two substances that are sticky or gluey. Any attempt to box one theory or one substance into a compartment is never entirely complete, as contamination by one is always found in the other. The history of the mind–body problem is a matrix of intermingling of ideas that create a spectrum of beliefs and worldviews.

I am left with the sense that the modern mind has wrestled continually with the difficult mental task of understanding clearly these two fundamental aspects of the world and of grasping the meaning of their relationship in ways that are not laden with contradictions. This struggle appears to result in a general trend of reasoning: First, it is discovered that there are two aspects or qualities in the human condition (psyche and soma), and, second, the problem "arises" as to how they are related. Third, various means of explaining the relationship are tried on.

The first attempt includes the variations of duality: Perhaps a causal or an acausal relationship can describe the relationship between the mental and the physical. When these descriptions don't entirely hold together, one begins to imagine that one quality of being is primary and that the other is a secondary property of the first. This second attempt includes the variations of monism, including materialism and idealism. Complications are still inevitable, and so one turns to a fourth solution: Perhaps these two qualities are, in a fundamental sense, the same thing after all. Double-aspect theory says that psyche and soma are both secondary qualities to "another thing," which itself must be primary. However, this fourth solution is untenable to the basic precepts of the Western mind in several ways. First, it undermines the spirit–matter split. Second, it displaces human reason from its autonomous and central position in philosophy. Third, it denies the possibility of a mechanical (causal) universe and implies a pre-Socratic notion of meaning or order (teleology). As discussed later, this kind of solution is largely characteristic of the post-modern mind and its embracing of subjectivity and relativity. Although there are many subtle variations on the four themes listed earlier, this general division of mind–body solutions provides a framework within which the research may now investigate the platform of psychoanalytic thought: Sigmund Freud and his theories.

PHILOSOPHICAL AND CULTURAL FOUNDATIONS
OF PSYCHOANALYSIS

This section covers Freud's major philosophical, cultural, and medical influences in an attempt to synthesize existing thought as to Freud's own relationship to the mind–body problem. An investigation of Freud's personal influences and psychological theory is saved for Chapter 3. The intersections between philosophy and Freudian metapsychology are explored in depth to answer the question of what may be unconscious within Freud's theories regarding the body and its relationship to psyche due to the historical and cultural context in which he lived. This task is accomplished by following the theological and philosophical influences on the framework of depth psychology, which appear to reinforce the suspicion or devaluation of the body.

Setting the Stage: Priest Versus Doctor

For these purposes it is useful to look back as far as psychology's ancestry in primitive medicine. Here one finds early disease theories and treatments that demonstrate no distinction between physical, emotional, and spiritual elements of the human being. For instance, a disease was thought to be caused by object intrusion, loss of soul, spirit intrusion, or breach of taboo. The physical symptoms of disease were treated through psychological or spiritual means such as soul retrieval or exorcism (Ellenberger, 1970). These characteristics of early healing and surrounding belief systems seem distant and unrelated to contemporary psychotherapy in many respects. However, as we look forward in history, it becomes apparent that some tenets of depth psychology find their roots in these early structures. In particular, it is out of this matrix of the physical–spiritual–psychological model that future generations and cultures struggle to define the distinction, or lack thereof, between physical and psychological illness.

Around 4,000 BC, emerging religious structures greatly informed the initial distinction between medicine in the physical sense and the medicine of the spirit or soul. The traditional medicine man became the priest, whereas the lay healer—typically a person with lesser knowledge and training—became the physical doctor (Ellenberger, 1970). In the West, philosophic schools and sects were forming with their own strict mental training and initiatory rites.

As time progressed, these mental disciplines became quite separate from physical medicine and more closely aligned with and affected by political fluctuations of the church (Ellenberger, 1970). The shift from a world that used poetry, myth, and story to explore the nature of human life to a world that relied on rational discourse was heightened by the political influence of the Catholic church. Rationalist thinking served the omnipotent power of the church by divorcing science from the sensations of the physical body. Rationalists claimed that the senses could not be relied on to provide true and reliable data; if the sensate functions could not provide scientific data, then the body was spiritually devalued by the institution of the church, which was now backed by academic science. The fit between the two institutions was heightened by the Catholic value of denying the influence and desires of the flesh. In these early political affiliations between scientific thought and the church, one can see how the future of a scientific discipline dedicated to psyche—later to become depth psychotherapy—is implicitly governed by a science of reason and a rejection of direct experience of the physical body.

Here researchers see a complex summation of influences on the roots of psychology. Psyche, from the Greek *psukhe*, originally referring to breath, carries the connotation of soul or spirit, and in the 19th century came to be used in reference to mind (Ayto, 1991). On the one hand, healers of the intangible aspects of person, including spirit, soul, and mind, belonged to the realm of the church and were distinguished from physical medicine; on the other hand, the church began to align itself with the doctrines of physical science and empiricism. Healers of the soul, therefore—who in the West were priests and philosophers—were now aligned with the scientific doctrines of Copernicus, which placed humans at the center of the theological universe. This doctrine was completely overturned by the principles of depth psychology. A dynamic psychology directly implied a metaphysical framework, which displaced human reason from the center of the universe; it was only within such a framework that the concept of unseen and universal forces at play on the human condition could be accepted. The idea of unconscious energies or magnetic fields that made up the universe placed humans in relationship to physical, mental, or spiritual forces that were not directly regulated by the institution of the church. This move greatly threatened the political and supposed scientific platform the church had enjoyed and explained an incredible resistance to the ascription of power and force to unconscious or physical energies.

Perhaps this tension plays a part in the ambiguous distinction between the scope of practice of the physician, analyst, and priest today. For instance, the analyst's practice deals with traditionally spiritual matters in a medical way. Likewise, medical matters are treated using what might be considered a spiritual approach. To the degree that one inherits a Christian psyche, psychological analysis is historically at odds with the institution that traditionally cares for the soul. The entire history of dynamic psychology is characterized by an underlying tension that acknowledges the attempt to address psychospiritual matters in a theological framework, which contradicts the platform of the church and much of the scientific doctrine. Although modern depth psychology occupies a very different metaphysical framework from 17th-century Catholicism, the founding father of psychoanalysis was not entirely separate from this worldview, but, rather, his assumptions were in part historically inherited.

Hypnotism and the Unconscious

Of interest to this study is what assumptions, regarding the continuity or discontinuity between the energies of the unconscious and that of the organic world, lie at the heart of psychoanalytic theory. I suggest that the nature of the relationship between the unconscious and the physical world is ambiguously defined and understood in psychoanalytic theory and that to avoid unconscious assumptions stemming from one's implicit inheritance and occupation of a dualistic world, a conscious investigation of the theories in this light is necessary. I begin with an investigation of the origins of the concept of the unconscious. As Ellenberger (1970) stated, "Historically, modern dynamic psychotherapy derives from primitive medicine, and an uninterrupted continuity can be demonstrated between exorcism and magnetism, magnetism and hypnotism, and hypnotism and the modern dynamic schools" (p. 48).[3] Specifically, implicit notions regarding the nature of the unconscious as Freud imagined it lie in the historical matrix out of which this concept emerged.

In the mid-18th century, Mesmer developed a system for the treatment of hysterical patients, based on the exploration of the unconscious energies (Ellenberger, 1970). Mesmer produced a number of "miracle cures" and attributed his success to his ability to rebalance the magnetic energies of the body. He postulated that the universe was made of and bound together by magnetic tides of animal gravity. It is very interesting to note that Mesmer was primarily a physician treating both mysterious physical symptoms and what researchers would consider psychological disturbances. The orthodox medical establishment, however, was very suspicious of his claims, and he eventually fled Italy to find a more receptive audience in the people of Paris. Mesmer's widespread

---

[3]From *The Discovery of the Unconscious: The History and Evolution of Dynamic Psychiatry*, by H. F. Ellenberger, 1970, New York, NY: Basic Books. Copyright 1970 by H. F. Ellenberger. Selected quotes reprinted with permission.

authentic healing successes are questionable at least (Ellenberger, 1970). Nonetheless, Mesmer seemed to have stumbled on some effectiveness, and some of his ideas carry forward into psychoanalysis. Magnetic fluid is such an unusual idea that researchers may have to branch outside of Western thought to find a correlate. I attribute Mesmer's influence to his having touched on what is referred to as *Qi* in Chinese medicine. Mesmer's description of a "magnetic fluid" that is universal to all organic life is remarkably similar to the following description of Qi by Ted Kaptchuk (2000):

> The idea of Qi is fundamental to Chinese thinking, yet no one English word or phrase can adequately capture its meaning. We can say that everything in the universe, organic and inorganic, is composed of and defined by its Qi. But Qi is not some primordial, immutable material, nor is it merely vital energy, although the word is occasionally so translated. Chinese thought does not distinguish between matter and energy, but researchers can perhaps think of Qi as matter on the verge of becoming energy, or energy at the point of materializing. (p. 35)

In the Chinese system, Qi, which can be moved with the use of hands or specifically designed acupuncture needles, composes the manifest world and can be manipulated toward physical and mental health (Kaptchuk, 2000). To consider the substance of Mesmer's work, like Qi, as bearing influence on and belonging to both the material and the immaterial dimensions, sheds light on the earliest conceptualizations of the "unconscious" of dynamic psychiatry. It also becomes apparent that these early conceptualizations of an unconscious assume a worldview consistent with a double-aspect theory of the mind–body. The unconscious is part of the underlying level of reality that can result in manifest phenomena on the physical or the emotional and mental levels.

Marquis de Puysegur, a French aristocrat believed to be the founder of hypnotism (Ellenberger, 1970), carried Mesmer's magnetic forces into the realm of the psychological. De Puysegur equated this hypothetical "fluid" with unknown psychological forces, a concept that would carry through in modified form into Freud's work in the next century. There is an important connection here that must not be overlooked if as psychologists we are to understand the subtle relationship between what we now study as unconscious energies and forces and the physical body and the subtle duality inherent in the psychological traditions. The concept of the unconscious originates with Mesmer and de Puysegur's' borderline-physical substance that composes the physical body and all living things. As stated earlier, one way to conceptualize that which is both substantial with real physical properties and also proper to mental or insubstantial phenomena has been formulated by the Chinese concept of Qi. De Puysegur appeased the disgruntled feelings of the medical establishment by agreeing that this mysterious fluid did not exist—that is, that the phenomenon did not have physical properties or implications—and explained magnetic trances as a psychological phenomenon.

Here again one can clearly see the want in the Western mind to define the matter of study as either physical or psychological in nature. There is a notable discomfort when a physical substance may be related to or responsible for psychological phenomenon, or vice versa. The future of psychological thought rests on this distinction, which separates psychology from physical medicine. This discrimination between the physical and the psychological falls in line with the dualistic theories of Descartes, which underlie modern science. Inasmuch as modern psychiatry is defined as a field of medicine that strongly adheres to the principles of the natural sciences, an "unconscious" that implies a dual-aspect position on the mind–body problem might have been pressurized to be transmuted into an unconscious, which implies a dualistic position on the mind–body problem. In other words, Freud's later concept of the unconscious was conceived of as primarily biological, although the origin of the concept is both biological and psychical.

What Mesmer and de Puysegur began as the study of magnetic fields and fluids became known as *hypnotism* when physician James Braid coined the term in 1843 (Ellenberger, 1970). A crucial transition occurred here, which more poignantly illustrates the subtle duality inherent in the psychological traditions. Braid continued the adaptation begun by de Puysegur, who adapted the French theory of magnetism based on fluid theory, called it hypnotism, and postulated that the phenomenon was based on brain physiology. This translation of the theory from a romantic notion of a universal substance to a theory suitable to the positivism and scientific rationalism dominating the scientific and medical field made the idea accessible to Sigmund Freud in the later part of the century. As Tarnas (1991) stated, "with Freud . . . who throughout his life obsessively collected archaic religious and mythological statuary, the romantic influence was often hidden or inverted by the Enlightenment–rationalist assumptions that pervaded his scientific vision" (p. 384).

Modern depth theories of psychogenesis and illness are strongly linked to Mesmer and de Puysegur's early theories. The fluid theory and other magnetic terminology gave way to theories of will and other psychological forces, such as nervous energy, urges, and drives. Central to all practices of this time period is the concept of rapport (Ellenberger, 1970). Mesmer and de Puysegur thought of rapport as a magnetic channel—a phenomenon with a physical dimension—between patient and doctor, through which all therapeutic action occurred. De Puysegur saw beyond the physical realm to the psychological implications of this relationship. I find these theories of magnetic rapport interesting because I believe they live on in our collective myths about the nature of the therapeutic relationship and about a chemistry that exists in the therapy room and they inform our unconscious notions of who the therapist is and the role he or she plays. It was believed that the magnetized patient was ultrasensitive to the magnetizer; in other words, a certain "magnetic reciprocity" (Ellenberger, 1970) occurs, for which there is no scientific recipe or direct, tangible evidence. These early descriptions of the magnetic field gave way to the terms *transference* and *countertransference* in modern dynamic psychology (Ellenberger, 1970). If one does not forget that these ideas stem from the notion of a magnetic fluid or universal energy that composes both the manifest and intangible worlds, it follows that the "transference relationship" has not only emotional and mental components but, in conceptual origin, is also not entirely distinct from the physical world. Practically speaking, such an awareness might inform the clinician's attention to the subtleties of body language and somatic symptoms or events in the therapeutic process.

From the time the phenomenon of rapport or magnetic reciprocity was articulated, an erotic component was noted (Ellenberger, 1970; S. Freud, Masson, & Fliess, 1985; Grosskurth, 1991; Hughes, 1994), and I believe this speaks directly to modern experiences of the therapeutic relationship and abuses thereof in the acting out of sexual and romantic relationships. Perhaps the fear of such abuses contributes to the therapist's and theorist's wish to attend to the mental aspects of the transference relationship singularly.

Empiricism and Romanticism

It is relevant to consider the cultural and social movements of the times as they intertwine with and influence notions of the psychological nature of mankind. Here I explore two major social trends and the major thinkers within each, which influenced Freud at the dawn of his theorizing about the unconscious. These two general influences, empiricism and romanticism, are at odds with each other in fundamental respects and can be linked with the competing sensibilities of the sciences and the humanities. To comprehend Freud's own potential conflicts in ideology lends an understanding of the conflicts and struggles within the theory that Freud was to develop in regard to drives, his fundamental theoretical building block.

The 16th and 17th centuries marked the birth of modern science and empiricism. Here the scientist became the technician who ascribed to a formal system of knowing and verifying factual information. The birth of science and empiricism served to further the divide between the priest and the doctor. For the doctor to abide by the rules of factual evidence, he or she must divorce the medical practice from the realm of religious or spiritual beliefs. Here marks the beginning of a deepening chasm between the realm of the soul and the realm of medicine. The interesting contradiction for psychology is that, although officially a branch of science, it initially claimed to be a way of healing the mind and soul (Ellenberger, 1970). Today there is still disagreement about whether psychology is a science of behavior and measurable data or a discipline of subjective healing and meaning making, or both.

The contrasting and to some extent reactionary philosophical movement is romanticism, originating in 18th-century Europe, which values the irrational, emotional, and intuitive. The idealists, led by Hegel and including a subset of romantic philosophers such as Schelling, believe that there is a level of reality beyond the immediate experience of the senses, which can be realized through the value of intuition, imagination, and feeling:

> According to Hegel the telos was the complete realization of all that could be known . . . . Both schools maintained that humans were not just another form of static being like physical objects, but were dynamic beings that became. (Horne et al., 2000, p. 111)

Depth psychology works from the premise that it is a matter of *psychic* importance. Again, the implications of psyche are ambiguous but include a reference to the mind and the soul. Hence, the tradition of depth psychotherapy has a foot on either side of a great divide that began with the early separation between physical science and a romantic, soul-oriented philosophy that originally held its place in the church but was complicated by the political affiliations of the church with rationalistic scientific thought. The birth of dynamic psychology—that is, a psychology based on a premise of unconscious forces or principles—occurred at a time when psychology or the forbearers of depth psychology had not yet defined themselves on one or the other side of this split. Tarnas (1991) described Freud and Jung's depth psychology as

> a fruitful middle ground between science and the humanities—sensitive to the many dimensions of human experience, concerned with art and religion and interior realities, with qualitative conditions and subjectively significant phenomena, yet striving for empirical rigor, for rational cogency, for practical, therapeutically effective knowledge in a context of collective scientific research. (p. 385)

The field of psychiatry tended toward systems and classifications as the Baroque was declining and the Enlightenment was rising. The mark of medical psychiatry was symbolized by "a contestation in 1775 between Gassner, a devoted priest and exorcist, and Mesmer, the enlightened layman and would-be scientist" (Ellenberger, 1970, p. 195). Reason triumphed and there remained great opposition and suspicion in regard to ignorance, error, superstition, imposed beliefs, passions, and fantasy; hence Freud's hesitancy to be associated with any form of mysticism. As stated earlier, the ability to reformulate "magnetism" into a theory of "physiology" carried the romantic notions underlying the concept of the unconscious into a 19th- and 20th-century medical psychiatry. The question arises as to whether the new conceptualization of unconscious was in large part a reformulation that served to dichotomize the mind–body and mind–brain. It appears to me that this is true and that such a dichotomization must be investigated in regard to its implicit influence on the future of psychoanalytic theory.

The romantic movement is characterized by idealists such as Friedrich Wilhelm Joseph von Schelling and Georg Wilhelm Friedrich Hegel (Kremerling, 2001). These thinkers emphasized a reverence for and a felt connection to nature, the desire to penetrate intimate regions of emotional life such as dreams, parapsychology, fate, the valuing of symbols as real forces instead of abstract ideas, and an attunement with the processes of becoming and unfolding; here the "ideal man" is one who possesses intuition, inspiration, and a longing for something indefinable and extraordinary. Among the important notions of romantic philosophy are the sense of a meaningful continuity and unity between nature and human spirit and the notion that the unconscious is not just forgotten memories but a fundamental condition of humanity and the world—a notion that suggests a meaningful bond between humans and nature. For instance, romantic philosopher Gotthilf Heinrich von Schubert felt that humans originally lived in harmony with nature but severed this relationship to return to a state of unity in a conscious form. Such statements speak to the ways in which romantic philosophy can be roughly classified as understanding the mind–body problem under the umbrella of double-aspect theories discussed earlier.

Consequently, the nature of medicine during the romantic movement differed greatly from that of the Enlightenment and general notions of empirical science. The nature of illness was seen as more symbolic and with deeper meaning in relation to the whole of nature than a physical problem to be solved (Ellenberger, 1970). The basic conflict represented by the empirical versus the romantic is one of subjectivity versus objectivity and teleology or meaningful relationship versus mechanical causality. The question is whether the individual and the disease are meaningfully important in relation to a greater cosmos, in stark contrast to a strict interest in and adherence to natural laws that uniformly explain all activity and dictate all cures.

It is apparent that the conflicting currents in social and political thought might have created much tension. A period of combat ensued between science and religion, in which science was equated with atheism but major progress was made in terms of hygiene, anesthesia, and the like, which quite literally changed the biological experience of mankind. The experience of the body was less direct and more under scientific control (Ellenberger, 1970). It is my belief that the scientific advances of this time and the corresponding experience of control in relation to the body are extremely important in the next chapter of the ongoing dialogue between mind, body, matter, and spirit and the eventual placement—or displacement—of the body in the analytic framework. Increased scientific control over the body via alleviated pain and uncontrolled death allowed for a dissociation from the direct experience of the body, a move that must have eased much of the tension between romantic notions of a unity between humans and nature—which obviously would include the physical body—and the Christian adherence for and longing to surpass the desires and experience of the flesh. The medical advances of the 19th century did elevate Western man from the flesh in a very real way, thereby making real and attractive the Christian doctrine of asceticism and ascension. Such notions were reflected in both empirical science and philosophy. Such an example is Schopenhauer's idealistic idea that the "ultimate goal of human life was to escape, via asceticism, from the power of the will" (Horne et al., 2000, p. 111). The general sense of the modern era is that mankind can and ought to gain a measure of objectivity from the material world, the subjective world of the senses, and even the structure of perception and thought itself (Tarnas, 1991). Medical advances made this a more realistic achievement.

Schopenhauer is an important voice in the idealist stance, influenced heavily by Kant and Plato, who in turn influenced Freud (Bischler, 1939; Horne et al., 2000; Proctor-Gregg, 1956; Young & Brook, 1994). Although there is debate over the direct influence of Schopenhauer on Freud, there is a consensus in the literature in regard to the relevance of Schopenhauer on the zeitgeist of the age, and more specifically on Freud's concepts of the id and the unconscious. Schopenhauer and Freud share in a romantic trend that runs counter to the advances of empiricism and reductive pessimism: With Schopenhauer and Freud, the primacy of human reason was displaced by an acknowledgement of what Schopenhauer called *will* and what Freud called the *id*. Schopenhauer's concepts of the will as the primary influence on man and the goal of gaining mastery over the passions of the will are reflected in Freud's concept of the id and the ego's developmental task of gaining mastery over the instinctual passions.

This move restores a displacement of human reason that can be likened to early mythological worldviews. The presence of something irreducible to the mechanical laws of empiricism is restored by the idealistic move. In this sense, idealism is not reductive but denies God or an underlying intelligence of the universe. Rather, what underlies the phenomenal world is an essential drive to exist. This concept is present in Freud's models concerning sexuality and the sexual instincts. Although the term *sexuality* is used in "at least three different and incompatible ways . . . in the broadest of his three usages, the term 'sexual' refers to what Plato calls Eros: all the forces that seek life, build structure, and synthesize psychic material" (Young & Brook, 1994, p. 6). The idealist stance is in some ways a compromise between the reductive world of dualism or materialism and the inherently meaningful, symbolic, or subjective world of double-aspect theory. Idealism is not ultimately reductive; the will and the unconscious are essentially mysterious in the sense that they cannot be entirely grasped, controlled by, or predicted on ego consciousness. However, idealism does not give itself readily to teleology or cosmology.

There is a debate in the literature over whether Freud was a reductionist or a mind–body interactionist (Meissner, 2003a, 2003b). Many of these arguments revolve around the difference between Freud's metapsychology and his clinical theories. As well,

> Freud's theory went through many modifications. He had two main models of the mind. In the first model which was the most deterministic, he thought of consciousness as being impelled by the unconscious sexual instinct which he called libido . . . . By the time of his second, the structural model (Freud 1923), he had added aggression as a second instinct (Freud 1920). In this model, instinctual expression was brought under control by the super-ego, the repository of cultural attitudes . . . Although all these models were deterministic there was a teleological element implied in the concept of sublimation in that its activity, by implication, led to an increasingly more mature ego. More teleological still were Freud's concepts of identification as an outcome of the oedipal conflict, and of secondary narcissism which lead to the desire to live up to the goals of the ego ideal. . . . However . . . Freud was firmly opposed to all teleological concepts of God. He maintained that there was no divine reason, plan, or purpose in nature. Nor was there a lasting order in human nature. (Horne et al., 2000, pp. 112–113)

It becomes apparent that Freud's theory was at times in conflict with itself in regard to the underlying assumptions inherent in his concepts. The investigation as to his empirical and romantic influences in Chapter 3 suggests that he was indeed a man of his time. This time was one in which empirical and romantic notions about the world were intermingled as Western systems of thought struggled to clarify a worldview consistent with the advances of modern science.

These sometimes contradictory ideas revolve in part around core issues of causality. Such issues of teleology versus causality that were so potently activated in the opposing approaches of empiricism and romanticism are indirectly related to the mind–body relationship. A mechanical universe is ostensibly reducible to its causally related elements and necessarily implies the absence of teleology implied in romantic notions of an underlying order or intelligence, which humans can seek to know through the interior and subjective means of feeling or intuition. A materialistic approach is reductionist and negates teleology. Idealism is more flexible and contributes to what Tarnas (1991) called depth psychology's medium ground between empiricism and romanticism. For instance, Schelling falls under the general category of idealism in that the primary nature of reality is the intangible, the noumenal. However, a teleological organization can be thought to imply meaning or not.

Schelling believed that there was a unifying organization of meaning. Schopenhauer, on the other hand, also an idealist who believed the primary nature of reality is the intangible, deduced not meaning or purpose at the heart of the universe but rather the will to become.

As Chessick (1980) stated, although Freud's psychoanalysis was modeled on Newtonian physics, it has come to be thought of as a form of hermeneutics. This issue remains one of hot debate. Freud's foothold in the natural sciences and his early desire for a reducible theory of the mind and neurophysiology point toward a dualistic or materialistic worldview in which the body is either secondary to the mind or the raw material of the mind. The second option is more compatible with Freud's neurological training and is emphasized by his interest in the brain and the physiology of the nervous system. Such a notion implies a lack of meaning ascribed to bodily symptoms and adheres closely to ideas of mechanical causality.

Freud's later work, on the other hand, emphasizes the meaning of symptoms such as in the hysteric patient's repression of forbidden wishes resulting in psychosomatic symptoms. These notions do not equate with a materialistic view of the world but are more closely related to the idealist stance.

> For example Freud says that the ego, in order to reduce anxiety, represses a wish. These theories have a teleological flavor and as such are not very popular among scientists. Both types of theories presuppose a metaphysics. The descriptive theories presuppose a materialistic mechanistic positivistic theory, which based on a trust in the order of nature, that nature can be described mathematically, for example. (Chessick, 1980, p. 499)

Freud's later work therefore implies a belief that what is primary is psyche and that the physical world is a secondary by-product. As mentioned earlier, the idealist stance is flexible and can be developed toward different conclusions regarding the nature of reality and the nature of the mind and world. To deduce Freud's particular philosophical inheritance, I look to those who influenced him personally (in Chapter 3).

As Chessick (1980) summarized,

> there is a tension-ridden paradox running all throughout Freud's work in his wish that psychoanalysis be a rigorous empirical science and his being forced to straddle the natural sciences and *Geisteswissenschaften* (studies of the mind or spirit such as in theology and philosophy) together. (p. 505)

This dispute has not been resolved. I assert that individual practitioners or schools of thought must attempt to consciously engage this problem within their own theories in order to avoid the earlier mentioned unconscious assumptions and contradictions regarding the nature of bodily experience and the relationship between the unconscious and the somatic pole of experience.

POST-FREUDIAN AND POSTMODERN CONSIDERATIONS

Psychoanalytic theory has undergone substantial revisions in the 20th century. Gill (1994) discussed the sum movement within psychoanalysis over the previous century: "The changes from a natural science to a hermeneutic science and from positivism to constructivism embody a new metapsychology that supplants Freud's physicoenergic framework" (p. 155). Phenomenology, constructivism, hermeneutics, and intersubjectivity have deeply influenced psychoanalytic theory in the neo-Freudian era. This section underscores the philosophical shifts inherent in the major theoretical moves from Freudian drive theory to object relations theory and intersubjective or relational perspectives.

Postmodernism

The 20th century has entertained a core of philosophical challenges to the basic assumptions of the so-called modern mind. The shift in philosophical worldviews revolves around

> the deepening relativisms introduced not only by Einstein, Bohr, and Heisenberg, but also by Darwin, Marx, and Freud; by Nietzsche, Dilthey, Weber, Heidegger, and Wittgenstein; by Saussure, Levi-Strauss, and Foucault; by Gödel, Popper, Quine, Kuhn, and a host of others—radically magnified that effect, altogether eliminating the grounds for subjective certainty still felt by Kant. (Tarnas, 1991, p. 351)

The inescapability of relativism and the recognition of the deep subjectivity of the human mind ushered in a new period, often referred to as the *postmodern,* in which Cartesian certainty, a foundation for the modern confidence in human reason, is no longer defensible. Existentialism and phenomenology became the emerging trends in philosophical and psychological thought, which represent a recognition of the contextuality of meaning and the uncertainty of metaphysical propositions that speculate about the nature of reality beyond the perceptual field of the human mind; "there was no all-encompassing or transcendent or intrinsic 'deeper' order in the universe to which the human mind could legitimately lay claim" (Tarnas, 1991, p. 354). A review of the basic tenants of the postmodern sensibility forms a philosophical framework in which Chapter 4 may investigate contemporary shifts in psychoanalytic theory.

Tarnas (1991) named Friedrich Nietzsche as the philosopher who sits at the turning point of the postmodern mind with his articulation of

> radical perspectivism, his sovereign critical sensibility, and his powerful, poignantly ambivalent anticipation of the emerging nihilism in Western

culture . . . . What is called postmodern varies considerably according to context . . . . Out of this maelstrom of highly developed and often divergent impulses and tendencies, a few widely shared working principles have emerged. There is an appreciation of the plasticity and constant change of reality and knowledge, a stress on the priority of concrete experience over fixed abstract principles, and a conviction that no single a priori thought system should govern belief or investigation. It is recognized that human knowledge is subjectively determined by a multitude of factors; that objective essences, or things-in-themselves, are neither accessible nor positable; and that the value of all truths and assumptions must be continually subjected to direct testing. (pp. 395–396)

The postmodern sensibility is rooted in the sense of perspectivism, which finds its philosophical lineage in the likes of Hume, Kant, Hegel, and Nietzsche and culminates in the schools of pragmatism, hermeneutics, and deconstructionism.

Phenomenology

Abram (1996) called phenomenology "the Western philosophical tradition that has most forcefully called into question the modern assumption of a single, wholly determinable, objective reality" (p. 31). Phenomenological philosophy investigates the nature of experience and awareness themselves and thus initiated the turn toward subjectivity in the postmodern era. Phenomenological philosophy is the line of thought inspired by Brentano and carried through Husserl, Heidegger, and Maurice Merleau-Ponty, among others. It is these thinkers whose thought represents the shift in the philosophical foundations of contemporary psychoanalytic theorizing (Atwood, Orange, & Stolorow, 2002; Stolorow, Orange, & Atwood, 2001b, 2001c).

The phenomenological move has important consequences as to the meaning of the physical body. An investigation into the subjective nature of experience necessarily leads one to an awareness of the body; there is no human experience not experienced in a body. Abram (1996) summarized the new place of the body for phenomenology:

Husserl struggled long and hard to answer [the question] how does our subjective experience enable us to recognize the reality of other selves, other experiencing beings? The solution seemed to implicate the body— one's own as well as that of the other—as a singularly important structure within the phenomenal field. The body is that mysterious and multifaceted phenomenon that seems always to accompany one's awareness, and indeed to be the very location of one's awareness within the field of appearances . . . . In this manner, carefully describing the ways in which the subjective field of experience, mediated by the body, opens onto other subjectivities—other selves besides one's own self—Husserl sought to counter the charge of solipsism that had been directed against his phenomenology. (p. 37)

Phenomenologist Robert Romanyshyn echoed this sentiment:

> I do know that what links us to the rest of creation is the common field of the body, which, in all of its variations and permutations, is the locus or the site where we appeal to and address each other (in Johnson & Grand, 1998, p. 56).

Likewise, Abram (1996) noted that "the living body is the very possibility of contact, not just with others but with oneself—the very possibility of reflection, of thought, of knowledge" (Abram, pp. 45–46). Phenomenology at once counters the powerful stance of human reason and the primacy of objective science and opens an investigation of experience and consciousness themselves. This new investigation embraces the inherent subjectivity of being and of knowledge and in so doing returns the experience of the body to a place of value in the quest for knowledge and knowledge of being. Such a valuing of bodily experience has been absent in the whole of Western philosophy simply because the subjective nature of sense data is called into question by a system of knowledge that seeks objectivity above all.

However, Brentano and Husserl evolved out of the German idealistic stance, and Abram (1996) claimed that "Husserl was unable to drop the transcendental, idealist aspirations of his early philosophy" (p. 45). Despite the general move of phenomenology that found the locus of its study in the physical body, Husserl's philosophy contains a sharp division between the world of experience "inside" the body and that of the world "outside" the body and therefore fails to overcome the transcendent idea of an ego that is ultimately separate from the physical body.

> The body remained a mere appearance, albeit a unique and pivotal one, in Husserl's thought. The body was, to be sure, the very locus of the experiencing subject, or self, in the phenomenal world . . . but the self was still affirmed, by Husserl, as a transcendental ego, ultimately separate from the phenomena that it posits and ponders. (Abram, 1996, p. 45)

It was Maurice Merleau-Ponty who "set out to radicalize Husserl's phenomenology . . . [to] draw us into the sensuous depths of the life-world" (Abram, 1996, p. 44). Merleau-Ponty (La Phénoménalogie de la Perception [The Phenomenology of Perception], Merleau-Ponty, 1962; and Le Visible et L'invisible [The Visible and the Invisible], Merleau-Ponty & Lefort, 1968) applied Husserl's phenomenological methodology to the mind–body relationship.

> Merleau-Ponty rejected dualism and diagnosed a pervasive ambiguity in the character of human life. Attributing all consciousness to prereflective

sensual awareness of the corporeal, Merleau-Ponty tried to overcome the traditional dichotomy between objective and subjective elements of human experience. (Kremerling, 2001, "Merleau-Ponty, Maurice," para. 1)

Don Hanlon Johnson (Johnson & Grand, 1998) related his training in phenomenology to his valuing and attention to bodily experience in psychotherapy:

> I came to those sessions after years of schooling in the phenomenology of Edmund Husserl, Martin Heidegger, and Maurice Merleau-Ponty. From them, I had learned the significance of attending to the body as the manifestation of the self. And to the full manifestation of bodily experience, not simply emotional expressions, nor the mechanistic muscular pulls, but the unending intricacies embedded in the awareness of breathing, peristalsis, the movements of the little finger and toe . . . before, those body-respecting notions were for me more in the realm of hoped-for possibilities than *actualities of my living*." (p. 3)

Phenomenology lends itself to body-based psychotherapies in their inclination to view the living body as a primary and valid expression of the self and as a legitimate domain of knowledge. These psychologies and philosophies embrace the living, dynamic body above the objective body, which has been the study of science and medicine. Romanyshyn (1989) referred to this body, which has been "reduced to an inanimate thing" as the "specimen body" or the "pornographic body" (p. 174). Phenomenology is the philosophical quest to inhabit the body and the world; it is immanence in place of transcendence. Phenomenology is also the foundation of the major turns in contemporary psychoanalysis, because of the interest in the intersubjective nature of experience and of the self.

Such a stance takes the Western mind full circle toward its beginnings at the dawn of dualism. Merleau-Ponty's attributing of consciousness to prereflective sensual awareness of the corporeal is a harkening back to the pre-Socratic embedded-in-the-world consciousness that does not assume a fundamental separation from the physical world. This move is echoed by the philosophical shift toward dual-aspect theories regarding the mind–body problem mentioned earlier. The historical pattern is that of returning to a recognition of the relatedness and embeddedness of consciousness–world and psyche/soma. However, one does not return to the original state unchanged. Rather, the trajectory of the Western mind has been one of discovery. The nature of the mind, of experience, and of the material world has been "discovered" by philosophy, psychology, and science. The gift of dualism is that of reflexive consciousness. Dualism creates the chasm in which subject and object, psyche and soma, reflect one another. The danger is that the self identifies with a disembodied consciousness, or as Walker Percy said: "In the end the self becomes a space-bound ghost which roams the very Cosmos it understands perfectly" (Percy, 1983, p. 17). Phenomenology is the revision of knowledge for the Western mind; Phenomenology seeks experiential, subjective, embodied knowledge. Chapter 4 uses this basic understanding of phenomenology and intersubjectivity to explore the changing meaning of the body in contemporary psychoanalytic theory.

Philosophy Meets Neuroscience

Chapter 6 of this volume explores the currently evolving field of neurobiology, cognitive science, and attachment theory as they are impacting psychoanalysis. It is worth noting here the works of Antonio Damasio, a Portuguese-born behavioral neurologist and neuroscientist now researching and writing in the United States on both neurology and philosophy. His neurobiological research has focused on the biological or neurological basis for emotion and the role of emotions in decision making and thinking. Damasio drew and expanded on the works of Spinoza and the earlier mentioned double-aspect theory of the psyche/soma interaction to propose a solution to the mind–body problem that is not only philosophical but scientific. Damasio (2003) noted that

> until recently the mind–body problem remained a philosophical topic, outside the realm of empirical science. . . . Only in the last decade has the problem finally entered the scientific agenda, largely as a part of the investigation of consciousness. (pp. 183–184)

Because of the empirical evidence that mind and consciousness are directly dependent on activities in the physical brain and body proper, dualism has become empirically and philosophically outdated. Damasio (2003) noted that although dualism is outdated scientifically, "it is probably the view that most human beings today would regard as their own" (p. 187).

Damasio observed in his research that the *process of the mind* requires that the mind have at its disposal a body representation, drawn from sensory data, in which to ground itself. Without this grounding of the mind in the body, the human being falls into "mental disarray," and if extended, loses consciousness, such as in a psychotic break or an epileptic seizure. Damasio called this "pulling the rug from under the mind." Based on these empirical observations and the neurobiology that underlies them, Damasio proposed a perspective on the mind–body problem closely related to but expanding on Spinoza's double-aspect theory. Double-aspect theory supposes the mind and body are inherently unitary, composed of the same essence. Neurobiology and Damasio's model of somatic mapping provide a more detailed model for how such a unitary essence might manifest properties of a physical body and the processes of mind and consciousness.

Damasio's work and the related theory of *embodied cognition* or *embedded mind* have been used by psychoanalysts Fonagy and Target (Fonagy & Target, 2007) in the weaving together of attachment theory and psychoanalysis. The embodied cognition or embodied mind model supposes that the nature of the mind is determined by the form of the body and that all aspects of cognition are shaped and influenced by the body and the experience of the body. The embodied cognition model in philosophy references the "embodied embedded cognition" position in cognitive science, which states that intelligence itself can only exist in the context of a body that is in contact with the sensory world. This position draws on the philosophical history of Kant and Merleau-Ponty, a natural evolution from the phenomenological approach outlined earlier and underlying the more recent evolutions in psychoanalysis. It appears to me that the interaction of these fields of philosophy, neuroscience, and attachment theory within psychoanalysis provides a doorway into a cohesive theory of the mind–body system. However, a critical analysis of metapsychological principles, in light of this system, is necessary in integrating the sensibility of this model. Chapter 6 seeks to begin such an investigation.

CONCLUSION

In this chapter, I have laid out a philosophical and historical framework within which the history of psychoanalytic theorizing regarding the psyche/soma relationship can be analyzed. The history of philosophy reveals a general trend described earlier: Psyche and soma are separated, attempts are made to describe how the two are related via various forms of interactionism or monism. In the process, science learns a great deal about the functioning of the physical body per se, and philosophy and psychology gain insight as to the nature of mental experience itself. What is emerging in contemporary trends in philosophy and psychology reflects a reunion of psyche and soma; however, the new combination is entirely different from the first because it has gained the reflective knowledge made possible by the dualistic chasm. Phenomenology, mainly Merleau-Ponty's radical phenomenology, is the first philosophical turn in the history of the Western mind, which enlivens the physical world and bridges the spirit–matter divide set in motion at the dawn of Western civilization. As such, it is a useful backdrop and language system for an embodied psychoanalytic metapsychology.

Reflections as to the origins of psychoanalysis and the Western mind reveal the basic character of the Western mind and the inherent interplay between the history of philosophy and the history of medicine upon the birth of psychoanalysis. In particular, contextualizing Freud's theorizing within the historical context in which he lived reveals the global and subtle influences on the way he sought to reconcile the problem of duality in regard to medicine and psychology.

Freud lived at a time in which he was subject to the philosophies of the German idealists and romantics as well as the emerging power of Enlightenment-style science. The basic conflict is equated with the philosophical problem encountered by Kant in 1781 and is symbolized by the gap between Freud's metapsychology and his clinical psychology.

The conflict is represented also by the empirical, hermeneutic, and romantic inclinations:

> Nobody has been able to reconcile these apparently contradictory aspects of reality. How can one harmonize man as a machine, with even his mind as ruled by causal laws, and man as a joyous creature creating and reaching out for transcendence. (Chessick, 1980, p. 497)

These problems are relevant to clinical psychology because

> unlike science, philosophy examines not our conclusions but the basic conceptual models we employ and the kinds of concepts and ordering patterns that we use. . . . We are forced in the practice of psychotherapy to make certain philosophical assumptions and conceptions. These differ and conflict, and our choices will affect our clinical work. (Chessick, 1980, p. 496)

The particularities of Freud's theory and its development over time are explored in the Chapter 3. The following discussion begins with the understanding that Freud was influenced by a dualistic worldview in which both materialism and idealism were heavily employed to explain the relationship between the newly divorced psyche and soma.

Inherent to the conflicts of Freud's time in history is the pervasiveness of the belief in a causal universe and the distancing from teleological implications associated with religion and mythology of previous times. Conversely, the origins of the concept of the unconscious can be traced to the romantic roots of hypnotism, whose healing power was first assumed to be related to the borderline mental–physical properties of magnetic fluid. At every turn there are contradictions and unconscious conflicts of philosophical presuppositions and worldviews. Chapter 3 investigates how these conflicts in ideologies influence Freud's actual theories. Chapter 4 follows with an investigation of contemporary moves in psychoanalysis that is informed by the earlier understanding of the basic challenges to Western philosophy that have been instigated in the previous century.

3

PSYCHE AND SOMA IN THE WORK OF SIGMUND FREUD: THEORETICAL FOUNDATIONS

This chapter explores the founding concepts of psychoanalysis through the lens of the body and the mind–body relationship. The aim of this part of the research is to answer the questions: "What role does the body occupy in the founding constructs of psychoanalysis?" and "What were Freud's fundamental assumptions regarding the mind–body relationship?"

In Chapter 2, I explored Freud's cultural and philosophical influences and pointed to a conflict between positivistic and romantic worldviews, which each held some weight at the end of the 19th century. In this chapter, I investigate the particulars of Freud's psychological constructs, in an effort to estimate how these influences were reconciled in Freud's clinical and metapsychological thinking. There are several opinions as to Freud's stance on the mind–body problem in the literature: Barry Silverstein (1997) summarized the debate: "Freud has been portrayed as a materialist-monist-biological reductionist (Amacher, 1965), a monist–nonreductionist, emergentist (Parisi, 1987), and a materialist, dual-aspect monist (Wallace, 1992)" (p. 369). Silverstein's (1989) thesis was that Freud's approach was essentially dualist–interactionist (see also Silverstein & Silverstein, 1990). Though critics of Silverstein (Macmillan, 1997; Wallace, 1992) disagree, Freud himself stated that "if the present speaker had to choose among the views of the philosophers, he could characterize himself as a dualist" (in Nunberg & Federn, 1975, p. 136). Meissner (2003b) portrayed Freud as developing from a dualistic parallelism toward a dualistic–interactionist position. Meissner also concluded that there is ambiguity in Freud's thinking on this seminal issue. Particularly, the ambiguity and vagueness are in regard to the nature of the interaction between mind and body within Freud's varying interactionist statements. Again, one thing is clear: "Contemporary interpreters of Freud cannot agree on the meaning of Freud's statements" (Silverstein, 1997, p. 369).

Clearly, there is not a consensus in the literature as to Freud's position on the mind–body problem. This book emphasizes the trends in the ways in which Freud's ideas have been interpreted by psychoanalysts to address the primary aim of this book. In other words, one cannot come to an absolute truth as to Freud's conceptualization of the body in psychoanalysis. Rather, I am interested in how Freud's ideas have been generally utilized by psychoanalytic thinkers.

The literature can roughly be characterized along a spectrum between those who see Freud as a materialist–reductionist and those who see Freud as a hermeneutic scientist. Silverstein (1985) argued against the idea that Freud could be understood as primarily a neurobiologist who never abandoned the quest for an organically based psychology:

> Several historians already have rejected the "need to neurologize" theme in viewing Freud's work prior to 1898. Anderson (1962) notes that Freud had moved from an organic to a psychological explanation of neuroses by 1894. Stewart (1967) argues that by 1894 Freud saw psychological explanations of neuroses as separate from, but equal in dignity to, physiological explanations. Levin (1998) points out that from 1886 until 1894 Freud consistently emphasized psychological interpretations of his clinical data, but that he resorted to physiological speculations from 1895 to try to account for neurasthenia and anxiety neurosis, which appeared to him to have an organic base. But Sulloway (1979) takes the point of view that Freud remained a cryptobiologist because even though Freud moved away from concepts derived from reductionistic physiology after 1895, his theory building was significantly dependent upon concepts borrowed from organismic and evolutionary biology. However, none of these authors systematically explores Freud's early views on the mind–body relationship, nor do they consider the implications of Freud's early adherence to a mind–body interactionist position in shaping the direction of his theory building. (pp. 204–205)

Silverstein (1985) argued for Freud's development from an empirical scientist into a humanistic science of hermeneutics and that ultimately Freud's theories were best understood as hermeneutic rather than empirical. The common understanding of Freud in this light argues that he was not a reductionist but rather evolved from his early positivistic–scientific background to elaborate a humanistic and hermeneutic psychology based on a mind–body interactionist position. Central to this view is Freud's conviction that the mind itself possessed a property of intentionality; this idea is clearly incompatible with a materialist–reductionist stance, which would rather characterize mind as an emergent property of the brain. Here we see that Freud is distinguishing the physiology of the brain and states of consciousness attributed to the mind; the first understood in a deterministic manner according to mechanical laws and the latter not simply determined by mechanistic laws but rather engaged in a bidirectional influential process. Here one sees the evolution of a dualistic position closer to double-aspect theory of relationship: The mind is integrated with the brain "in a manner although not knowable, must be lawful" (Silverstein, 1985, p. 209).[1]

Silverstein emphasized that Freud's comprehension of psychosomatic phenomenon and later his theory of sexuality clearly rely on this assumption that the mind has a property of intentionality or will. This conception is clearly in line with a dualist–interactionist approach to the mind–body problem and is closely aligned with idealist ideas stemming from Freud's association with Brentano, "who rejected the view that psychology must be based upon physiology. . . . Brentano's influence may have been a decisive counterforce against the scientific materialism Freud encountered in his medical training" (Silverstein, 1985, pp. 209–210). Silverstein cited Freud's 1890 article "Psychical (or Mental) Treatment" as a clear statement on behalf of an interactionist view of the mind–body problem:

> The relationship between body and mind . . . is a reciprocal one; but in earlier times . . . the effect of the mind upon the body found little favor in the eyes of physicians. They seemed to be afraid of granting mental life any independence, for fear of implying an abandonment of the scientific ground on which they stood. (p. 284)

Hughes (1994) took a similar position to Silverstein and emphasized the fact that Freud himself actively distanced himself from philosophical problems in and of themselves and that in so doing he "gave a new twist to traditional problems" (p. 2). Hughes explored how the idea of the unconscious and a metapsychology based on the unconscious encountered the mind–body problem on its own terms; Hughes essentially concluded that Freud's early works, such as *On Aphasia: A Critical Study* (1891/1953) described the mind–body relationship in terms of parallelism but that Freud backed away from this position by 1915 in *The Unconscious*. Hughes emphasized that the evolution of Freud's thought was an evolution toward the deliteralization of his neurobiological scientific

[1]From "Freud's Psychology and Its Organic Foundation: Sexuality and Mind-Body Interactionism," by B. Silverstein, 1985, *The Psychoanalytic Review*, 72, pp. 203–228. Copyright 1985 by Guilford Press. Seleted quotes reprinted with permission.

background and into a humanistic science of meaning. Meissner (2003b) took a similar stance, although he emphasized the interactionist position in Freud's later work; this position retains a more direct interest and question about the actual body and its actual effects on or capacity to be affected by the mind.

Sulloway (1979) represented the strongest case for the ultimately reductionistic nature of Freud's metapsychology. However, Sulloway distinguished between mechanical reduction and organismic, evolutionary reduction to emphasize that, although Freud "did abandon his initial dream of devising a neurophysiological, and hence *purely mechanical,* theory of defense (repression) . . . he never abandoned the assumption that psychoanalysis would someday come to terms with the neurophysiological side of mental activity" (p. 131). Although the goal of the *Project for a Scientific Psychology* was to coordinate psychoanalysis with the standard of "hard sciences," physical–chemical reductionism, with the specific problems of defense and repression it became necessary to renounce a physicalist–reductionist prejudice in favor of organic and evolutionary explanations (Sulloway, 1979). This is a mild but important evolution in the philosophical and scientific foundations of psychoanalytic metapsychology as Freud understood it, for it portends a view of the mind–body relationship that underlies and influences all future conceptualizations. Sulloway contended that it is "often assumed, erroneously, that there is only one form of reductionism in science—to the laws of physics and chemistry. But in certain sciences, particularly the life sciences, there are two major forms of reductionism—physical–chemical and historical–evolutionary" (p. 131). The two forms support and supplement the other, for no one theory alone is able to explain the phenomenon of living organisms. Sulloway went on to argue that it was this historical–evolutionary reductionism that Freud ultimately leaned on to explain the etiology of the neurosis, the Oedipal complex, and the theory of sexuality.

As illustrated in Chapter 2, Freud's intellect was stimulated and influenced by contradictory forces. Here I draw attention to the language of Freud's clinical thinking that often appears conflictual and contradictory. Indeed, historians and analytic scholars have argued strongly for very different interpretations of Freud's ultimate stance on the mind–body problem and, consequently, the ultimate meaning of Freud's founding concepts of psychoanalysis. Here I attempt not to resolve the question but to explore the conflict itself to answer the primary question: What is unconscious within the theory of psychoanalysis regarding the relationship of mind and body? At this point I find it most likely to ascribe the fact that Freud's writing has been left open to vastly different although equally well-researched interpretations to the idea that Freud may have either maintained conflicting allegiances or lacked a certain clarity regarding his philosophical allegiances. It becomes clear as one investigates the evolution of Freud's thought that he began with his clinical observations—especially those of the psychosomatic symptoms of the hysteric—and attempted to build a theory that might explain living phenomena. He did not begin with a philosophical certainty but instead began with conflicting inspirations. I now turn specifically to the explicit and implicit assumptions in Freud's original ideas about the neurosis and, subsequently, about the unconscious.

FREUD'S CHRONOLOGICAL DEVELOPMENT

It is my position that because Freud's theories were developed over a period of nearly 60 years, during which Freud himself learned and developed, it is necessary to contextualize any of Freud's statements within the period of time in which he was writing. To comprehend the historical development of Freud's ideas is to comprehend the impetus for his changing views and allows one to tease out the arguments of the authors mentioned earlier.

Freud's Mentors

The discussion in Chapter 2 regarding the cultural and philosophical tensions of Freud's time can be underlined and detailed through an investigation of Freud's personal influences. The following is a summary of Freud's early personal and professional relationships. The story is told here and hermeneutically interpreted from the vantage point of the above questions; that is, what were Freud's biological, psychological, romantic, and scientific empirical influences, and how might they have influenced his early conceptualizations of the unconscious and of drives in relation to the physical body?

Ellenberger (1970) stated that "a knowledge of the first period [of Freud's career] is necessary for a full understanding of the origin of psychoanalysis" (p. 474). More specifically relevant to the investigation of the meaning of the body in the origin of psychoanalysis, Sulloway (1979) asserted that

> Freud, through the years, has become a crypto-, or covert, biologist, and that psychoanalysis has become, accordingly, a crypto-biology. It is my contention that the hidden biological roots of Freudian psychoanalytic thought must first be understood if one is to comprehend fully many of Freud's most extraordinary and controversial claims about the human mind. Significantly, these biological roots of Freudian thought were not originally as cryptic as they are today. (p. 3)

Freud's early area of study progressed from zoology to physiology, anatomy, histology, and neurology. Sulloway (1979) attributed Freud's

> basic scientific views to his studies with the foremost Viennese luminaries in the fields of zoology, anatomy, and physiology. During his crucial

years of discovery as a psychoanalyst (1890–1895), Freud therefore found it perfectly natural to place man as a biological entity at the very heart of his psychoanalytic system. But he was also highly ambivalent about admitting the true extent of his intellectual debt to the field of biology. Indeed, once he had finally achieved his revolutionary synthesis of psychology and biology, Freud actively sought to camouflage the biological side of this creative union. (p. 4)

Sulloway (1979) and Ellenberger (1970) both suggested that Freud's need to be seen as original and independent played a part in his later denial of the biological inspiration and implications of psychoanalytic theory. Biographical interpretations of Sigmund Freud (Ellenberger, 1970; Jones, 1961; Sulloway, 1979) and interpretations of psychoanalytic theory (Gill, 1994; Hughes, 1994; Ricoeur, 1970; Sulloway, 1979) differ in their understanding of the metapsychological meaning of Freud's early work in regard to the natural science of the body. However, all agree that Freud began with the intention of creating a *scientific psychology*, one based on a neurological model of the physical body and later described his theory as *pure psychology*. This research is concerned with the ways in which Freud's training, values, temperament and worldview contributed to the meaning of the body in the founding ideas of psychoanalysis. One begins to comprehend these influences in an investigation of Freud's early mentors.

The first 20 years of Freud's career were spent studying anatomy and neurology (Ellenberger, 1970). His first research in Professor Claus's Institute of Comparative Anatomy was conducted via microscope and required years of strict training aimed expressly at removing the bias or self-deception of the perceiver. The first important influence on Freud was a distinct belief in the objective observer who is separate from the subject of scientific study. Such a relationship between the scientist and the science was highly sought after and understood as the path to knowledge. Clearly, the values of empiricism and logical positivism lie at the heart of Freud's scientific indoctrination during the last 20 years of the 19th century.

Yet, Ellenberger (1970) cited the intermingling of Freud's romantic character with his scientific character. In fact, Freud's choice of vocation has been self-described as inspired by the 1873 reading of the poem "*Nature*, ascribed to Goethe" in a lecture by zoologist Carl Bruhl—"for many young men at that time, the study of medicine was a means of satisfying their interest in the natural sciences" (p. 430). Ellenberger also characterized Freud as belonging to the romantic Germany of Goethe and claimed that the key to Freud's personality lay in his "identification with Goethe" (p. 466). Ellenberger cited a number of Freud's behaviors that exhibited an intensely romantic disposition: Freud's exalted letters to his fiancée, his passionate relationship with Fliess, his identification with "the Byronic figure of the lonely hero struggling against a host of enemies and difficulties," (p. 465) the Wednesday evening meetings, the secret group of six chosen disciples, and the wearing of the secret ring. Most important,

> much philosophy in psychoanalysis can be understood as a revival of the concepts of the philosophy of nature and romantic medicine. . . . Both Goethe's idea of beauty and interest in art and archeology, as well as his concept of science with its search for archetypal patterns, can be found in Freud. Freud's literary style is modeled after Goethe's; the influence of Goethe can be found in Freud's predilection for certain words, such as "international" (in the sense of supranational). (Ellenberger, 1970, p. 466)

Ellenberger (1970) captured the mix of romanticism and empiricism in Freud in the context of Freud's repeated reference

> to the fact that the great poets and writers had preceded psychologists in the exploration of the human mind. He often quoted the Greek tragedians, Shakespeare, Goethe, Schiller, Heine, and many other writers. No doubt Freud could have been one of the world's foremost writers, but instead of using his deep, intuitive knowledge of the human soul for the creation of literary works, he attempted to formulate and systematize it. (p. 467)

The notion of systematizing intuitive knowledge is in itself a tension and speaks to the tension in Freud's own personality between that which is subjectively or intuitively known and that which is objectively, impersonally, and factually known. The earlier discussion of the romantic nature of the origin of the unconscious in contrast to Freud's conscious identification with the medical establishment highlights this tension as it existed at the dawn of dynamic psychiatry.

Freud was himself deeply affected by a handful of mentors who are worth mentioning for the sake of understanding the mental stance toward the world that Freud valued and worked within. Ellenberger (1970) and Amacher (1965) credited Freud's intellectual stance in the *Project for a Scientific Psychology* as stemming from Herbart, Fechner, Heinrich Sachs, Ernst Brücke, Meynert, and Exner.

> Herbart is credited with the "initial dynamic speculative philosophy," whereas the greatest part of its energetics to Fechner. The principle of inertia and the principle of constancy are very similar to what Fechner called absolute stability and approximate stability. Fechner had already connected the pleasure–unpleasure principle with the idea of approach and retreat from approximate stability, and he also equated quality of perception with the periodicity of the stable movement. These Fechnerian principles were later complemented by Heinrich Sachs with his alleged law of the constant quantity of psychic energy. (Ellenberger, 1970, p. 479)

Ernst Brücke became Freud's esteemed laboratory professor when Freud left Carl Claus early in his medical studies. Brücke studied in the tradition of esteemed German physiologist Johannes von Muller,

> who marked the shift from philosophy of nature to the new mechanistic–organistic trend inspired by positivism . . . Brücke rejected the kind of vitalism or finalism in science, but strove to reduce psychological processes to physiological laws, and physiological processes to physical and chemical laws. (Ellenberger, 1970, p. 431)

Brücke, Meynert, and Exner were reductionist and strove toward a scientific orientation in psychology based on a neurological model. Brücke "explained the entire functioning of the nervous system as a combination of reflexes" (Ellenberger, 1970, p. 479). It is also in Brücke's laboratory that Freud met Dr. Josef Breuer, who would later become the colleague with whom Freud would collaborate on the case of "Anna O."

Theodor Meynert headed the Psychiatric Department at the Viennese General Hospital during Freud's employment there in 1883. Meynert was a brain anatomist questioned as a "brain mythologist," a trend in describing "psychological and psychopathological phenomena in terms of real or hypothetical brain structures" (Ellenberger, 1970, p. 434). Although Freud's association with Meynert was short-lived, Freud followed Meynert's method of scientific investigation of "build[ing] a theoretical model and see how the facts fit in, on order to recast the model if necessary" (Ellenberger, 1970, p. 477) as opposed to first gathering facts and then deducing laws and generalizations. Meynert also shared Freud's description of "psychological processes in terms of quantities of excitation and of reflex neurology" (Ellenberger, 1970, p. 479).

Exner was another of Freud's neurological teachers, whom Ellenberger (1970) considered

> a synthesis of Brücke's and Meynert's systems. In the meantime, though, the neurone theory had appeared, and Exner discussed how quantities of excitation could be transferred at the junctions between neurones, where he believed that summations of excitations took place . . . He described emotion centers, particularly the pain, or unpleasure, center. Under the name of instincts, he described associations between ideas and emotion centers. He extensively developed his neurological psychology, giving explanations of perception, judgment, memory, thinking, and other mental processes. (pp. 479–480)

Here one sees that the basic language system of Freud's metapsychology, including instincts, pleasure–unpleasure, excitation, associations, and the system of energetics, were all drawn from his early training as an empirical neuroscientist.

However, the story is far from reducible to this fact. Another important early influence for Freud is Charcot, whom Freud first met in 1885 at the Paris Salpêtrière. Freud was enamored of Charcot, who was interested in hysteria and hypnosis:

> From the beginning Freud had been under the spell of Charcot . . . Freud left Paris on February 28, 1886, with the impression of having met a great man, one with whom he would keep in touch for the translation of his books, and who had provided him with a world of new ideas. (Ellenberger, 1970, p. 436)

It was in the context of the relationship to and idealization of Charcot that Freud first began to think about the physical phenomena of hysteria and to develop a system of distinguishing between organic and hysterical symptoms. Charcot was an anatomist and neurologist, a specialist in hysteria, and a strong proponent of hypnotism. Charcot's position as a famed neurologist of respected empirically based study is uniquely combined with an interest in things such as faith healing and a realization in his late career "that a vast realm existed between that of clear consciousness and that of organic brain physiology" (Ellenberger, 1970, p. 91). Charcot represented a unique blend of empiricism and romanticism. For instance, he founded two of the first journals combining art and medicine, and "Charcot was the man who had explored the abysses of the human mind, hence his nickname 'Napoleon of Neurosis.' He had come to be identified with the discovery of hysteria, hypnotism, dual personality, catalepsy, and somnambulism" (Ellenberger, 1970, p. 95).

Silverstein (1985) quoted a telling moment in Freud's personal conflict around these ideas: Charcot, in response to a small group of German physiologists challenging him on the point, "But that can't be true, it contradicts the Young-Helmholtz theory," stated that "theory is good, but it does not prevent things from existing" (S. Freud, 1893/1966e, p. 13). What is striking is the sense that Freud's empirical scientific background was a strict training to begin with what is observed and to then work logically toward the universal laws that most aptly describe the phenomenon. Freud appeared loyal toward this scientific tradition; yet his encounter with Charcot seemed to reveal phenomena—the hysterical symptoms—that were not entirely true to the anatomical and neurological laws he knew. These observations led Freud toward an attempt to extrapolate metapsychological laws that might explain hysterical symptoms.

Charcot and Freud share a scientific training in anatomy and neurology, which led both to a passionate interest in the neurosis via hysteria and in the relationship between the conscious and unconscious mind. It is also Charcot who had shown that there was a symptomatic distinction between traumatic paralyses and organic ones, demonstrated by his ability to artificially reproduce nonorganic paralyses with hypnosis. The same distinction was established between organic and traumatic amnesia. Freud explicitly credited Charcot with impressing upon him the psychogenic nature of hysterical symptoms: "M. Charcot was the first to teach us that to explain hysterical neurosis we must apply to psychology" (Freud, 1893/1966e, p. 171). Freud also emphasized that this concept was at first foreign to his identity as a physician trained in the Germanic tradition with its emphasis on a physiological interpretation of symptoms. It was out of Freud's relationship to Charcot that the notion of psychosomatic symptoms was born. In 1893, Freud concluded that hysteria "behaves as though anatomy did not exist or as though it had no knowledge of it" (p. 169) based on his observation that the cerebral paralyses of hysteria occurred at anatomical locations not proper to organic paralyses. These discoveries are important to the story of Freud's founding ideas about the body and the unconscious because they were the initial glimpse Freud had of the dynamics of the unconscious at work and, especially, because these symptoms were visible through the flesh of the body and the peculiar physical phenomena of hysteria.

The period between 1886 and 1896 marks a great turning point in Freud's career:

> Freud's scientific evolution during those ten years is shown by the fact that in 1886 he was mainly a neurologist who completely accepted Charcot's theories of neurosis, whereas by 1896 he was no longer interested in neurology, and after having given up Charcot's and Bernheim's ideas, had slowly come to elaborate his own system. (Ellenberger, 1970, p. 443)

Freud named this new system of psychology *psychoanalysis* and published the studies in *Hysteria* and *Project for a Scientific Psychology* between 1895 and 1896. Freud's thought had been influenced by the zoologists Brücke and Breuer as well as the neurologist Charcot in profound ways; however, he was now defining his own ideas and laying the groundwork for the new science of psychoanalysis.

Freud's indirect mentors include those who influenced him philosophically rather than personally. Although Freud spoke little of philosophy and did not acknowledge any direct influence, the philosophers most commonly linked to Freud include Schopenhauer (W. Aron, 1964; Bischler, 1939; Mann & Lowe-Porter, 1947; Proctor-Gregg, 1956; Young & Brook, 1994), Nietzsche (Faber, 1988; Mann, 1956; Southard, 1919), and Spinoza (W. Aron, 1964). It is through these links that we can deduce the particular form of idealism that was impressed on Freud. Bischler (1939) noted that Freud and Schopenhauer shared a "dynamic, energic and pessimistic conception of life . . . and their tendency to attribute ills to dominance by animal and egoistic instincts . . . born of an unconscious creator" (p. 88). Young and Brook (1994) affirmed these shared attributes and emphasized the Germanic 19th century themes of the will and the unconscious.

Sigmund Freud, like the field of depth psychology, was profoundly influenced by the competing sensibilities of romantic philosophy and Enlightenment style science. The romantic side of Freud's influence—Goethe, Bruhl, Schiller, Charcot, Schopenhauer, Nietzsche, and Spinoza—generally takes the soma to be a secondary property of the psyche, which is primary. The scientific influence, on the other hand—Claus, Fechner, Sach, Brücke, Meynert, Exner, and Breuer—tends to view the biological as primary. It is reasonable to conclude that Freud did not have a clear position on the mind–body problem or on the psyche–soma relationship, but rather that he sought a metapsychology and a clinical methodology that might explain the phenomenon he witnessed. In the process, he entertained dualistic, materialistic, and idealistic solutions. At times he may have combined opposing notions unconsciously; this is a question detailed later.

1885–1894

As noted earlier, the late 1800s were marked by Freud's encounter with Charcot. This was the time in which the science of the nerve was greatly expounded upon, hysteria was of major concern, and hypnotism was controversial. Freud's noted works prior to the *Project for a Scientific Psychology* (1895/1966d) include *Hysteria* (1888/1966c), *Hypnosis* (1891/1966b), *On Aphasia: A Critical Study* (1891/1953), *Some Points for a Comparative Study of Organic and Hysterical Motor Paralyses* (1893/1966e), and *The Complete Letters of Sigmund Freud to Wilhelm Fliess* (*Fliess Papers*; Freud, Masson, & Fliess, 1985).

From these works we gain a sense of Freud's early thoughts; these are the ideas he was most impressed by on the journey toward his culmination of work on the *Project*. Freud's interest in psychology and in the unconscious began with the problem of the hysteric and is marked in history by the event of Freud's time with Charcot in Paris from 1885 to 1886. It is of no small importance that the primary symptoms of the hysteric were psychosomatic, which impressed upon Freud the possibility that ideas lay at the heart of the hysteric's physical symptoms rather than organic causes (Silverstein, 1985). Relative to Freud's materialistic and empirical education, this was a revolutionary idea that clearly steered Freud in an entirely new direction; Freud wrote to his fiancé from Paris that

> Charcot, who is one of the greatest physicians and a man whose common sense borders on genius, is simply wrecking all my aims and opinions . . . when I come away from him I no longer have any desire to work at my own silly things . . . no other human being has ever affected me in the same way. (Freud et al., 1985, p. 196)

In 1885, Freud's "own silly things" were the endeavors of brain anatomy and neurology as guided by the Helmholtz school of medicine. Freud's encounter with Charcot, hypnotism, and the idea that ideas might cause somatic symptoms mark a decisive turn away from the contemporary science of popular medical training at the time.

Freud's work brought him head-to-head with the mind–body problem from the beginning. In *On Aphasia: A Critical Study*, Freud (1891/1953) "argued that investigators must distinguish what is psychical from what is physical" (Silverstein, 1985, p. 211). Freud was discovering, through hysteria, that there were psychic processes not under conscious control or not in the realm of conscious awareness and that these contents and processes played a role in symptom formation. Freud set out to develop a metapsychological model of the mind that could account for this:

> How could he discuss and describe unobservable psychical processes and distinguish them from what was physical? How did they interact to produce neurotic symptoms? In . . . 1888 [Freud] discussed the idea of a threshold of consciousness that might be crossed by a mental image. The mental image might be a sensory perception of an exterior object, or a perception of the achievement of a satisfaction of a need by means of an imagined movement. Thus, he saw that unconscious psychical process might be motivated, directed intentionally toward achieving satisfaction of body needs through motor actions. (Silverstein, 1985, pp. 210–211)

Freud was attributing a degree of independence to the psychic relevant to the somatic, and he also could not localize mind processes in anatomy, and thus the possibility for a monist reductionism fell out of reach. In addition, "he could not account completely for such phenomena as the quality of imagery, subjective meaning and intentionality, and conflicts over goals and purposes and their resolution through his knowledge of mechanistic physiology" (Silverstein, 1985, p. 211). It is indeed the psychosomatic symptom that first challenged a materialistic psychology and brought Freud directly to the heart of the mind–body problem, despite his reported (Ellenberger, 1970; Hughes, 1994) aversion to philosophical problems. Freud, in 1893, asserted

> that the lesion in hysterical paralyses must be completely independent of the anatomy of the nervous system, since in its paralyses and other manifestations hysteria behaves as though anatomy did not exist or as though it had no knowledge of it. (p. 169)

In other words, hysterical paralyses did not occur at the anatomically correct locations. This was a striking observation: If ideas in the mind can produce a symptom in the body, yet this symptom does not follow the known channels of neurobiology, there remains little possibility that mind is simply an emergent property of the brain and nervous system or, consequently, that a monist biological reductionist model could explain the neuroses. Seen in this light, both Silverstein's and Sulloway's arguments are initially intelligible.

Freud retained his allegiance to the scientific paradigm and in so doing expanded the scope of his theory to account for that which he observed and was ostensibly not reducible to neurobiological laws. From here, Sulloway claimed that Freud turned to the laws of evolutionary biology, whereas Silverstein claimed that Freud turned to hermeneutics as the basis for the building blocks of psychoanalysis.

By 1894, Freud, while continuing his work on *Project for a Scientific Psychology*, worked on the problem of anxiety and deduced that anxiety was at heart a physical phenomenon, because it occurred in patients with anesthesia or paralysis:

> [an] extremely important point became established for me. . . . Anxiety neurosis affects women who are anaesthetic in coitus just as much as sensitive ones . . . it can only mean that the source of the anxiety is not to be looked for in the psychical sphere. It must accordingly lie in the physical sphere: it is a physical factor in sexual life that produces anxiety. (Freud et al., 1985, p. 190)

He further concluded that anxiety was sexually related and began the basic concepts of drive theory: Physical sexual tension, if not discharged in a sexual act, builds up and either accumulates as physical tension (anxiety) or psychical tension. The term *psychical libido* came to designate the resulting psychical tension. Accordingly, the anxiety neuroses evolve when this physical energy cannot become psychical. The *Project for a Scientific Psychology* is largely an attempt to describe exactly how physical energy becomes psychical energy. In other words, as Freud abandoned a monistic position and moved toward a dualistic position, he began to clarify whether his now dualistic model of the mind was a dualistic parallelism or interactionism (Meissner, 2003b).

1895: *Project for a Scientific Psychology*

The notebooks that Freud mailed to Fliess in 1895 elaborating his ideas of a neurological model of psychological functioning, although never published by Freud himself, have become known as the *Project for a Scientific Psychology*. The manuscript is highly controversial among Freudian scholars, both as to the meaning of the work itself as well as to how completely or incompletely Freud abandoned the *Project* after 1896. The manuscript is essential to a conversation regarding Freud's conception of the body as it is closely linked to neurophysiological constructs and because these constructs form the early basis for drive theory. Meissner (2000) claimed that the *Project* "must be seen as an extremely important and seminal work . . . [it] determined the shape that psychoanalytic principles were to take" (p. 10). The *Project for a Scientific Psychology* is perhaps the best representation of Freud's thought at this potent and transformative moment in his career. It represents the profound influence of a reductionist natural science of neurology and anatomy, yet it still carries an aura of romanticism in Freud's fascination with a theory that would unite the mysteries of the psyche with the inner workings of neuroanatomy.

The primary principles originating in the *Project* are that of Q, the neuron doctrine, and the *constancy principle*. Q is a quantitative measure of neural activity contained in and transmitted between cells. The neuron doctrine is the idea that the basic units of the nervous system, the neurons, were "separated from each other yet in contact with one another through 'contact barriers'" (Meissner, 2000, p. 11). These *contact barriers* were confirmed by science and given the now common name of *synapse*. The constancy principle is modernly known as *homeostasis*; it is the property of the nervous system—and living systems in general—to keep themselves "free from excitation" (Meissner, 2000, p. 11). Neurons can then receive and move Q along neural pathways. Once a threshold of excitation is reached, neurons seek to discharge this energy in order to return to a range within the homeostatic range. "The principle of constancy serves as the economic foundation stone for Freud's instinctual theory" (Meissner, 2000, p. 11). Stimulus for the accumulation of Q does not arise spontaneously but can originate in the external world or from within the body itself (endogenous stimuli). This endogenous stimulus produces a demand on the body to discharge as an action, leading to the satisfaction of a physical need and a resulting return to neurological homeostasis.

> Thus, at the root of his thinking, Freud explicitly stated a theory of the nervous system as passively responsive to external sources of stimulation and motivated in terms of drive or tension reduction. His view . . . was decidedly Helmholtzian; that is, reality consisted of nothing but material masses in motion. (Meissner, 2000, p. 12)

The conceptualization of the threshold below which no energetic discharge was necessary was later referred to as a "stimulus-barrier, the primitive analogue of defense" (Meissner, 2000, p. 13). Likewise, Silverstein (1985) claimed that the neurological threshold of stimulation is akin to the somatic–psychical boundary, which, if crossed, results in the arousal of psychical libido and the consequent instinct-satisfying behaviors.

These concepts place the *Project* and the origins of drive theory in the framework of Newtonian energy theory and a deterministic neurology. However, the problem of qualitative experience and consciousness permitted Freud from resting here:

> How, Freud wondered, could a thought process construed in quantitative terms acquire the quality necessary to become perceptible to consciousness? (Consciousness he conceptualized as "a sense-organ for the perception of psychical qualities"—only by being highly saturated with sensory content could an idea attract consciousness to itself. (Hughes, 1994, p. 18)

This problem reflects Freud's confrontation with the mind–body problem. How could his neurological stimulus-discharge model account for either the perception of external reality or the origin of internal images, thoughts, and feelings?

> Freud solved this difficulty by appealing to the special system of perceptual neurons whose excitation gave rise to the experience of different qualities in the form of conscious sensations. . . . He was unable, however, to provide a satisfactory account of either defense or consciousness . . . he thus introduced into his system a major concession to vitalism, an observing ego. (Meissner, 2000, pp. 13–15)

Meissner and Silverstein agreed on the idea that Freud's observing ego assumes a quality of intentionality to the psyche, which defies a reductionistic science. The fact that the *Project* contains elements attributable both to reductionistic science and to vitalism opens the building blocks of psychoanalysis to divergent interpretations.

Sulloway (1979) believed that the *Project* was not simply a neurological document but

> indeed little more than a projection of previously formulated psychophysicalist constructs onto hypothetical neurophysiological structures. Hence it follows that much of the continuity between the Project and Freud's later theory of the mind stems just as naturally and inevitably from these constructs as from anything unique to the ostensible neuroanatomy of the document itself . . . that in the course of writing the Project, Freud did abandon his initial dream of devising a neurophysiological, and hence purely mechanical, theory of defense (repression). Inasmuch as this ambition was Freud's most immediate and practical concern in the Project, his long-range goal of developing a truly mechanical model of the entire psychical apparatus soon began to strike even him as "a kind of aberration." Still, he never abandoned the assumption that psychoanalysis would someday come to terms with the neurophysiological side of mental activity. (pp. 130–131)

Sulloway's comments represent the line of criticism insisting that the notion of psychical libido "fails to meet the most minimal criteria of accepted scientific methodology. Specifically, it is internally contradictory and lacks consistency; it presents a logically closed system that misinterprets metaphor as fact" (Meissner, 2000, p. 15).

Silverstein (1985), on the other hand, argued for the metaphorical and hermeneutic aspects of Freud's thinking in these early documents, which are ultimately meaningful to psychoanalysis. He argued that although

> Freud's initial motivation was "to see how the theory of mental functioning takes shape if quantitative considerations, a sort of economics of

nerve-force, are introduced into it (Origins, p. 119), Freud introduced the work by stating his intention "to represent psychical processes as quantitatively determinate state of specifiable material particles—the neurons are to be taken as the material particles (1985a, p. 295). Here the key word is *represent;* it is *psychical* processes Freud was concerned with and, metaphorically, he represented psychical processes as increases in the quantity of excitation flowing through systems of neurons, in the direction of motor discharge . . . Ideas were not actually neurons, rather the intensity of affectively charged ideas and the motivated, intentional quality of psychical processes could be represented *as if* they were the build-up of quantities of energy within specific structures. (p. 222)

Silverstein (1985) believed that Freud's clear statement against localizing mental functions in the brain spoke to the general trend of deliteralization in his thinking: "Freud used the available concepts of the 19th-century neurology to conceive the principles that governed his hypothetical neuronal apparatus, but he added something of his own to the model when he confronted the enigma of consciousness" (p. 223). Silverstein was referring to Freud's concept of the Omega system, a group of neurons to which Freud attributed consciousness. Freud asserted that a lack of consciousness would change the neurological system; consciousness was not a mechanistic by-product of biology.

Freud reviewed two available options for understanding the mind–body relationship. The first position viewed consciousness as an appendage added on to the physiological–psychical events, which did not in any way alter or direct these mechanical events. The second position was a double aspect theory, which viewed consciousness as the subjective side of the mechanical physiological–psychical processes, not something that might alter or direct them. Freud rejected both these positions and proposed one that he saw as lying between the two (1895). Consciousness was a variable that paralleled certain *qualitative* features of the excitation in the Omega system, but altered and directed the flow of excitation in unconscious, mechanical, parallel physiological–psychical process. This mind–body interactionist position is consistent with Freud's (1888) earlier position in which intentionality or will is attributed to psychical processes that could stimulate and direct processes in the mechanical sphere. (Silverstein, 1985, pp. 223–224)

Silverstein interpreted Freud's Omega system as a group of *metaphorical neurons* to account for that which did not appear consistent with a mechanical universe or a monist–reductionist mind–body solution: consciousness, the intentionality of mind, and the subjective qualities of experience. It is important that Freud began to explore the directive or intentional quality of mind or consciousness. This exploration is important and complicated: Is the driving or motivational force a biological one, or a psychic one? Or, if it is both, as Meissner (2009) and Damasio (1994, 1999, 2003) postulated, is the generative capacity linked to "something else"—which implies theological questions and concerns? These complications become more evident as later theorists struggle with the mind–body problem in metapsychology. Silverstein, like Hughes (1989), argued that Freud later settled on sexuality as the lynchpin to hold this theory together and to account for the connection between psychological meaning and physical energy—psychosexual drives were both physical and psychical.

In an 1898 letter to Wilhelm Fliess, Freud stated that he had abandoned his quest to elaborate an organic base for psychology but retained a conviction that one existed despite his failure to solve such a puzzle (S. Freud et al., 1985). Some argued that this marked Freud's turn away from empirical science and toward a hermeneutic science—and that psychoanalysis, as the result of this turn, is a hermeneutic science (Gill, 1994; Meissner, 2000). Others said that Freud simply felt the neurobiological sciences of the times were insufficient to fully elaborate the basis for a dynamic psychology and that while he directed his focus toward the psychic apparatus itself, he continued to utilize the energetic terminology of the *Project* because he had not abandoned the ideas he had seeded there (Sulloway, 1979).

For instance, *cathexis* was originally conceived as a neurological event that occurred when there was enough energy (Q) to excite a neuron into synaptic communication with another neuron or neural system (Freud, 1894/1962). However, Strachey's introductions to the *Standard Edition* texts continually emphasized the idea that Freud gradually dismissed and then entirely dropped the neurological basis of the concept:

> The system of neurons were replaced by *psychical* systems or agencies; a hypothetical "cathexis" of psychical energy took the place of the physical "quantity"; the principle of inertia became the basis of the pleasure . . . principle . . . Some of the detailed accounts of psychical processes . . . owe much to their physiological forerunners and can be more easily understood by reference to them. (Strachey, in Freud, 1895/1966d, p. xviii)

This trend toward a metaphorical use of the terms of the *Project* is common in the literature. However, the idea that an endogenous, somatic stimulus (i.e., an actual stimulus) was involved with instinctual drives remained in Freud's *Interpretation of Dreams*. Only by examining the evolution of Freud's theory can psychologists look back to the *Project* with some idea of what it has ultimately meant in the history of psychoanalysis.

1900: *The Interpretation of Dreams*

The Interpretation of Dreams is considered one of Freud's most important works; some scholars cite this work as the marking point of the origination of psychoanalysis. As Meissner (2000) pointed out, the psychic model that Freud presented in 1900 was, taken schematically, an elaborate construction based on a basic notion of a stimulus-response mechanism . . . The energic conception of these drives followed the basic economic principles laid down by the *Project*. They were elevated states of psychic tension in which the energy was constantly seeking discharge according to the constancy principle and the pleasure principle. (pp. 60–62)

Meissner (2000) went on to elaborate the basic assumptions in Freud's thinking that demonstrate the continuity between the *Project* and *The Interpretation of Dreams*:

> The first assumption was that of "psychological determinism," which held that all psychological events . . . are caused by . . . a preceding sequence of causal events. This assumption was derived from Freud's Helmholtzian convictions and represents the application of a basic natural-science principle to psychological understanding; but it was also reinforced by Freud's clinical observation that apparently meaningless hysterical symptoms, which had been previously attributed to somatic etiology, could be relieved by relating them to past, apparently repressed, experiences . . . . The inherent determinism of psychoanalysis is generally accepted as resting on such psychological causes involving motive and meaning, usually on an unconscious level. (p. 64)

Two other assumptions include that of unconscious psychological processes governed by laws and rules and that of unconscious psychological conflicts. Further,

> the final assumption of the topographic theory was that there existed "psychological energies" that originated in instinctual drives . . . It was suggested, therefore, that a . . . quantity of energy was involved in the psychological process responsible for symptom formation . . . The assumption of psychic energies served Freud as an important heuristic metaphor. The usefulness of the metaphor and its necessity as a basic assumption of analytic theory are currently in question. (Meissner, 2000, p. 65)

These four assumptions illustrate the basic compliance of Freud's topographic model and drive theory, which became visible in *The Interpretation of Dreams* to be relatively consistent with the basic principles outlined in the *Project*, namely, that of a psychic apparatus governed by Newtonian energetics governed by causal determinism and mind–body dualism.

Freud claimed that there are four potential stimuli for dreams: external sensory stimulation, internal sensory stimulation, internal somatic stimulation, and purely psychical stimulation (S. Freud, 1900/1961e, p. 22). The idea is that "during sleep the mind attains a far deeper and wider sensory consciousness of somatic events than during the waking state" (Meissner, 2000, p. 33); here we see the general correlation between the sensory experience of the body and the unconscious embedded in Freud's fundamental assumptions. Sleep lowers the stimulus barrier or the threshold between somatic–psychic content. The mind then has access to what is in normal waking states unconscious; this unconscious content is equated with the "somatic events." Somatic events are, as discussed above, the prepsychological (i.e., without the quality of consciousness) origination of psychological events. Meissner (2000) referred to dream content as "essentially a form of gratification of an unconscious instinctual impulse in fantasy form" (p. 50).

Further, Freud (1900/1961e) went on to surmise about a "singular aetiology for dreams and mental disease, whose manifestations have so much in common; for coanesthesic changes and stimuli arising from the internal organs are also held . . . responsible for the origin of the psychoses" (pp. 35–36). Freud's parallel between dreams and psychosis hinges on the soma: Psychosis and dreams are both the result of unmediated somatic stimuli. The underlying assumption is that the causal force in the psyche originates in the soma and that psychological life is attained when this somatic stimulation can become psychical.

Freud reviewed the current debate as to the origin and meaning of dreams. His detailed discussion of the debate revealed the inherent struggle between dreams as somatically stimulated process or as mental process, and consequently as meaningless or meaningful events in a psychological sense:

> Anyone who is inclined to take a low view of psychical functioning in dreams will naturally prefer to assign their source to somatic stimulation; whereas those who believe that the dreaming mind retains the greater part of its waking capacities have of course no reason for denying that the stimulus to dreaming can arise within the dreaming mind itself. (S. Freud, 1900/1961e, p. 64)

Freud pointed out that the popular description of dreaming as a somatic process "is intended to show that dreams are unworthy to rank as psychical process" (S. Freud, 1900/1961e, p. 78). There seems to be a general conflict between assigning meaning to dreams and the idea that dreams are a somatic process, that is, "not mental at all" (S. Freud, 1900/1961e, p. 96). Scientific theory appears to assume that mental acts by definition cannot be a somatically linked process and that a somatic process is not a mental act. It seems to me that this is an implicit assumption rooted in a historically inherited worldview that contains an essential splitting between psyche/soma and spirit–matter. The aim of this research is to name such implicit assumptions.

Toward the end of the book, Freud reviewed the debate in light of his conclusions:

> I have found myself faced by a topic on which, as has been shown in my first chapter, the opinions of the authorities were characterized by the sharpest contradictions. My treatment of the problems of dreams has

found room for the majority of these contradictory views. I have only found it necessary to give a categorical denial of two of them—the view that dreaming is a meaningless process . . . and the view that it is a somatic one. (S. Freud, 1900/1961e, p. 588)

Freud seemed to have decided that dreams are meaningful and primarily a psychological process; he found it necessary that dreaming could therefore also be a somatic process. However, a seeming contradiction appears when, a few pages later, Freud (1900/1961e) did not eliminate the somatic element in his dream theory:

Internal organic sensations, which have commonly been taken as a cardinal point in explanations of dreaming . . . have retained a place, although a humbler one, in our theory. Such sensations . . . provide a material which is accessible at any time and of which the dream-work makes use, whenever it has need of it, for expressing the dream-thoughts. (p. 590)

It appears that, on the one hand, Freud assumed that psychologically meaningful content was inherently not somatic and vice versa. On the other hand, it is as if psychological content used to be somatic and that it had become psychological. Psychological content arose from the somatic base; dream-work provided a sort of retrospective view into the relationship between the two.

Instincts (1913–)

If there is a defining idea in Freud's psychology, it is that of instincts or drives. However, the concept itself is debated among psychoanalysts as to its literal or biological relevance and its ultimate place in psychoanalysis.

The first issue of confusion is Freud's use of the German word *Trieb:*

The term has usually been translated into English, especially in the normative *Standard Edition,* as "instinct." One might ask why *Trieb* was not simply translated as "drive"? The reluctance to do this was apparently based on the fact that the drive concept had been rather widely abused in behavioral sciences. There was presumably a wish on the part of psychoanalytic theorists to maintain some distance between their own basic concepts and the notions of drive that were used by behavioral theorists. Moreover, Freud assumed that the *Triebe* were based on innate givens; that is, preformed biological potentials present at birth. This aspect of the concept was reflected in the English term "instinct." Nevertheless, in an attempt to avoid the semantic pitfalls involved in the term "instinct," general usage currently prefers to use the term "instinctual drive" to express the Freudian notion of *Trieb.* (Meissner, 2000, pp. 75–76)

Classical drive theory is based on the topographic model, which in turn derives from the *Project.* The topographic model is governed by a basic dualism between "the forces and contents of the mind that were viewed as repressed and unconscious and those forces and mental agencies that were responsible for the repression" (Meissner, 2000, p. 70). Freud's investigation of the former preceded his investigation of the latter; the study of instincts and the idea of the id preceded Freud's ego psychology. Consequently, Freud's early writings are much more concerned with the soma via the somatic source of instinctual drives. This historical progression is often interpreted as Freud's development away from the natural sciences and toward a hermeneutic psychology (Ricoeur, 1970; Silverstein, 1985).

Meissner (2000) outlined the use of the term *instinct* by animal behaviorists as a

> Pattern of species-specific behavior that is based mainly on the potentialities determined by heredity and is therefore considered to be relatively independent of learning . . . Such usage resisted successful physiological explanation and tended to introduce a strong teleological connotation . . . Freud adopted this usage unquestioningly, but its validity has been questioned even by strong proponents of instinctual theory among animal behaviorists. (p. 74)

Freud's adoption of a biologically based notion of instinct ties his psychological theory to the somatic dimension. The question remains as to the nature of the connection between the somatic and psychological; the degree to which Freud emphasized a psychological tie to the *actual* versus the *metaphorical* body is ambiguous in his own writings and widely debated by psychoanalysts. Meissner (2000) addressed this issue:

> The instinct, then, is a psychic representation of internal stimuli, and the stimuli represent physiological needs. The physiological needs, as for example hunger, which can be described in such physiological process terms as lowering of blood sugar or emptying of the stomach, cannot be confused with the psychic representation, whether that representation be conscious, preconscious, or unconscious. Freud's notion of instinct, however, embraces all of these in varying degrees and with varying emphasis. (p. 75)

Freud's notion of instinct was rooted in a physiological model; he adopted this concept of instinct but transformed it in his own formulation. In 1915, he said that

> an "instinct" appears to us as a concept on the frontier between the mental and the somatic, as the psychical representative of the stimuli originating from within the organism and reaching the mind, as a measure of the demand made upon the mind for work in consequence of its connection with the body. (Freud, 1915/1961b, pp. 121–122)

This description appears to draw directly from the fundamental model of dynamic psychiatry proposed in the *Project*. This model proposes that there are energetic forces present in the soma and that these forces exert a pressure on the mind. Psychological life occurs when this energetic force is transformed into mental content, which is the mind is able to respond to the somatic pressure in order to make cognizant steps toward tension-reducing activities. The instinct became the concept for this frontier between psyche and soma; instinctual drive embodies the process by which somatic process become psychological. The literature converges around the idea that Freud felt that there was not enough scientific knowledge to describe this process of transformation between psyche and soma; he nonetheless maintained this conceptual model. At the heart of Freudian metapsychology and therefore at the heart of psychoanalysis lies the idea that the causal or driving energy of human life exists in the soma; psychological life is presumed, in the most basic sense, to arise as the energetic force of the soma exerts a "pressure" on the mind.

There are numerous philosophical and scientific problems with this formulation (Meissner, 2000; Sulloway, 1979). Psychoanalysis generally responds to the lack of clarity around the process of transformation from somatic to psychological by utilizing this model as a metaphorical as opposed to an actual transformation. Nonetheless, this basic assumption of a "soma–psyche hierarchy" underlies Freud's most fundamental ideas: Psychological life is a more advanced form of somatic life, and psychological or psychosomatic problems arise when the "advance" from soma to psyche is inhibited.

Psychosexuality (1905–)

From the publication of "Three Essays on Sexuality" in 1905 (Freud, 1905/1961f) to the end of his career, the idea of psychosexuality became a theoretical lynchpin for Freudian psychology.

> For when he encountered hysterical patients, that is, patients suffering from somatic symptoms for which he could find no organic cause, he could not duck the mind–body problem. He reached an impasse. He . . . turned to sexuality and reconceptualized it as psychosexuality. In similar fashion, when in his clinical practice he tried to sort out the value of memories, how the mind appraised the external world and stored that appraisal, he came up against epistemological riddles. A standoff ensued. Once again psychosexuality . . . proved the fruitful approach. (Hughes, 1994, p. 2)

The idea that somatic energy exerts a demand on the mind for psychological work was retained and solidified in a way that linked the mind and the body for psychoanalysis. "Freud rethought the mind–body problem and included the body as a source of meaning in the unconscious . . . he rethought the subject–object problem and included the object world again as a source of meaning in the unconscious" (Hughes, 1994, p. 2). Psychosexuality is both a somatic and a psychological concept that most directly accounts for the role of the body in Freud's clinical theories. In *Psychoanalytic Terms and Concepts* (Moore & Fine, 1990), published by the American Psychoanalytic Association, psychosexuality and erotogenicity are described as firmly anchored in the realm of the actual body:

> Freud postulated erotogenicity as a quantitative factor, capable of increase or decrease and displacement from one part of the body to another. Perceptions, feelings, ideas, or actions may, because of this erotogenicity— that is, because of their readiness to be a source of sexual excitation— activate the sexual system. Such excitement spreads to other mental and biological systems, leading to states of mind . . . [that] are colored by sensuality. (p. 68)

Judith Hughes (1994) explored in depth Freud's case histories in the development of this concept. Freud's abandonment of seduction theory, the role of fantasy, the development of conversion theory, and the advent of the structural model all played a role in the historical development of psychosexuality.

> Freud may have dreamed of running a causal sequence from the soma to the psyche, and he may have wished to discover the solid organic ground for his psychology, but in waking life he was obliged to admit that he could not fit together the organic and the psychological. Paradoxically, his turn to sexuality had the effect of reinforcing his commitment to the psychical. (What other bodily process so readily suggested that a "demand" was being "made upon the mind for work?") Freud's view of sexuality as psychosexual, as a linkage between somatic sexual excitation and psychical sexual ideas . . . made possible a crucial step: his conceptualization of the erotogenic. An erotogenic zone was initially bound up with something somatic, with a vital bodily function; subsequently it became separated from bodily needs; it became an archive of experiences of satisfaction. . . . The body had ceased to be merely physiological. . . . The erotogenic . . . could endow the ego with more than one meaning. (pp. 164–165)

The erotogenic linked the mind and body because it was both physiological and meaningful. The above definition of psychosexuality links the psyche to the soma in a rather literal and causal sense. An actual energy of the soma is assumed to act upon the mind. On the other hand, authors such as Hughes (1994) claimed that psychosexuality links the mind and body not causally but metaphorically; Hughes emphasized the metaphorical meaning that the soma can take on in response to psychosexual development to foster the argument that Freud developed from a natural scientist to a hermeneutic one in the 20th century.

It appears that the concept of psychosexuality references both the actual soma and the psychological meaning associated with the metaphorical somatic—that is, the meaning that somatic symbols take on in the psychological world. Psychoanalytic thought converges around the idea that the soma can take on metaphorical meanings relevant to the psyche. However, the place of the actual soma in psychoanalytic theory is less clear. As discussed earlier, many writers tend toward the idea that the "pressure" exerted on the mind from the body is a metaphorical one rather than the Newtonian energetic one arising from actual physiological needs or neurological processes.

The struggle between the actual and the metaphorical body is illustrated in Freud's attempts at explaining psychosomatic symptoms. Conversion theory, which Freud entertained from 1894 to the early 1900s, supposes that mental contents split from consciousness become converted into physical expressions rather than psychological ones. By 1909, Freud regarded hysterical conversion as a "'leap from a mental process to a somatic innervation' that could 'never be fully comprehensible.' By 1926 he had come to the conclusion that this incomprehensibility offered 'a good reason for quitting such an unproductive field without delay'" (Hughes, 1994, p. 34). Although Freud apparently gave up on the comprehension of this mysterious leap from mental to somatic (or visa versa), the notion of this very leap, embedded in conversion theory, had begun a correlation between the body and what would come to be defined as *unconscious*. As Hughes (1994) stated: "The invitation had been indirect, the kind of invitation one extends to the significant other of an intended guest" (p. 35).

In other words, the incomprehensibility of the process by which somatic energy might become psychological led Freud away from the actual body toward the metaphorical body. Hughes pointed out that although conversion theory itself was abandoned, an important implicit assumption of psychoanalysis had been laid down: The body had become equated with the unconscious. I believe that it is precisely these "indirect" or inadvertent associations that have misplaced psychoanalytic comprehension of the body.

Conversion theory follows directly from the basic suppositions of the topographic model: A qualitative and somatically existent energetic force exerts a pressure on the mind to transform this energy into psychological energy or content. The process can proceed in reverse, whereby it is named *defense*: Psychological content intolerable to the organization of consciousness can be repressed back into the somatic realm. The underlying model is the Newtonian energetic model outlined in the *Project*, which entertains a somatic–psychical barrier on either side of which a qualitative energic force can exist with differing qualities—somatic or psychical. By 1926, Freud had become frustrated with his inability to adequately back up such a model with a clear description of the transformation implied. The question remains as to whether he ever replaced this model, and if so, which of the assumptions in the old model were carried over in to the new?

1920–1939: Ego Psychology

In *Beyond the Pleasure Principle* (S. Freud, 1920/1966a) and *The Ego and the Id* (S. Freud, 1923/1961d) Freud's structural theory was elaborated and presumed to replace the topographic model. The topographic model is described by Moore and Fine (1990) as referring

> to the description of the relative positions and elevations of a place or region. Using the topographic view, Freud characterized mental phenomena according to their relationship to consciousness. He postulated three regions, neither anatomical nor spatial, but metaphorically arranged in the "psychic apparatus" on a vertical axis from the surface to the depths. (p. 196)

This model is that referred to by Meissner (2000) as the basic idea that the mind is a dynamic play between the repressed and the repressing. The structural model is slightly more complex yet not entirely a departure from the topographic view, which

> has been supplemented and largely overshadowed by a second topography, the tripartite model (id, ego, superego) of Freud's 1923 structural theory . . . the topographic model continues to influence thought and technique in that most of the conflict analyzed is related to unconscious ideas, and interpretation proceeds from the surface to the depths. (Moore & Fine, 1990, p. 196)

To examine the evolution from the topographic to the structural from the vantage point of the body, however, reveals a sense of Freud's having become a step removed from the soma. Although the topographic model tends to be interpreted metaphorically in reference to the "depths" versus the "surface" of consciousness–unconsciousness, there is a historical precedent and assumption based on the notion of somatically originating instincts, which tends to correlate the unconscious and the depths with the somatic. The structural model, on the other hand, claims that not only the id, which "is compromised of the psychic representations of . . . instinctual drives" (Moore & Fine, 1990, p. 186) can be unconscious, but that portions of the ego or superego may be unconscious as well. This model lends itself less directly to the correlation between the somatic and the unconscious.

Freud's *Ego and the Id* (1923/1961d) explores the ramifications of the ideas set forth in the 1920 text. In this work the ego becomes the primary focus of interest and may be said to be the founding work for ego psychology (Meissner, 2000). However, Strachey pointed out in the introduction that "the forerunners of the present general picture of the mind had been successively the 'Project' of 1895, the seventh chapter of *The Interpretation of Dreams* and the metapsychological papers of 1915" (in Freud, 1923/1961d, p. xxix).

Freud's first chapter began with the idea that "there is nothing new to be said" (p. 2) regarding consciousness and unconsciousness. He reiterated that psychoanalysis "is obliged to regard consciousness as a quality of the psychical" (p. 3). In other words, what is conscious is necessarily psychical. What is psychical, however, can be either conscious or unconscious. The id, the psychic representations of instinctual drives, is psychical. It is the unconscious element of the psychical that contains representations of the instinctual drives.

This leaves me to wonder, what has become of the actual soma in Freud's theory? Contemporary Freudians continue to speak of instinctual drives as a demand on the mind from the body (Meissner 2000; Mitchell & Black, 1995; Moore & Fine, 1990; St. Clair, 2000). Freud himself spoke of the ego's function as controlling "the discharge of excitations into the external world" (S. Freud, 1923/1961d, p. 8) and went on to describe "internal perceptions [which] yield sensations . . . in the deepest strata of the mental apparatus. Very little is known about these sensations and feelings . . . They are more primordial, more elementary, than perceptions arising externally" (pp. 14–15). Freud had abandoned his attempts to describe the path from the nervous system to the psychic apparatus, yet he continued to utilize the terminology and the general precepts outlined in the *Project* through the end of his career. The earlier-mentioned authors who included the notion of instinctual drives in their understanding of Freud typically emphasized the transition from the actual to the metaphorical to explain this aspect of Freud. This interpretation suggests that the body is present in classical Freudian theory only insofar as the body can take on metaphorical meaning for the psyche. This is in line with the claims that Freud evolved from a natural scientist to a hermeneutic one and that psychoanalysis is primarily a hermeneutic investigation of psychological meanings (Hughes, 1994; Ricoeur, 1970).

I then wonder about the place of the actual body for psychoanalysis and about the potential for a psychology to become disembodied if it loses a tie to the actual body that a human being must actually live in. I now turn to a reflection on the tension between the psychological capacity to symbolize and the dynamism of the actual or literal body in the durational themes of Freud's theory.

THEMATIC CONSIDERATIONS

I turn now to two thematic considerations in the works of Freud, which cannot be isolated in time but which appear to pervade the evolution of Freud's thought. It appears to me that these two themes—the idea that words can form a link between the unconscious and the conscious, and the idea of displacement or projection—portray the existence of certain philosophical assumptions regarding the body within Freudian theory and are therefore worthy of examination.

Words as the Link Between Unconscious and Conscious

In 1891, Freud wrote that "the word itself was a complex presentation constituted of auditory, visual, and kinaesthetic elements" (1891/1966b, p. 73). We know that in the 1890s Freud conceptualized sense data as having a quantitative and energetic quality in the nervous system of the body. He also conceptualized consciousness as a quality proper to the psychical. These ideas raised the question of how sensory stimulus in the nervous system became psychical. The idea that words were composed of kinaesthetic elements provided a link between the soma and the psyche. By giving words to sense data, perceptual stimuli could become available to consciousness. Hughes (1994) recognized the role of words for Freud throughout his career as flowing directly from the neurologist mentor Jackson, who "made the difference between consciousness and unconsciousness hinge on the word" (p. 18). Indeed, this hinge location of words was employed in the *Project* as he struggled to conceptualize how data constructed of quantitative qualities might "acquire the quality necessary to become perceptible consciousness" (p. 18). Freud was conceptualizing consciousness as the sense organ for the perception of psychic qualities; the sense organ was assumed to register these psychic qualities if a threshold of saturation with sensory content was reached, essentially attracting consciousness to itself. This capacity to "attract consciousness" is fundamental in *The Interpretation of Dreams:* Just as words link sense data with psychically registered thing presentations, day residues can attract unconscious wishes and thereby make them accessible to the consciousness of the dreamer. Here we see Freud developing a metatheory for the means by which unconscious and conscious interact, side by side with a metatheory for how sensory and psychical interact. The two are interwoven in a very particular and telling manner. In the topographic model, the word provides the link between the unconscious and the conscious—which seems to be correlated to the soma and the psyche to the extent that the kinaesthetic elements of words include perceptual sense data of the neural system.

This idea remained intact as Freud moved into the structural model. In 1923, Freud answered the question, "'How does a thing become conscious' . . . and the answer would be: 'Through becoming connected with the word-presentations corresponding to it'" (1923/1961d, p. 12). It seems that the role of the word in forming a link between what is unconscious and what is conscious remained intact throughout Freud's career.

However, the evolution from the topographic to the structural model lends itself less to simplifications regarding the body. In the topographic model, the basic conflict was between the conscious and the unconscious; in the structural model, the basic conflict was also within the unconscious itself—between unconscious aspects of the ego, superego, and id (Mitchell & Black, 1995). The topographic model historically correlates with Freud's emphasis on the nervous system and the qualitative nature of sensory stimuli. In this model, words are a borderline concept between soma and psyche and between unconscious and conscious.

Freud's abandonment of a biological basis for his psychology seems to have had the net effect of describing the unconscious as less directly associated with the soma. By the 1920s, the unconscious was conceived of as psychical content without the quality of consciousness, rather than simply somatic elements. Words are still assumed to be involved in the transformation between unconscious and conscious; yet there is a deemphasis on the kinesthetic role of words, which corresponds to the deemphasis on the strict correlation between the psychic and the conscious. However, the implicit assumption is that the body is itself entirely unconscious, and this assumption appears to remain embedded in psychoanalytic theory. In other words, the somatic is correlated with the unconscious, whereas the psychic is correlated with the unconscious and the conscious, depending on whether psychic contents have reached a threshold of perception.

It can be said that a basic assumption of psychoanalytic theory and practice is that, by putting words to experience, we endow that experience with the quality of consciousness and it becomes a psychic perception. Freud's earlier models speak directly to a threshold around which a transformation between unconscious and consciousness occurs, and he associates words with this transformation. Drive theory explicitly correlates the soma with the unconscious, as the requisites of drives are somatic events. The added complexities of the structural model broaden the imagined contents of the unconscious but do not negate the primary assumption that the somatic dimension is entirely unconscious.

What is interesting about words in regard to the body is Freud's initial observation that words themselves are composed of kinesthetic elements. The spoken word is itself a threshold between symbolization and actual experience: Spoken words have a sensory sound composed of a kinesthetic vibration that reverberates in the physical, sensual body, and they are signifiers for mental contents. In this sense words occupy a unique role in the human capacity for consciousness, reflection, and symbolization of the literal or actual world of sensory experience.

However, words themselves can move from the spoken realm to the written realm and thereby attain a quality of abstraction from the literal world. Abram (1996) argued that the modern evolution toward the use of the written word results in a reliance on abstractions and an abandonment of a qualitatively essential element of our human sensibilities. That is to say that a move too far into the symbolic capacities of the human psyche can obscure or render invisible the actual nature of the experience we are symbolizing. To grasp the nature of this qualitative shift, I turn to an exploration of this embedded-in-the-world quality of experience gained through the capacities of the senses themselves.

Metaphorical Versus Actual Space

One of Freud's first moves away from a literal science of psychology was his abandonment of equating brain anatomy with psychological functioning. This move away from anatomy and toward metaphor is a recurrent theme in Freud's evolution. As early as 1888, Freud was diverging from two popular scientific trends: to localize conscious anatomically and to equate psychic functioning with purely conscious activity. Thus, Freud was obliquely confronting the mind–body problem. His leaning away from localization of consciousness within the nervous system foreshadows the metapsychological development of the topographic model, in which related levels of consciousness are assigned to psychic "localities" that do not correspond to "actual space." Freud did, however, rely on physical metaphors to represent this psychic "space." (Silverstein, 1985).

The move from an anatomical model to a hypothetical psychical apparatus described metaphorically is again recognized as a developmental theme in the history of psychoanalytic thinking. Yet, as Milton Horowitz (in Wallerstein & Applegarth, 1976) pointed out, "quantitative assumptions are so embedded in analytic theory that they cannot be abolished without undue violence to the theory as a whole" (p. 648). This paper, which summarized a panel entitled "Psychic Energy Reconsidered," held at the fall meeting of the American Psychoanalytic Association in New York City in December 1975, captured the theoretical debate regarding quantitative versus qualitative and mechanistic versus metaphoric uses of bodily terms. A central theme in the conversation was whether energetic models are actually metaphorical models, and if so, what are energy and psychic space metaphors of?

I believe this is a relevant point, one that leads me to question the ideas of displacement and projection as they pertain to the body. Both concepts involve the metaphorical movement of psychic material onto another person or object. For example, a fear of sexuality can be displaced onto a fear of snakes, or one's longing for intimacy can be projected onto another person. The idea that a "psychical location" can exist independent of an anatomical location in time and space is inherent in the concepts of displacement and projection. Projection is a displacement of psychical contents incongruent to the organization of consciousness into a "metaphorical space," in the sense that it is "located" outside of consciousness. Central to the psychodynamic thinking about psychosomatic symptoms is the idea that these contents, which are not "made psychical," can become located in the metaphorical "space" of the body in such a way that the content is expressed by a physical symptom in the anatomical location (e.g., McDougall, 1989).

I find that this idea raises some interesting considerations best illustrated by viewing Freud's ideas in the larger historical and philosophical contexts outlined in Chapter 2. Abram (1996), in his investigation of the temporal and spatial dimensions in the Newtonian and phenomenological worldviews, distinguished between actual place and abstract space. He defined abstract or "featureless" space as a new development of the modern Western mind; space without a place is an abstract notion, a

> retreat of the senses . . . from the diverse places that had once gripped them, cleared the way for the notion of a pure and featureless "space"— an abstract conception that has nevertheless come to seem, today, more primordial and *real* than the earthy places in which we remain corpo- really embedded. (Abram, 1996, p. 185)

Likewise, Abram (1996) argued that abstract or linear time is a modern conceptualization that differs experientially from what we might call a circu- lar or cyclical time–space frame of oral cultures. As Abram pointed out, this notion is "difficult to articulate on the page, for it defies the linearity of the printed line" (p. 186).

Abram's (1996) writing is an experiential journey into the qualitative shift of experience that occurs when one can step out of the modern *Weltanschauung* (worldview) and into an experience of one's consciousness as embedded in the spatiotemporal world derived from sensory experience. The qualitative shift from *space to place* and from *present to presence* is the subject matter of phenom- enology. It is also the shift from what Romanyshyn (1989) referred to as the pornographic or abandoned body into the enlivened body.

Romanyshyn (1989) said:

> perhaps it is all the more surprising that the living, human body should have been reborn in the context of psychoanalysis through the work of Freud. . . . Freud, trained in the tradition of the abandoned body, knew very well the body of anatomy . . . the body which belongs nowhere and to no one, that anonymous body with neither a history nor a situation. (p. 208)

Romanyshyn was speaking to the resurrection of the living body that Freud witnessed via the psychosomatic symptoms of the hysteric. It was in the hysteric that Freud witnessed phenomena that could not be explained in the context of linear time. As Hughes (1994) pointed out, it was the psycho- somatic symptom that suggested to Freud that the past infuses the present. Freud linked the pieces of linear time with his conceptualization of an unconscious that contains past experiences, allowing them to resurface in the present field of experience via symptoms and dreams. It was this phenomenon of the hysteric that first revealed the body as a living presence that behaved "as if anatomy did not exist." Romanyshyn argued that the hysteric carried the cultural–historical expression of the exiled living body. The theme of the living, sensuous body exiled in the course of Western history and speaking through the symptom of the hysteric is a common one explored in the writings of Romanyshyn (1989), Abram (1996), Berman (1998), Goldenberg (1990), Lowen (1967), Kidner (2001), Johnson and Grand (1998), and Sheets-Johnstone (1992).

Yet, as Romanyshyn (1989) pointed out, Freud ultimately "disappoints" the living body in the conceptualization of a "cure." Not surprisingly, the goal of psychoanalysis was to eliminate the symptom of the hysteric; effectively this meant that the presence of the living body was to be brought into the present, to conform to the *Welschtang* of the scientific body. In so doing, the past becomes separate from the present; the body is merely an object of anatomy that can function in the modern world. This body has conformed to consensual reality of the modern world consisting of a present and a space. Certainly this is a desired state for those wishing to live and work in the world. What is sacrificed, however, is the living presence of sensory-embedded body, the quality of consciousness in which one is in contact with the "qualitative matrix, a pulsing or potentized field of experience, able to move us even in its stillness" (Abram, 1996, p. 190).

Freud's conceptualization of psychosomatic symptoms and their cure is an interplay between the enlivened body and the mechanistic body. The metaphorically "empty" body is the mechanistic body that has been cleansed of pre-Socratic or even romantic notions of vitalism. Likewise, it is the mechanistic body that Freud sought to return to the hysteric in search of a "cure."

I see another assumption subtly existent in the conceptualization of psychosomatic symptoms as a defense. The notion that psychological material, if insufficiently integrated as mental contents, can become deposited in the soma in the course of defense—or brought back into the psychical in the course of analysis—assumes a developmental hierarchy between the somatic and the psychical. This idea is consistent with Freud's topographic model: Psychological contents that cannot be "thought" proceed in a regressive or defense path toward a less mature manifestation in the soma as unconscious impulses or Id derivatives. Because the capacity to symbolize and reflect is indeed a necessary and developmentally mature capacity of the human psyche, one can understand how this hierarchy may be taken for granted. I argue, however, as did Abram (1996) and Berman (1998), that our reflective and symbolic capacities are themselves diminished when they become disembodied from the actual experiences one is making meaning of. If this is true, a subtle hierarchy of value between the somatic and the psychic is not helpful for a theory of psychological advancement, and it may be important to recognize whether psychoanalysts subtly hold such an implicit value system.

CONCLUSION

The fundamental goal of this chapter has been to name the implicit and explicit assumptions regarding the body in the work of Freud. In this critique of Freud from the point of view of the body, it is recognized that scholars and psychoanalysts have interpreted Freud's position on the body in greatly varied ways. This chapter of research reveals that Freud's theory developed and changed in important ways over the course of his life but that certain thematic assumptions appear to underlie psychoanalysis in a basic sense. These implicit assumptions, although fraught with philosophical and theoretical difficulties, cannot be extracted from the fundamental principles of instinctual drive theory, which embodies Freudian interpretations of clinical material.

In the most basic sense, psychoanalysis is defined by the idea that there is an unconscious at play in the psychology of human beings. From the beginning, the discovery of the unconscious was entwined with the quest for a model to describe the relationship between consciousness and unconsciousness. This quest brought Freud directly into contact with the mind–body problem, and his early models nearly equated unconscious–conscious with body–mind. Freud's initial attempts to describe the unconscious–consciousness relationship hinged on an energetic and quantitative model of neurological events in the soma, which could "become" psychic events. This is a monistic, reductionistic model that failed to become coherent, and Freud moved away from the literal processes of the body and toward a metaphorical model of the mind still using neurological terminology. This retention of biological language while adapting it to dualistic models of the mind–body is an ongoing source of debate and confusion regarding Freud's position on the mind–body problem.

This chapter has explored this evolution of thought in regard to implicit assumptions regarding the body. The most general of these assumptions appears to me to originate in the topographic model; this model assumes a continuum between the somatic and the psychical. Somatic stimuli can become psychical and psychological problems—especially psychosomatic symptoms—arise when this course of action cannot be completed due to psychological defense. The implicit assumption is that the psychological is an advance from somatic and portrays a subtle but persistent hierarchical value system of psyche over soma. The idea flows in reverse with the idea of psychosomatic symptoms as defense: Psychological contents exiled from consciousness can regress toward the somatic. I argue that such a model rests on the assumption that the soma is itself unconscious and an empty or disembodied space and that this model inherently exists in a worldview inherited from a split between matter and spirit or psyche and soma. Likewise, I argue that, in the context of a larger historical and philosophical perspective, consciousness itself has to some extent become exiled from the sensual and somatic world. This historic trend is visible in Freud's picture of a cure for the psychosomatic symptoms of the hysteric, in which the living body is brought into accord with the mechanistic body of the modern world.

Another key point that bears direct influence on our comprehension of the somatic lies in Freud's theory of motivation. For Freud, the human being is motivated from the somatic dimension. The body, via its instinctual drives, is motivated toward a state of homeostasis. This general disposition, retained throughout Freud's writings, ascribes certain attributes to the somatic dimension: The soma is the source of needs that secure the ongoing survival of the human being, and the human body programs the mind primarily to meet these physiological needs. This idea is to be fundamentally challenged by later theorists.

I have explored the ways in which the soma has been either literally or metaphorically equated with the unconscious. The point to become more clearly explicated by later theorists is that Freud's body is not only unconscious but not primarily relational. In other words, the body is related to or seeks relationships only to meet physiological needs of survival and pleasure related to survival. The implied assumptions in this correlation include the valuing of the psychic over the somatic, mentioned earlier. Although I do not contest that there is validity in the maturational value of symbolic capacities, I point out that these capacities themselves are strengthened when positioned within the experiential matrix of the actual body and world in which humans experience themselves. I now proceed to ask: In what ways has this soma/psyche hierarchy and somatic–unconscious association been either challenged or not challenged by the advances of the increasingly relational schools of thought?

4

KLEIN AND OBJECT RELATIONS: CONTEMPORARY DEVELOPMENTS

How have the shifts and evolutions in psychoanalytic thought since Freud's initial formulations altered the role of the body for psychoanalysis? To answer this question, I begin by examining some of the major trends in popular contemporary thought. The emphasis is on the works of those theorists who have most substantially challenged or revised the role of the body via the shift away from Freud's instinctual drive model. This includes the shift from the drive-structural model to the relational–structural model ostensibly initiated by Melanie Klein and more fully manifest in the object relations school.

MOTIVATION: DRIVES TO OBJECTS

Perhaps some of the most comprehensive accounts of shifts in psycho-analytic theory are compiled in Greenberg and Mitchell's (1983) *Object Relations in Psychoanalytic Theory*, Mitchell and Black's (1995) *Freud and Beyond: A History of Modern Psychoanalytic Thought*, and St. Clair's (2000) *Object Relations and Self Psychology: An Introduction*. These texts explore the dynamism of psychoanalytic theory over the previous century to provide the reader with a sense of the commonalities as well as the irreconcilable differences in the broad range of thinking falling under the umbrella of psychoanalysis. Meissner (2000) explored the prominent mind–body positions of several ego psychologists and the emerging trends of neuroscience but did not address the major metapsychological shifts explored in this chapter. This chapter begins with a review of the major principles subject to change within this historical evolution. It is then possible to review the nature of these changes in regard to the primary research question as to the place of the body in psychoanalytic theory.

As reviewed in Chapter 2, the general trends of philosophical inquiry and assumptions regarding the nature of reality and human experience have shifted from a sharp and objective division between that which is experienced as inner and outer or self and other toward an appreciation of the subjective and the reciprocity between inner and outer or self and other in the continual cocreation of experience. It appears to me that the body, as the frontier and the fluid boundary between that which is inner and that which is outer, that which is self and that which is other, bears the burden of these philosophical and clinical ambiguities. Idealism, transcendence, and the ascension myth lend themselves to the interpretation or experience of the body as an*other* of the mind-centered self. In this way the body has an ambiguous place in psychoanalytic theory. For Freud, it was both the precursor to the mental and an other to the mind upon which the mind might displace or project psychological contents. Yet, from Freud's initial observations of transference phenomenon, psychoanalysis has observed that the distinction between self and other is less than straightforward:

> The concept of the transference suggests that the "object" of the patient's experience . . . is at best an amended version of the actual other person involved. People react to and interact with not only an actual other but also an internal other, a psychic representation of a person which in itself has the power to influence both the individual's affective states and his overt behavioral reactions. (Greenberg & Mitchell, 1983, p. 10)[1]

The evolution of object relations has simultaneously investigated the interpenetration not only of self and other but also of inner and outer. Movement and change within psychoanalytic theory over the previous century appears to have been at its core driven by this fundamental observation and attempts to account for the interpenetration of subjective worlds:

> The term "object relations theory," in its broadest sense, refers to attempts within psychoanalysis to answer these questions, that is, to confront the

---

[1]From *Object Relations in Psychoanalytic Theory*, by J. R. Greenberg and S. A. Mitchell, 1983, Cambridge, MA: Harvard University Press. Copyright 1983 by J. R. Greenberg and S. A. Mitchell. Selected quotes reprinted with permission.

potentially confounding observation that people live simultaneously in an external and an internal world, and that the relationship between the two ranges from the most fluid intermingling to the most rigid separation. (Greenberg & Mitchell, 1983, pp. 11–12)

Greenberg and Mitchell (1983), as well as St. Clair (2000), argued that although psychoanalytic theoretical developments are diverse and irreducible, the trend of development appears to have gradually shifted the fundamental notion of human motivation. That is, whereas classical psychoanalysis emphasizes instinctual drive theory as the essential accounting for motivation, object relations, self-psychology, interpersonal psychoanalysis, intersubjectivity, and feminist psychoanalysis, each to some degree emphasizes the role of relatedness over that of instinctual drives in motivation. Greenberg and Mitchell (1983) pointed to the work of Fairbairn and Sullivan as the turning point between Freud's drive-structural model and the relational–structural model employed to some degree by the preceding schools of thought. These terms are employed "as a means of highlighting the differences between the models in their metaphysical commitments concerning the underlying content of mind" (Greenberg & Mitchell, 1983, p. 20).

The basic motivational polarity between these two models is that of the bodily needs and relational needs. Drive-structural models follow Freud's basic supposition that bodily needs exert a pressure on the mind from which flows the basics of mental life. Relational–structural models, on the other hand, view the body as secondary, a vehicle of expression for the more primary human need to be related. In these models, psychological relatedness is primary, and the body becomes secondary as a vehicle for the literal and symbolic expression of these needs.

Although Fairbairn is considered to have authored the first form of a relational–structural model, that is, abandoning drives altogether, most psychoanalytic theories can be understood as existing on a continuum somewhere between a clear statement of one or the other motivational system. Each of these two theories of motivation infers a mind–body position: Drive-structural theory, via the primacy of somatic impulses and bodily needs, cannot escape the implicit if not absolute adherence to a materialist stance. Relational–structural theories, on the other hand, imply an essentially idealist stance; the primacy of psyche, the secondary nature of soma, and the reliance on the archetypal structure of mind and its images to explain the structure of experience reflect a philosophical idealism. These two polarities of psychoanalytic motivation can be seen as a reflection of the essential Western mind–body dilemma explored in Chapter 3, as symbolized by the differences between the philosophies of Plato and Aristotle. We recall Raphael's *The School of Athens*, in which Plato points upward toward the heavens and the transcendent while Aristotle motions toward the earthly and tangible. It appears that the struggle between somatic drives and relational needs reflects a similar dilemma in psychoanalytic theory:

> Of Freud's metapsychological points of view, the economic is both the most problematic and the most resistant to change. Acceptance of the idea of drives which set the activity of the psychic apparatus in motion and serve as the crucial bridge between mind and body has become the litmus test for the "orthodox" psychoanalyst. . . . From the early dissents of Jung and Adler, though the heterodoxy of Fairbairn and Sullivan, to the current controversy over Kohut's "psychology of the self," a theorist's attitude toward the drives determines his place in psychoanalytic circles. (Greenberg & Mitchell, 1983, p. 304)

Indeed, a study of the history of psychoanalysis reveals intense and often passionately vehement personal struggles over what theory holds as essential truths (Grosskurth, 1991). Likewise, for theorists who opted to include some of each motivational system somewhere in their metapsychology, we might ask if and how they have overcome this dichotomizing tendency in ways that are either contradictory or reveal creative moves beyond the either-or dilemma. An analysis of some of the key thinkers of the 20th century serves to lead into such an analysis.

MELANIE KLEIN

Modifying Drives

Mitchell and Black (1995) stated that Melanie Klein "has had more impact on contemporary psychoanalysis than any other psychoanalytic writer since Freud" (p. 85). As Greenberg and Mitchell (1983) claimed, Klein's role is that of a key transitional figure in the eventual modification of drive theory: "For Freud the drives originate as physical forces, although they have psychological manifestations and consequences. For Klein the drives are essentially psychological forces, which utilize the body as a vehicle of expression" (p. 138). As stated earlier, this moves psychoanalysis from an essentially materialist position to an essentially idealist one.

Greenberg and Mitchell, as well as Hughes (1989) and St. Clair (2000), showed that Klein's innovations begin a line of theoretical shifts regarding the nature of drives, which trends increasingly toward the idea that drives are primarily relational rather than biological. In other words, Freud assumed that instinctual drives originating in the body were primary and that they secondarily became related to objects as a means to gratify the tension-reducing aim of the drive. Klein, on the other hand, conceived of drives as psychic phenomena (Greenberg & Mitchell, 1983). Klein did not dismiss the notion of drives, but she did modify their essential nature. Klein's model incorporated the body in an entirely new way. Rather than a correlation between the unconscious or the Id and the soma, which generates the energetic quantities of drive derivatives, the soma becomes a vehicle for expression of the psyche in its primitive state:

> Where, then, does the body come in? The body, in Klein's theory, if not the originator of the drives, is the most effective means of their expression. Picture the young infant as seen by Klein. He experiences profound love, overwhelming hate, and desolate dread and horror in relation to those around him; yet, has no verbal or motoric means for expressing these passions. He cannot speak them; he cannot act them out, except in very crude and inchoate fashion. His understanding of the workings of the world is limited essentially *to his own body* [emphasis added]. Therefore, the parts and functions of his body become signifiers in a primitive grammar of physical expression. He uses this bodily lexicon to put into effect his driving passions of love and hate. (Greenberg & Mitchell, 1983, pp. 140–141)

The explication of this bodily lexicon of the infant mind is a central and unique feature of Klein's work. Klein believed that "the child develops elaborate fantasies concerning the inside of the mother's body and the mysteries it contains—including food, feces, babies. . . . The outer world stands for the mother's body" (Greenberg & Mitchell, 1983, p. 124).

Woven into Klein's modifications of instinctual drives is her differing views on anxiety from that of Freud and her emphasis on phantasy (Hughes, 1989). Although Klein struggled to maintain her loyalty and allegiance with Freud in the face of her innovative ideas (Greenberg & Mitchell, 1983; Grosskurth, 1995; Hughes, 1989), the way in which Klein spoke of the body and the nature of drives in her clinical writing implicitly shifted the psychoanalytic view of somatic experience. In the broadest sense, Klein's ideas emphasized the idealism present in Freud's metapsychology while simultaneously downplaying the materialistic notions implicit to instinctual drives and the economic model of the mind. This shift in attitude appears to be a telling forecast of many psychoanalytic thinkers to come.

An aspect of this shift is evident in Klein's new formulation of the oedipal complex; "Klein's view of the very nature of the Oedipus complex changed from a struggle over illicit pleasures and the fear of punishment, to a struggle for power and destruction and the fear of retaliation" (Greenberg & Mitchell, 1983, p. 125). In shifting the oedipal conflict from that of drives versus society to one of inherently relational matters, Klein had begun the shift away from what (Greenberg & Mitchell, 1983) called the "beast metaphor" of Freudian psychology, in which mankind's essential nature is driven by antisocial urges, toward a view of human nature as essentially social.

Historicity

Klein modified Freud's oedipal complex by placing its origination much earlier in the development of the child. In making this move, Klein ventured into an arena of the psyche that is not governed by historicity; infants and toddlers do not experience linear time in the fashion of adults. In fact, as Juliet Mitchell (Klein & Mitchell, 1987) pointed out, it is the resolution of the oedipal conflict that ushers in the possibility of past and future:

> Psychically speaking, there is no past until after the repression of Oedipal wishes by the castration complex. The castration complex destroys the phantasy of an eternally satisfying relationship with the mother, it introduces the command that the Oedipus complex be over and done with: if you accept it as past you will be able to have a new version (be a father in your turn with a woman of your own) in the future. . . . The castration complex, bearing the injunction of human history, inaugurates history within the individual. (p. 26)

This new way of thinking about infant experience adds a new dimension to psychoanalytic thinking. Inasmuch as the infantile mode of experience is not seen to vanish but to coexist alongside more developmentally mature processes (Klein & Mitchell, 1987; Ogden, 1989), Klein had introduced a dimension of the human psyche that extends beyond the referents of the modern Western mind. That is, Klein had introduced a mode of experience that is nonlinear both in time and space, commonly described as a moment-by-moment sensory-motor existence. She termed this mode of experience the *paranoid–schizoid mode*, which is assumed to be the predominant experience during the earliest months of life.

It is notable that the elements of nonlinearity, ahistoricity, and a sensory-dominated experience coexist in this mode. Embedded in this formulation appear to be a number of implicit assumptions regarding the role of somatic experience in psychoanalytic metapsychology. By this I mean that somatic experience is equated with that which is *psychologically primitive*. In this sense Klein's formulations are in line with those of Freud, despite the differences in each theoretical organization. What is psychologically primitive is, by Klein's definition, lacking in a linear organization of time and the capacity for reflexive thinking. This issue is taken up again by the contemporary Kleinians discussed later. Although I do not doubt that this area of psychoanalytic thought is a highly useful, creative exploration into the somatic dimension of psychological experience, I believe that it is necessary to name the assumptions embedded in this model; it appears that Klein had built her new model around Freud's existing equation of the somatic with that which is prepsychological. Each acknowledges a connection between the somatic and psychical and constructs the somatic as the less developed underpinnings of psychological experience, which requires transformation and organization to be considered "psyche."

Images, Archetypes, Phylogenetic Inheritance

Like Freud, Klein was said to have relied on humankind's phylogentic inheritance to account for what psychoanalysis observes to be innate patterns of relatedness (Greenberg & Mitchell, 1983; Sulloway, 1979). Klein used this concept in particular to explain the infant's innate developmental capacity to become related:

> My hypothesis is that the infant has an innate unconscious awareness of the existence of the mother. We know that young animals at once turn to the mother and find their food from her. The human animal is not different in that respect, and this instinctual knowledge is the basis for the infant's primal relation to his mother. (Klein & Mitchell, 1987, p. 22)

This notion that the human psyche is composed of a reservoir of unconscious images from which fantasy may draw is an essentially idealistic notion drawing on Plato's notion of archetypes. Thus, Klein's focus on the infant psyche's phylogenetic inheritance is a key factor in the reconception of drive as something of primarily somatic inheritance to something primary to psyche. Sulloway (1979) argued that Freud came to essentially the same conclusion toward the end of his career to explain the nature of the oedipal complex and the socialization of the ego. However, it seems to be Klein who articulated this notion and whose theory is presented in this light in the bulk of psychoanalytic writing. Whether it was Freud or Klein who initiated this stance, psychoanalytic history can be seen as moving from a materialist toward an idealist stance in the movement from classical theory toward Kleinian and eventually object relations theory. On the whole, the idea that a physical energy produces a force that produces mental work is replaced with the idea that mental forms are preexistent and that they draw on the somatic experience to find expression and meaning.

CONTEMPORARY KLEINIAN CONTRIBUTIONS

The following is an exploration of the ideas of Wilfred Bion and Thomas Ogden, two theorists who have built on the work of Klein with a marked influence from a particularly postmodern perspective. By this I mean a de-emphasis on notions of order, certainty, objectivity, and positivism, with an inclusion of notions such as subjectivity, intersubjectivity, and local truths. I believe that these writers are of particular importance in that each wrote specifically about the role of the somatic and the psyche/soma in their meta-psychological formulations. We see these ideas expressed most explicitly in Bion's concept of the protomental or beta elements and in Thomas Ogden's development of the autistic-contiguous position.

Wilfred Bion

Bion is perhaps best known for his interpersonalizing of the concept of projective identification (Mitchell & Black, 1995), and this predilection is a telling sign of his forays into a particularly postmodern approach to psycho-analytic problems. For instance, Bion focuses on the analyst's affective experience and ability to contain disturbances and anxieties—as opposed to what might be considered a more modern quest for order and certainty. Symington and Symington (1996) claimed that in this regard Bion's theory was a radical departure from his predecessors; "he was concerned to comprehend the life of the mind itself" (p. xii). Symington and Symington (1996) contrasted this approach to other schools of thought that focused on pathology; in this way I believe that Bion's writings yield a particular presentation of the body that is easily overlooked when one's perspective is focused on bodily phenomena primarily as manifest defensive organization.

Central to Bion's formulations is the notion that the pursuit of knowledge is a predominant motivation (Greenberg & Mitchell, 1983). This is an idea initiated by Klein: "Libidinal development for Klein is closely related to the child's drive to know" (Greenberg & Mitchell, 1983, p. 124). Symington and Symington (1996) claimed that the centrality of this notion displaces and overrides many of Freud's original assumptions within Bion's metapsychology. Particularly, Bion rejected those parts of Freud's thinking that were rooted in determinism: Causal notions such as drives and instincts in particular are rejected as the primary motivational drive in human psychological organization. Bion rejected Freud's use of the term *mechanism* to explain psychological processes, on the principle that there is nothing inanimate about the human psyche. This is a revealing statement; Freud's quest to link the subjectivity of the psyche with what he assumed to be the objective and scientific life of the body drove his quest for a scientific psychology. Bion, on the other hand, spoke about the psyche/soma as a completely animate phenomenon; he is not attempting to causally link an inanimate soma with an animate and subjective psyche but rather to explore the animate life of the psyche/soma as the deep underpinnings of the mind.

Bion's 1961 *Experiences in Groups, and Other Papers* outlines the concept of the protomental, which Symington and Symington (1996) claimed foreshadows the later concept of beta elements, which is embedded in Bion's condensed conception of the grid, developed between 1953 and 1967. Bion was intensely interested in the intersection between the individual and the group, and his 1961 publication is an exploration into the presence and/or the loss of an individual's capacity to have independent thoughts in a group situation. He uses his experience of military groups and group therapy to explicate this phenomenon wherein relative degrees of homogony of ideas and perceptions can become apparent. Bion observed that this phenomenon can take on a pathological quality in that it maintains a significant denial of some portions of reality—and therefore can result in the ostracization or idealization of ideas or individuals. This interest led Bion to the heart of the psychoanalytic inquiry regarding the relationship between self and other, inner and outer; I believe it is of utmost importance that this inquiry led Bion also to the relationship between psyche and soma. Bion formulated the concept of the protomental, a layer of the psyche that individuals share with one another, to account for these group phenomena. To understand this concept, the metaphor of coral or aspen trees can be used—these are organisms that appear as individuals but are actually interconnected (below the surface of the earth as in aspen trees or within a reef structure as in coral) and communicate behavior within this system of interconnectedness.

In 1961, Bion stated:

> The proto-mental system I visualize as one in which physical and psychological or mental are undifferentiated. It is a matrix from which spring the phenomena which at first appear—on a psychological level and in the light of psychological investigation—to be discrete feelings only loosely associated with one another. . . . Since it is a level in which physical and mental are undifferentiated, it stands to reason that, when distress from this source manifests itself, it can manifest itself just as well in physical forms as in psychological. (Bion, 1961, p. 102)

Bion was investigating an aspect of the psyche to which Klein perhaps opened the psychoanalytic door; Klein, in her study of early infant states of mind and the paranoid–schizoid and depressive modes of experience, opened the door to the level of human experience that is assumed to be largely constructed of undifferentiated somatic elements. Bion implied that this level of the mind is the generative and motivational source of physical and psychic energy. Klein and the contemporary Kleinians seemed to imagine these early infant states in a particular way, as ones dominated by raw sensory perceptions that are originally chaotic and gradually organized into recognizable patterns, which eventually form the foundation of the body schema and the continuity of the sense of self (Klein & Mitchell, 1987; St. Clair, 2000).

Bion (1961) went on to investigate the relationships among disease, symptomatology, the individual, and the group:

> It is these proto-mental levels that provide the matrix of group diseases. These diseases manifest themselves in the individual but they have

characteristics that make it clear that it is the group rather than the individual that is stricken. . . . To make my meaning still clearer I shall take an analogy from physical medicine. . . . Let us assume the case of the patient who is suffering from anxiety symptoms . . . In ordinary parlance it would be said that the disease had a physical origin. I would prefer to say that the matrix of the disease lay in the sphere of proto-mental events . . . in my option the sphere of proto-mental events cannot be understood by reference to the individual alone. (p. 103)

I believe that Bion made a radical statement that profoundly altered the role of the body in his model. He stated that this place where psyche and soma are one and the same—more accurately, where there is only psyche/soma— is also an inherently group state. The psyche/soma is both interpersonal and transpersonal. What is radically new about this configuration is that the spirit–matter divide has been definitely undone, if we take spirit to include an intelligence beyond the personal and shared by or accessible to all people. The physical matter of the body in this model is synonymous with the interpersonal intelligence of group phenomena. I find this concept better suited to the term *soma–psyche*; for the first time the soma is granted its own intelligence—albeit a "prepsychological" (i.e., not known), or "primitive" kind of intelligence.

For Bion, psyche/soma is the place where there is no such thing as the individual mind. Perhaps this is why Bion is referred to as the "psychoanalytic mystic" (Eigen, 1998), for he has trespassed into the hallmark of the Western worldview and Freud's longstanding insistence that psychoanalysis had nothing to do with mysticism but was instead an empirical science.

Symington and Symington (1996) stated that this "mystical" quality of Bion's is largely responsible for the suspicion and rejection he faced in the Kleinian group. In fact, Winnicott appears to have encountered similar attitudes in response to his late-life interest in mystic states (Rodman, 2003). It appears that the intensity of Freud's desire to build a psychology that could be seen as sufficiently "scientific," combined with his drive to create an enduring legacy in strict agreement with his theory (Grosskurth, 1991, 1995; Roazen, 1992), created an atmosphere in which anything that might discredit psychoanalysis's claim to the "hard" sciences was "almost fanatically opposed" (Symington & Symington, 1996).

I now challenge Bion's formulations to consider the ways in which this creative inclusion of the somatic in his metapsychology might contain inherited assumptions from Freud's early positivism in the *Project for a Scientific Psychology* and drive theory. Symington and Symington (1996) claimed that Bion rejects the pleasure principle and drive theory. However, they went on to describe the "genetic development of thoughts" with direct reference to Freud's model laid out in the *Project*, which includes a neurological transformation of the physical to the psychical:

Beta elements . . . are not in a condition to be thought about. They cannot be verbalized and are not able to yield their meaning, but they can be transformed so they become suitable for use in thinking, in other words they must become processable by the mind. For this to happen, they must be submitted to the unknown process of alpha function. . . . Alpha function endows the mind with a sense of subjectivity . . . . Without alpha function a person can abstract the sensory data pertaining to the external world but not to those of internal emotional experience. (Symington & Symington, 1996, p. 39)

The development of thoughts in Bion's model includes "an unknown transformation" from raw sensory data into progressively more abstract perceptions and conceptualizations that constitute developed psychological life. This unknown transformation is strikingly similar to that described by Freud in the *Project* and contained in the later concept of "instinct" as a frontier between the somatic and the psychical, discussed in Chapter 3 of this volume. Freud described an unknown transformation—whose mechanism eluded him—between the somatic and the psychical. The constancy principle explained the threshold of somatic energy that would tip the balance toward this transformation. Both Freud and Bion were attempting to deal with the philosophical problem of the relationship between inner and outer, subjective and objective. For both theorists, the mysteries of the psyche/soma come to represent this essential problem, and both theorists referred to a mysterious process by which sensory data "become" psychical.

The difference is that Bion's somatic elements are also primarily psychological, and this is a profound difference. He postulated a level of the psyche at which somatic and psychic are undifferentiated, directly implying a dual-aspect perspective on the mind–body problem. Where a dual-aspect solution to the mind–body problem is employed, the spirit–matter question is inevitably called into the dialogue: What is the nature of this layer of the psyche, especially if it is transpersonal, in the sense that it is shared by all individuals? It is essentially the generative field of biological and psychological life, and thus activates one's own or one's cultural understanding of this dimension as potentially spiritual or religious. It appears to me that psychoanalysis is historically and presently hesitant to engage such theological concerns. Recalling the priest–doctor division discussed in Chapter 2, we can comprehend the historical thrust behind this hesitancy. However, the scope of practice of the psychotherapist—the suffering and meaning of human experience—necessarily includes a model that acknowledges these concerns.

However, it seems to me that several of Bion's conceptualizations appear to construct a developmental model leaning toward ever-increasing levels of abstraction and potentially disembodiment. For example, in Bion's grid, progression through the rows of thought development are considered growth "both in complexity and degree of abstraction . . . The *concept*, row F, is derived from the conception by purifying it of anything that would stop it from representing the truth" (Symington & Symington, 1996). Eventually, even words become replaced by the greatest abstractions of mathematics in row H to allow for greater flexibility, symbolism, and closer approximations of an "ultimate truth" expressed by Bion in the term *psychoanalytic object*.

The psychoanalytic object, or O, is the ultimate reality or ultimate psychological truth that Bion understood to be the goal of psychoanalytic inquiry. Symington and Symington (1996) stated that there are "three axes which intersect and interpenetrate in Bion's thinking. They are ultimate reality, the difference between sensuous and psychic reality, and the way an individual comes to knowledge" (p. 175). Symington and Symington structured their argument around a Platonic understanding of the difference between the manifest or sensuous world and the ultimate truth of the abstract world of ideas and knowledge. As discussed in Chapter 2 of this volume, this is an idealist perspective that views the primary or ultimate reality as beyond the senses. Sensual knowledge is essentially distrusted as illusory or a barrier to ultimate truth.

Symington and Symington (1996) related this movement to the mystical quality of Bion's work in that he was often viewed or feared as "quasireligious" in his understanding of psychic reality. This correlation highlights the presence of an underlying ascension myth present in the contemporary interpretation of Bion's work, if not in Bion's work itself. That is, there is an absolute reality of higher truth, which is encountered in a nonsensual dimension. One may utilize sensual perceptual data in the manifest world to begin to build models to know this ultimate reality—"To the question 'How is the analyst to penetrate through the sensuous to the psychic reality?', Bion's answer is that he waits until a pattern begins to emerge and that he *intuits* the psychic reality" (Symington & Symington, 1996, p. 178); but eventually we reach an inherent dualism in which the sensuous is polarized in a hierarchical relationship to the more valued psychical reality:

> Mysticism tends to be viewed pejoratively by those with a scientific attitude. Essentially mysticism is the record of the experiences of those who claim to have had close, even if not direct, contact with ultimate reality. True mystics always emphasize that this contact is not sensual but psychic. (Symington & Symington, 1996, p. 177)

Symington and Symington (1996) went on to confirm that the domination of sensory phenomena in the mind is a barrier to the perception of nonsensuous reality and that "we need to be freed from this" (p. 182). The sensuous and the somatic are repeatedly correlated to the "primitive within us, the primaeval chaos" (p. 183).

This line of thinking leads me to the observation that it was the tie to the biological sciences that Freud felt would protect psychoanalysis from devaluation as a mystical practice. It is in letting go of this tie that Bion is associated with that which is mystical. It appears that the evolution of psychoanalytic thought has been largely contained within the dualistic dilemma of psyche and soma: Psychoanalysts assume that they can be either somatically rooted or mystically bound. In either choice lies the psychoanalytic valuation of symbolization, words, and reflexive thought, which highlights the underlying motif of ascension in the mythological landscape inherited by the Western culture at large.

The aim of this research is to name these unconscious assumptions or mythologies guiding our metapsychologies. I now suggest a question psychoanalysis might ask in order to elaborate these assumptions and to perhaps think beyond the polarization of psyche and soma. In the context of Bion's terminology, is O or the ultimate psychological reality—as opposed to being most clearly apprehended distinct from the senses—perhaps most fully present and experienced as an embodied sensual reality? That is, if the psyche/soma matrix or beta elements are the source of human experience, is soma not also the root of human access to O or psychological reality? Can we humans challenge ourselves to think circularly rather than linearly, so as not to invest in a disembodied psychology? Perhaps we can conceptualize psychological development not as growing out of the distrusted medium of the somatic but as returning to the place where we "began"—with entirely new perceptual and reflexive capacities.

Joyce McDougall

Joyce McDougall drew on the work of Klein, Bion, and Winnicott, as well as Kohut and Kernberg, and is a specialist in the psychoanalytic treatment and thinking about psychosomatic symptomatology (McDougall, 1989). I mention McDougall here because she drew on Bion's concept of the mind–body matrix in her conceptualization of psychosomatic symptoms. In my opinion, Bion, in his original formulations, appears to move beyond two Western assumptions, whereas McDougall does not: the objective nature of individualism and the inanimate nature of physical matter.

McDougall (1989) developed a model for thinking about psychosomatic symptoms in which the body is seen as carrying out a nonverbal communication that has not been translated into symbolized thoughts and feelings that can be processed psychologically. This is a model of psychosomatic symptoms as defense; the defense can be either against a drive or conflict (in classical terms) or unmediated experiences of a primitive kind—such as Bion's beta elements. Psychosomatic symptoms are therefore a discharge or an acting out of that which cannot be thought about. This model is similar in structure to that of Bion's grid and the movement of elements of experience from beta to alpha elements or from lower to higher rows of abstraction. McDougall (1989) drew on developmental models and expanded on the Mahlerian notion that an infant is born in a state of merger with the mother, experienced as a total environment or "mother universe":

> Deeply buried within us all there is a longing to return to this illusory fusion, to become once again part of the omnipotent mother universe of early infancy, in which there is no frustration, no responsibility, and no desire. But in such a universe there is no individual identity either. We might say that the fulfillment of such a longing would be the equivalent of the loss of personal identity, that is, of psychic death. (p. 33)

McDougall was drawing on Mahler's (Mahler, Pine, & Bergman, 1975) model of separation–individuation, in which the original state of the mother–infant dyad is assumed to be experienced by the infant as a state of unity—"one-body fantasy" (McDougall, 1989, p. 33)—and that this state is both presymbolic and composed of raw sensory data.

McDougall (1989) referred to the developmental line as a "gradual 'desomatization' of the psyche" (p. 34). Although McDougall's clinical examples illustrate the usefulness of her model, I find the emphasis on desomatization and individualization, to illustrate again the unconscious influence of a hierarchical psyche/soma polarization along psychoanalytic developmental lines.

The portrayal of somatic symptoms as acting out or repression of psychological thoughts and feelings into their prepsychological form again underscores the assumptions pointed out in Chapter 3. The body is assumed to be an empty space, inherently without its own meaning, into which an entity we call the *mind* can displace or project unbearable contents.

The idea that the capacity for symbolization is gained simultaneously with the development of an individual sense of self out of the infantile union points again to the gain of reflexive thought and self-consciousness, which comes with distinguishing, separating, and creating "space." I suggest again that McDougall's contributions are useful models but that perhaps an unconscious overvaluation of individualization, verbalization, and desomatization could be counterbalanced with a developmental model that was less linear and more circular in nature.

Thomas Ogden

Ogden is another contemporary Kleinian writer who has applied Bion's interpersonalization of projective identification (Mitchell & Black, 1995) and who therefore represents the contemporary Kleinian movement toward a dyadic understanding of the analytic relationship. Again, we can understand these contemporary moves as reflecting increasingly postmodern views on the nature of reality, which emphasize a continual interpenetration of inner and outer, self and other.

Ogden (1989) placed his writing within the context of the development of the British psychoanalytic discourse:

> The exchange of ideas constituting the British psychoanalytic discourse of the 1930s to the early 1970s revolved in large part around the work of Klein, Winnicott, Fairbairn, and Bion . . . The history of the development of British object relations theory in the last twenty years can be viewed as containing the beginnings of an exploration of an area of experience lying outside of the experiential states addressed by Klein's (1958) concepts of the paranoid-schizoid and depressive positions. (p. 47)[2]

Specifically, Ogden cited the works of Esther Bick (M. Harris & Bick, 1987), Donald Meltzer (1967, 1973), Didier Anzieu (1989), Daniel Stern (1977, 1985, 1998, 2004), and Frances Tustin (1981) as beginning an exploration to a "more primitive" dimension of human experience: the somatic dimension.

Ogden introduced a concept that I find particularly interesting in light of the body in psychoanalytic theory in general and in contemporary Kleinian theory in particular. Ogden (1989) posited that, in addition to Klein's original formulation of the paranoid–schizoid and depressive modes, it is useful to think about a third mode of psychological organization: the autistic–contiguous mode. Ogden (1989) described this mode as existing developmentally prior to the paranoid–schizoid mode and as an ongoing dimension of all human experience:

> The conception of a dialectic of experience constituted exclusively by these two modes is incomplete, insofar as it fails to recognize an even more primitive presymbolic, sensory-dominated mode that I will refer to as the *autistic-contiguous mode*. The conception of an autistic-contiguous pole of the dialectic of experience represents an integration, interpretation, and extension of aspects of the work of Bick (1968, 1986); Meltzer (Meltzer 1975, 1986; Meltzer et al., 1975); and Tustin (1972, 1980, 1981, 1984, 1986). Each of these authors was strongly influenced by Bion's (1962, 1963) conception of the container and the contained, as well as by his theory of thinking . . . . The autistic–contiguous position is a primitive psychological organization operative from birth that generates the most elemental forms of human experience. It is a sensory-dominated mode in which the most inchoate sense of self is built upon the rhythm of sensation (Tustin, 1984), particularly the sensations at the skin surface (Bick, 1968). (pp. 30–31)

The articulation of this position endeavors to explicitly incorporate the role of the somatic not only in the form of body schema or ego identity

[2]From *The Primitive Edge of Experience*, by T. H. Ogden, 1989, London, England: Northvale. Copyright 1989 by T. H. Ogden. Selected quotes reprinted with permission.

formation but also as an ongoing process of experience generation. Ogden (1989) agreed with Eigen's argument that

> the depressive mode is too often viewed as the full realization of the human potential. In the depressive mode, it is held that the individual develops the capacity for abstract symbolization, subjectivity and self-reflection, concern for others, guilt, and reparative wishes, all of which lead to cultural production . . . such a diachronic conception of the relationship between the two . . . fails to appreciate the fundamental dialectical nature of their relationship. (p. 29)

I believe that Ogden was speaking to the bias of linear developmental theories that value abstraction and was positing that therapists rather attempt to think in terms of developmental theories that gain more options and flexibility: "The therapeutic process as I understand it involves the establishment, reestablishment, or expansion of a dialectical relationship between different modes of experience" (Ogden, 1989, p. 29). In this way Ogden was speaking to a circular or integrative model of development, as opposed to models that suggest a linear progression as described earlier.

The essential features of the autistic–contiguous mode of experience are related to the experience of shape and its boundedness, texture, rythmicity, and periodicy. The autistic–contiguous position is a

> way of conceptualizing a psychological organization more primitive than either the paranoid–schizoid or the depressive position. The autistic–contiguous mode is conceptualized as a sensory-dominated, presymbolic mode of generating experience which provides a good measure of boundedness of human experience, and the beginnings of a sense of the place where one's experience occurs. Anxiety in this mode consists of an unspeakable terror of the dissolution of boundedness resulting in feelings of leaking, falling, or dissolving into endless, shapeless space. (Ogden, 1989, p. 81)

Ogden went on to describe the particular forms of defense and ways of organizing experience in this position. I do not attempt here to reduce Ogden's full explanation of the nature and quality of this position but rather refer the reader to this text directly. For the purposes of this research, it is sufficient to understand that this position refers to the actual body and to the raw sensory data of the earliest developmental phase as imagined by psychoanalytic theorists and of what is referred to as the most primitive layer of the human psyche. It encompasses actual sensory experiences and the ability to organize and differentiate them in ways that are continuous and supportive to a sense of self-cohesion and boundedness.

A basic assumption of Ogden's work, continuous with his Kleinian foundations, appears to be that mental contents can be experienced as body parts in primitive states of mind. This assumption is built into the developmental view of the Kleinian school and carries an implicit message that the somatic dimension of experience correlates to that which is primitive or not psychologically developed. This assumption appears to be so embedded in developmental and metapsychological theories that it is difficult to question; indeed, it is a useful formula for the organization of clinical material, which is validated by the work of neuropsychological research by theorists such as Stern (1977, 1985, 2004).

What is implied by "primitive" in a psychoanalytic sense is an absence of subjectivity and symbolic or reflexive capacities. In other words, there is an absence of separation or the ability to distinguish between self and other, inner and outer, psyche and soma. Developmentally, "the infant's subjectivity in the autistic-contiguous position can be thought of as an extremely subtle, non-self-reflective sense of 'going on being' (Winnicott, 1956)" (Ogden, 1989, p. 54). I believe that it is necessary to unpack this developmental model to comprehend the implicit assumptions regarding the body.

What psychoanalysis refers to as infantile, primitive, or psychotic states of mind includes a "collapse" of the space of differentiation required for adult ego capacities. This lack of differentiation is apparent in the separation between self and other, inner and outer, psyche and soma. The Kleinian tradition is a pivotal one in a philosophical sense: It is that tradition that begins to explore the paradox of these differentiations. Object relations, with its roots in the Kleinian school, attempts to account for the fact that although the adult ego can experience the separation between self and other, the interpenetration of the two is an ongoing reality of the psyche.

It appears to me that Ogden's work subtly acknowledges that whereas the ego, to function in the adult world, must be able to ascertain a subtle differentiation between psyche and soma, it must also be able to understand their essential interpenetration. This is evident in the idea that the autistic–contiguous position is an ongoing mode of experience generation in the adult psyche and that the ego capacities are crippled without access to this organization. To fully comprehend this, it appears that one must understand the soma not as inanimate matter or empty space in which psyche can project but as an animate "going-on-being" in itself.

I believe that to embrace this notion fully, we are again called to confront the spirit–matter split that appears to be embedded in the history of the Western mind. It is difficult to comprehend the animate nature of the human body without subtly challenging the inanimate nature of the physical world of which the body is a part.

I am of the opinion that the language of Ogden's model gives subtle reinforcement to the inanimate nature of the physical world. I am particularly struck by the continual use of terms such as *floor*, *below*, and *primitive* in conjunction with the somatic dimension of experience. As Ogden (1989) pointed out, "collapse in the direction of the depressive pole involves a form of isolation of oneself from one's bodily sensations, and from the immediacy of one's lived experience, leaving one devoid of spontaneity and aliveness" (p. 46).

I wonder if an unconscious overvaluation of depressive mode capacities and the correlation between somatic and primitive invites a psychology devoid of this spontaneous aliveness. I find that the psychoanalytic valuation of language, symbolism, and abstraction invites a potential danger of a tendency toward an *ascension psychology* that polarizes itself within a hierarchical relationship of psyche over soma, and that this danger is heightened with the language utilized in Ogden's model. Likewise, the conceptualization of the autistic–contiguous mode as *presymbolic* and *nonreflexive* confirms the hierarchical status of soma as something necessary but necessarily outgrown in a quest for psychological maturity or psychoanalytic gain.

I propose that a psychoanalytic theory whose language lent itself less to models of ascension and more to models of integration might encourage psychoanalytic psychotherapy toward embodiment of the symbolic capacities we strive toward. I find this idea succinctly held in the phrase "we can be holistic when we are differentiated enough to know the difference between mind and body" (A. Panajian, personal communication, April 23, 2000). To this end, we might consider that the somatic pole of experience is the grounding medium of symbolic experience—as opposed to presymbolic. Likewise, we might consider that in developmentally mature states the soma is not merely a nonreflexive or inanimate container for psychic experience, but that the soma is the participatory medium of reflexive consciousness. This languaging, while less convenient, implies more directly that which is tempting to ignore of Ogden's implicit assumptions: that the physical world and the soma are the animate expression in which we know psyche.

THE BRITISH MIDDLE OBJECT RELATIONS SCHOOL

Far from being a unified concept, object relations theories refer to a broad spectrum of theories in which the subject's need to relate to objects occupies the central position (Rycroft, 1995). Object relations can be defined in the narrow sense as analysts of the so-called British Middle school, particularly the work of Ronald Fairbairn (1952, 1954), Donald Winnicott (1958a, 1971, 1992), and the theorists they inspired, whereas a less restricted conceptualization also includes the work of ego psychologists who have contributed to the theory (Hughes, 1989; Kernberg, 1995a, 1995b). In general, object relations theories are concerned with the investigation of the early formation and differentiation of what are considered to by psychological structures—inner images of the self and the other—and how these inner structures are manifested in interpersonal situations (St. Clair, 1996). Object relations then has grappled with the essential dilemma of the relationship between the inner world and the outer world, real people and an individual's inner experience of relationships. As St. Clair (1996) and Greenberg and Mitchell (1983) demonstrated, the object relations school in its entirety represents the movement away from Freud's instinctual drive theory.

W. R. D. Fairbairn is considered a pure object relations theorist in that he departs most completely from instinctual drive theory. A unique aspect of his position is the assertion that real contact with real people is the primary and developmentally mature mode of experience. He sees the world of internal object relations a necessary component of development but in the long run a pathological turning away from external reality, from actual exchange with others: "For Fairbairn, internal objects are not (as for Klein) essential and inevitable accompaniments of all experience, but rather compensatory substitutes for the real thing, actual people in the interpersonal world" (Mitchell & Black, 1995, p. 117).

Thus, the object relations school includes a broad range of interest in the relationship between inner and outer. The object relations school comprises many theorists, and although a complete discussion of them is beyond the scope of this research, it is helpful to understand that the spectrum of thinking is on the whole engaged in new ways to grapple with models of the developing sense of self and its relationship to the real or outer world—including the physical world. I now turn to an exploration of the two object relations theorists who dealt most directly with issues of the body and the somatic pole of experience in their metapsychological models and specific clinical interests: D. W. Winnicott and Marion Milner.

D. W. Winnicott

Winnicott saw himself as working within the traditions of Freud and Klein, but he is considered a unique and independent thinker who clearly differed from his predecessors in important ways (Greenberg & Mitchell, 1983; St. Clair, 2000).

Winnicott eventually broke with Klein both personally and theoretically over the issue of the relationship between what is inner and what is outer in infant development. The disagreement revolved around the role of the mother and early infant states of self and is summarized succinctly in Winnicott's (1975) famous statement, "There is no such thing as a baby," by which he meant that the interpersonal environment defines early states of mind (p. 98). Klein insisted on the inner reality of the baby and individual capacities being present from birth. Ultimately, Winnicott embraced the situation in a manner fundamental to his style as a psychoanalytic thinker: as a paradox. Winnicott's paradoxical thinking about the relationship between inner and outer proves useful in a discussion about the very nature of that which is the boundary between the two: the body.

Winnicott's writings emphasize the relationship between the environment and the evolving self and the quality of subjective, meaningful experience. Winnicott is perhaps best known for his article "Transitional Objects," published in 1953. This concept illustrates the ways in which Winnicott creatively embraced the core philosophical issues at play in the evolution of psychoanalytic theories: The relationships between inner and outer, real and unreal, tangible and intangible were approached with an attitude of playfulness and paradox (Rodman, 2003). In this way Winnicott both moved beyond the either–or dynamics of the contemporary theoretical battles and became relatively isolated in the history of theoretical development in that he ultimately felt exiled from Klein and her group and could not be clearly classified in his allegiances.

In 1949, Winnicott authored an essay titled "Mind and its Relation to the Psyche/Soma" (Winnicott, 1992), which spells out how he conceived of the role of the body in his theory of infant development and psychopathology. A pediatrician, Winnicott's ideas are interwoven with his picture of infant development and the mother–infant dyad.

> Let us attempt, therefore, to think of the developing individual, starting at the beginning. Here is a body, and the psyche and the soma are not to be distinguished except according to the direction from which one is looking . . . . I suppose the word psyche here means the *imaginative elaboration of somatic parts, feelings, and functions*, that is, of physical aliveness. We know that this imaginative elaboration is dependent on the existence and the healthy functioning of the brain, especially certain parts of it. The psyche is not, however, felt by the individual to be localized in the brain, or indeed to be localized anywhere. (Winnicott, 1992, p. 244)

Winnicott distinguished clearly between the mind and the psyche for depth psychology. It is as if the mind is the furthest extreme elaboration of the psyche-end of the original psyche/soma collaboration: "Mind is then no more than a special case of the functioning of the psyche/soma" (Winnicott, 1992, p. 244). The psyche/soma, a collaborative experience of embodied and enlivened experience, constitutes the essential going-on-being of the individual. The mind then appears to be the furthest abstraction of human experience; that is, mind contains the capacity for reflexive functioning. This reflexive ability of mind is often called the *observing ego* and inherent in the common implicitly valued capacity for psychological mindedness.

Winnicott appeared to articulate a new characterization of the mind–body relationship within the psychoanalytic tradition. He understood the infant as a psyche/soma continuum in which bodily experience is primary and essentially comparable with the earliest forms of psychological experience. This is a view approximated by most psychoanalytic developmental models, such as the Kleinian and neuropsychological models; however, Winnicott went on to speak of normal adult development in a manner I find creatively revealing of a potentially new paradigm. In defining psyche as an "imaginative elaboration of somatic reality," and defining mind as a particular manifestation of psyche, he placed all human experience and the components of the self-concept along a continuum capable of ongoing interplay. In my opinion, the language used here enables a leap outside of an implicit dualism often engaged by other writers. Like Bion, this model implies a dual-aspect position on the mind–body problem.

For example, Winnicott's writing conveyed the capacity for a psychological valuation of mind while recognizing the dangers of a mind that becomes dichotomized from the somatic. For example, he said that "there can develop an opposition between the mind and the psyche/soma" (Winnicott, 1992, p. 246), in response to an early facilitating environment that does not preserve the continuity of the psyche/soma experience. Here, "in reaction to this abnormal environmental state the thinking of the individual begins to take over and organize the caring for the psyche/soma" (p. 246).

I believe that Winnicott most clearly addresses this pivotal issue in the history of the Western mind–body problem when he addressed the *false localization* of the mind in the head. Winnicott (1992) asked "why the head should be the place inside which the mind tends to become localized by the individual, and I do not know the answer" (p. 247). He went on to address this question, and in so doing raised the issue of time and space in relation to the experience of a localized mind. I believe that this issue is directly related to the underlying philosophy of the mind–body problem in the Western paradigm.

Recall the philosophical statements about linear time as abstraction from spatial references discussed in Chapter 3; it is a unique capacity of the modern Western concept of linear time that results in the possibility of an abstracted space—that is, a space without a *place*. It is this capacity of the Newtonian world that enables the particular possibilities of displacement through time and space—and, therefore, the projection of psychological content *into* the body as described by Freud. This configuration appears to require or assume a localization of mind in the head, as Winnicott described and then questioned.

For Winnicott (1992), the falsely localized mind experienced as "other" is an element of psychopathology: "The psyche of the individual gets 'seduced' away into this mind from the intimate relationship which the psyche originally had with the soma. The result is a mind-psyche, which is pathological"

(p. 247). Winnicott was challenging what I find to be an inherent assumption in the Western worldview, inherited from an essential spirit–matter split, that the mind is a property of the brain—anatomically located in the head—and that the soma or the body as such is therefore in some way essentially "not mind."

Winnicott wrote about the body in a subjective way, about the psyche/soma connection and the inhabited body as essential to the fundamental aliveness of the self. As a relatively independent thinker, one who even claimed not to have read much of Freud (Rodman, 2003), Winnicott appears in many ways to have transcended what I have begun to construct as the essential assumptions of psychoanalysis regarding the body. In particular, his use of language circumvents the perhaps inadvertent tendency to polarize the psyche and the soma as opposites or as a duality in which the psychical part is assumed to be developmentally mature in a psychological sense. Rather, he portrayed the enlivened sense of self as necessarily embedded within the psyche/soma, and the defensive formation of mind–psyche polarized against soma as a pathological state.

Winnicott continued to weave this approach to the role of the body through his ideas regarding the *True Self* and his 1950s remarks on aggression in infancy. Rodman (2003) cited the 1949 essay "Mind and its Relation to the Psyche/Soma" as the origin of the idea of the True Self; the True Self at its earliest stage is later described as

> the theoretical position from which come the spontaneous gesture and the personal idea . . . . It is an essential part of my theory that the True Self does not become a living reality except as a result of the mother's repeated success in meeting the infant's spontaneous gesture or sensory hallucination. (Winnicott, quoted in Rodman, 2003, p. 265)

Here the early somatic experience and the mother's interaction with the sensory hallucination of the infant are inextricably interwoven with the emerging sense of self.

In "Aggression in Relation to Emotional Development," Winnicott (1958b) explored the relationship between the inner and the external nature of objects; an infant's initial physical mobility is understood as the primary manifestation of aggression in the broad sense of the psychoanalytic term. In other words, aggression is the result of the somatically impulsive gesture to reach out into the external world and to be met. The meeting of the impulsive gesture (i.e., a reaching of the arm being met by a caregiver's hand) is an affirmation of the reality of both the internal sense of agency and the external world. The caregiver's hand in this example is an "opposition" in that it is something to push against in order to discover boundaries and definition. Aggression has its roots in the soma, and the soma provides the medium by which a baby discovers its selfhood. The second part of this assumption is not out of agreement with Freud's famous 1923 statement that "the ego is first and foremost the bodily ego" (p. 25). It is Winnicott who reconfigured the role of aggression as the force by which an infant discovers the bodily ego and links the sense of reality with the expression of motility and aggression. In this way Winnicott elaborated another link between the actual body and ego development. Again, I find it notable that Winnicott's language does not give the impression of either polarization or a hierarchical positioning of psyche-over-soma that I have pointed out in other writings.

I suggest that although Winnicott's ideas might be echoed by other theorists, such as Klein, Bion, and McDougall, his capacity for paradox enables a new kind of dynamism to be portrayed between soma and psyche. In the final decade of his life, Winnicott became increasingly preoccupied with the nature of what is real, or the objective versus the subjective, and even the mystical. Rodman (2003) quoted a letter Winnicott wrote to John Wisdom in 1964 in which Winnicott felt that Bion was saying what he had been trying to say:

> It is important to me that Bion states (obscurely of course) what I have been trying to state for 2 ½ decades but against the terrific opposition of Melanie [Klein] . . . Bion uses the word reverie to cover the idea that I have stated in the complex way that it deserves that . . . *the mother lets the baby know what is being created.* (p. 296)

Reverie, the process through which "the mother lets the baby know what is being created," draws on a transpersonal layer of the psyche in which mother and infant communicate unconsciously or without words. Again, the image of the aspen tree or coral colony applies: It is as if there is a level of communication and organization that escapes the literal eye but goes on beneath the surface.

Winnicott alluded to the lifelong opposition he encountered from the Kleinian group, especially in regard to the places his theory reached toward the intersubjective nature of the mother–infant dyad and eventually toward what might be considered poetic or mystical. Again, it appears that the need for psychoanalysts to portray their science as positivistic and empirical results in a rigidity against trends toward the intersubjective precisely because the intersubjective alludes to or leads one toward something that feels "mystical." As both Winnicott and Bion's work suggests, these works also allude to new conceptualizations of the somatic dimension of experience, which are neither positivistic nor reductionistic. Rather, the physical body becomes the Mobius Strip of self and other, inner and outer, subjective and objective experience.

In my opinion, Winnicott speaks to both "the body as such," to the metaphorical language of the body, and to somatization with a linguistic style that subtly undermines the criticisms I have been raising in regard to the implicit assumptions regarding the body in psychoanalytic theory. For instance, Winnicott's position of psychosomatic disorders understands the symptomatology not as a regressive defense toward fantasied merger (McDougall, 1989) but as a problem of dissociation of psyche/soma.

In 1949, Winnicott (1992) asserted that "the psychosomatic disorders, half-way between the mental and the physical, are in a rather precarious position" (p. 244). Rodman (2003) explained that in 1962 Winnicott spoke about psychosomatic disease as essentially a "dissociation between mind and body. That vast continent of illness, so neglected even now, is an area of bewilderment for physicians and others unable to find a set of words and concepts that can do it justice" (p. 284). Rodman followed Winnicott's train of thought as he went on to examine

> the *positive value of somatic involvement* [emphasis added]. The individual values the potential psycho-somatic linkage. To understand this one must remember that defence is organized not only in terms of splitting, which protects against annihilation, but also in terms of protection of the psyche/soma from a flight into an intellectualized or a spiritual existence. (Quoted in Rodman, 2003, p. 295)

I find this to be a radically new understanding of psychosomatic symptoms from that of McDougall, for instance. The idea that somatization is the result of a dissociation of psyche/soma, which in health must be coordinated and unified, is a clear departure from the idea that somatization is a failure to symbolize because of a developmentally impaired or regressive slide from a mature state of differentiation (McDougall, 1989). It is interesting that aalthough Winnicott's ideas appear to undermine the deanimation of matter and soma and to undermine a one-sided valuation of individualization or differentiation, writers such as McDougall utilized his concepts in a way that reverse this creative movement beyond the basic Western assumptions regarding the body and the physical world. I interpret this failure to carry forward Winnicott's innovations into the greater field of psychoanalysis as an unrecognized allegiance to the philosophical assumptions embedded in Freud's original theories. I find support for this interpretation in the fact that although Freud himself appeared to venture beyond positivism and determinism in his shift from the topographical to the structural model in the 1920s, he is most commonly referred to in association with his earlier ideas (Greenberg & Mitchell, 1983; Meissner, 2000; Mitchell & Black, 1995; St. Clair, 2000).

Marion Milner

Marion Milner, a painter and later a psychoanalyst, was a close friend and colleague of Winnicott's who shared a propensity for the value of spontaneity, play, and the creative process (Rodman, 2003). I believe that Milner's work, although not as widely known or cited in the psychoanalytic literature, is worthy of note in a discussion of the body in psychoanalysis. Milner developed Klein's and Winnicott's ideas and addressed the topics of symbol formation and body awareness in ways that I find fresh for the field of psychoanalysis.

In her 1952 essay "The Role of Illusion in Symbol Formation," Milner (1987) articulated two uses of symbolization. The first, which she found commonly accepted in classical psychoanalytic literature, is the use of symbolization as defense. For example, a penis comes to be symbolized in a snake because the penis itself is taboo to the ego. The symbol in this sense is a method of concealing content from ego awareness and therefore impedes psychological progress. On the other hand, symbolism underlies any capacity to be related to the external world (Milner, 1987). Milner cited Klein as explicating this view and the role of primary identification in infancy as the developmental basis for symbolic capacity.

An obviously related issue is the symbolic role of words as understood by the psychoanalytic endeavor:

> The analytic rule that the patient shall try to put all that he is aware of into words does seem to me to imply a belief in the importance of symbolization for maturity as well as for infancy; it implies the recognition that words are in fact symbols by means of which the world is comprehended. (Milner, 1987, p. 105)

One recalls the important place of words in Freud's theory of the means by which unconscious and somatically perceived forbearers of psychological experience were carried across the somatic–psychic barrier to form psychological experience. Freud's emphasis on the kinaesthetic properties of words underscores the relationship between the body and symbol formation. Words are in one sense a symbolic transmission of sensory awareness into relational awareness; words are a vehicle for making somatic relatedness conscious for the psychical self.

Of the goals of psychoanalytic treatment, Milner (1987) echoed the common psychoanalytic aim of building a relationship between the ego and the unconscious; "but I think it is not only the repressed that is discovered, but also some sort of active direct feeling contact with a primary body awareness" (Milner, 1987). She believed that the achievement of Winnicott's True Self, or the inhabitation of one's own center of creativity and aliveness, is a "meeting of mind and body" (Milner, 1987, p. 235).

Milner (1987) distinguished that she is concerned with the here-and-now perception of one's own body,

> including the effects of deliberately directing one's attention to the whole internal body awareness and . . . the connection between this and both the creation of a work of art and the growth of a vital emotional involvement in the world around one. It is the direct sensory (proprioceptive)

internal awareness that I am concerned with; in fact, the actual "now-ness" of the perception of one's body, and therefore of the perception of oneself. (p. 237)

She went on to invoke the quintessentially psychoanalytic question engaged by both Winnicott and Bion of the "real thing" versus the symbolic in both art and bodily experience. She stressed

a highly important human capacity; that is the *non-symbolic direct sensory awareness of their own state of being alive in a body* . . . It is that I think we are here getting near to talking about a direct sensory internal experience of the integrating processes that *created and go on creating the body*. I believe this to be a *direct psycho-physical non-symbolic awareness*, although at the same time of course an experience which is inextricably bound up with the inner images of the relation to another person" [emphasis added]. (Milner, 1987, p. 237)

I believe that Milner was speaking here to the core of the dilemma regarding the role of the body for psychoanalysis. In speaking simultaneously of the here-and-now, inner sense of whole body proprioception, its role in the transference–countertransference relationship, and the relationship between what is symbolic—and therefore psychological in a psychoanalytic sense—and what is a "nonsymbolic sensory awareness," she called into question the "mind of the body." She spoke of the inner subjectivity of the embodied self as a source of intuition and spontaneous interpretation, yet at the same time she called this sensory awareness nonsymbolic.

Milner drew on Freud's notion that words are the basic symbolic capacity that makes "nonsymbolic direct sensory awareness" accessible to the reflexive capacities of psyche. It appears to me that what Milner was implying but not explicitly stating is that, when this meeting of mind and body occur—as in the discovery of the True Self—sensory awareness becomes more than presymbolic or prepsychological matter. The body in this process becomes animate; it is the body that is "going on being created" (Milner, 1969, p. 110) or, as Winnicott (1971, p. 100) said, is "imaginatively elaborated" in the process of creating psyche. This is a circular developmental model. It suggests that we return to the primary material of soma but that it has gained an entirely new perspective through the journey of the differentiation of psyche. Psyche/soma is a new entity all together; it is greater than the sum of mind and body.

Milner (1987) described this new state as

a real psycho-physical background to all one's conscious thoughts, something which can be directly experienced by a wide focus of attention directed inwards, such as in reverie—in contrast with the narrow kind of attention needed for discursive logical verbal thought. (p. 237)

I believe that Milner was speaking to the subtlety of experience and creative generation that comes with psyche/soma collaboration in which somatic awareness is perhaps more than raw sensory data or the presymbolic or pre-psychological dimension of human experience.

Milner (1987) addressed the profound newness of such a state:

> Also I suspect that the adjective "divine" . . . added to the word "ground" can be an accurate description (quite apart from any cosmological mean-ings) of what happens when the consciousness does suffuse the whole body; for it does seem that such a dialectic re-union, such a meeting of opposites, after the necessary division into mind and body, thoughts and things, that we have to make in order to take practical responsibility for ourselves in the world, it does seem to be an observed fact that such a reunion has, or can have, a marked ecstatic or "divine" emotional quality. . . . Thus it seems that, behind the states that are often rather loosely talked about by psychoanalysts as auto-erotic and narcissistic (and regarded as patho-logical) there can be an attempt to reach a beneficent kind of narcissism, a primary self-enjoyment which is in fact a cathexis of the whole body, as distinct from concentrating it in the specifically sexual organs; and which, if properly understood, is not a rejection of the outer world but a step towards a renewed and revitalized cathexis of it. (pp. 237–238)

Although Milner is not a widely known theorist alongside the ranks of Klein, Bion, or Winnicott, I find that these passages to speak toward a new par-adigm for the body in psychoanalysis. Milner is useful to this dialogue as a con-trast against which to understand the role assigned to the body by other, more influential theorists. Specifically, Milner has addressed a language and develop-mental model based on Winnicott's work which allows for an incorporation or integration of soma in a way that is more than presymbolic or prepsychologi-cal. Although she does not make metaphysical implications, she does acknowl-edge the felt sense that something "divine" is touched upon in this movement. In this way she has also crossed the spirit–matter split for psychoanalysis; she acknowledged that, through the psyche/soma collaboration, the individual can experience a sense of that which is larger than the individual.

CONCLUSION

This chapter has explored the thrust of the developments in psychoana-lytic theory in Kleinian and object relations theories through the lens of the body. Klein initiated explorations that moved away from somatic drives and the economic model and opened the door to the idea that humans are essentially and primarily relational creatures. This shift has two important implications in regard to the body. The fundamental shift from drives toward objects as the motivational bedrock is a shift from a view of the "body as a beast" with unruly and uncivilized drives that must be tamed by the mind toward a view of the body as a vehicle for the expression of the mind. In the latter view, the body is less feared and approached more with curiosity. It is essentially a move from a biological reductionist model toward a more idealistic perspective on the mind–body situation, in that the psychic is seen as the motivating source that animates the body toward its needs.

However, it might be said that the simultaneous interest in infantile states and this new view of the body result in another kind of fundamental assumption. The Kleinian school tends to correlate qualities of infantile states of mind with that which is primitive, psychotic, chaotic, presymbolic, prepsychological, and somatic. In object-driven models, the soma is not the "Id beast" of classical drive theory, but it is overwhelmingly grouped with that which is primitive and prepsychological. This association, paired with developmental models in which somatically informed states are often assumed to be outgrown or built over by more mature and thus more abstract modes of being or organizing experience, results in a linear developmental model aimed potentially toward disembodiment. These models emphasize differentiation, and I have argued for further attention to writers such as Winnicott and Milner who emphasize reintegration following differentiation.

This inheritance of linear developmental models, potentially coupled with an ascension myth, informs the scope of the psychoanalytic language and metapsychological models. It must also inform the unconscious messages therapists send to our clients: that the body is either a beast to be tamed by the mind (classical drive models) or a primitive form of experience to be outgrown (contemporary Kleinian models). However, I have elaborated the ideas of theorists such as Bion, Winnicott, and Milner who used language and models that appear to undo each of these assumptions to varying degrees. Within each of these theories I have explored the creative leaps beyond an essential hierarchical dichotomy as well as the subtle ways in which unconscious assumptions about the body tend to reemerge. It appears that the strength of the unconscious ties to these mythologies causes the creativity of these thinkers to be partially undone by their followers.

Bion and Winnicott both employed a dual-aspect perspective to the mind–body problem and therefore moved psychoanalysis beyond dualism toward a unified theory of body and mind. Bion confronted the spirit–matter divide, a move that resulted in conflict with the establishment of psychoanalysis and spoke to the hesitancy of the field to engage these questions and concerns. I have argued that Bion's language also lends itself easily to linear models of development, leading toward abstraction and potential disembodiment.

I argue that Winnicott's theoretical language is conducive to a more circular and embodied developmental model. Milner, in Winnicott's footsteps, addressed the important issue of symbolization, which can so easily be taken to be further and further levels of abstraction, and rooted this concept in the body.

In conclusion, I have explored the development of object relations as an exploration of the relationships between self and other, inner and outer, mind and body, and even spirit and matter. I have characterized the school of object relations as most essentially grappling with the differentiation and interpenetration of these dualities. Object relations has begun to explore the nature of objectivity and subjectivity within this interplay and in so doing has significantly altered the role of the body in psychoanalytic metapsychologies. Chapter 5 explores the role of the body for those schools of thought who venture further into notions of intersubjectivity and thus carry psychoanalysis further from its positivistic influences.

5

KOHUTIAN, INTERSUBJECTIVE, AND RELATIONAL THEORIES

This chapter explores the shifts and evolutions in contemporary psycho-analytic thought that depart most radically from Freud's metapsychologies. Heinz Kohut's construction of a psychology built around the concept of self-structure rather than drives marks an important event in the making of new myths for psychoanalysis. This chapter reviews Kohut's ideas through the lens of the body to further elaborate the role of the body in contemporary psycho-analytic thought. The investigation goes on to include the intersubjective and relational schools of thought in light of the role of the body. The discussion is focused around whether or to what extent these contemporary schools alter what I have previously raised as the fundamental unconscious assumptions regarding the body in classical psychoanalysis and object relations.

PHILOSOPHICAL SHIFTS IN CONTEMPORARY METAPSYCHOLOGY

Although Heinz Kohut began under clear loyalty to Freudian drive theory as represented by the American ego psychologists, it is accepted that his 1977 publication *The Restoration of the Self* marks "an originality that could no longer be contained by established metapsychology" (Detrick & Detrick, 1989, p. 176). In this way Kohut is another key transitional figure—much like Melanie Klein—in the evolution of psychoanalytic thought. Both Klein and Kohut initiate metapsychological shifts highlighted in this research because these shifts cast the body in new roles.

Masek (in Detrick & Detrick, 1989) pointed out that "the revision of a new philosophical foundation for self psychology is a project still to be completed" (pp. 177–178). Masek pointed out that Freud's discoveries had also "burst the boundaries of established philosophies and stood as an anomaly with respect to their ability to faithfully contain both the insights of psychoanalysis and its own self understanding" (p. 175) and argued that it was Maurice Merleau-Ponty's phenomenology that spoke toward a philosophy that would support psychoanalytic discoveries. Masek argued that self-psychology both elaborates and complements Merleau-Ponty's phenomenology and yet diverges from phenomenology's ultimate attempt to discover the world as it is, unencumbered by theoretical notions.

For the purposes of this research, Merleau-Ponty's emphasis is relevant in that he was focused on the meaning of "a person's lived bodily engagement with things" (Detrick & Detrick, 1989, p. 183). He approached the psychoanalytic question of the relationship between self and other as "an inseparable union of person and world being lived out within dynamic alterations of lived time and space" (p. 183). In other words, Merleau-Ponty's phenomenological approach takes as its base the notion that human experience occurs in a physical body engaged with the world. It is a philosophical position that there is no actual separation between mind and body, but that reality is a dynamic play of inseparable qualities of mind and body. Phenomenology underlies the shift in understanding of psychoanalysis as a positivistic science toward an understanding of psychoanalysis as a hermeneutic one—albeit one grounded in the empirical experience of the phenomenal world.

Merleau-Ponty's elaboration of the phenomenological view further elaborates the relationships among subjectivity, meaning, the body, and the physical world. Although it was Freud's classical models with which Merleau-Ponty personally dialogued (Detrick & Detrick, 1989), the full implications of this philosophical approach continued to be implemented by later theorists, particularly those of the intersubjective and relational schools (Chessick, 1980; Stolorow, Atwood, & Orange, 1999). The implications and contradictions of this new philosophical paradigm have been explored in the literature (Chessick, 1980). Two commonly noted metapsychological problems worth mentioning in this research are the implication of teleology in post-Freudian models and the changing use of *psychic energy*.

Teleology

Teleology is the idea that there is an underlying order or purpose driving all that exists. Teleological implications of a psychological theory inherently engage theological matters, which call into question whether psychoanalysis is strictly an empirical science. It is of consequence that Freud, in his adherence to a scientific paradigm that fully rejected animism in favor of determinism, clearly sought to develop a metapsychology devoid of teleological implications. Conversely, the deemphasis of instincts has by and large resulted in an implicit endorsement of teleology as the alternative organizational system. As Chessick (1980) pointed out, philosophy "examines . . . the basic conceptual models we employ and the kinds of concepts and ordering patterns that we use" (p. 496). Chessick went on to say that the development of "the psychology of the self . . . is also a step away from the descriptive science and toward teleology, which is what makes it so controversial" (p. 507).

This research has already explored the ways in which a mechanistic universe was the fundamental ordering pattern for Freud's drive theory. Likewise, I have mentioned the gradual emergence of theories that do not fit in this general schema. In fact, many schools of thought are differentiated from the classical school precisely over this issue:

> The interpersonal analysts also partly broke with Freud over the de-emphasis on instincts. Horney, in particular, was very explicit in her endorsement of teleology. Given the opportunity, she said, the human being would develop his/her full potential or real self. (Horne, Sowa, & Isenman, 2000, p. 114)

However, the articulation of a new ordering pattern, or *metapsychology*, which might contain relational or object-driven models, is fraught with its own complications.

Chessick (1980) outlined some philosophical implications of contemporary psychoanalytic theory. The fundamental evolution of psychoanalytic theories is one from an empirical science to a hermeneutic one and from a bioenergetic model toward a constructivist model, as epitomized in Kohut's abandonment of drives in favor of empathy and self. As well,

> object-relations theorists attempt to extend Freud in so-called modern psychoanalysis, but they introduce new metapsychological concepts such as splitting, and suffer from unclarity of definitions and new disputes, with the various authors using terms in different ways and introducing various modifications into metapsychology of differing extremes, ranging from Klein and Fairbairn, who offer quite radical revisions, to Kernberg, who stays closer to Freud. (Chessick, 1980, p. 508)

As explored in Chapter 4, object relations theory begins the shift from a structural conflict model toward a developmental deficit model.

> Freud views development in terms of instincts . . . Disturbance or psychological illness largely lies in conflicts between the different parts or structures of the personality . . . Theories of object relations and self psychology, in contrast to Freud, focus on earlier, preoedipal development. These theories see mental illness or pathology generally in terms of developmental arrest rather than structural conflicts. Developmental arrests result in unfinished and unintegrated structures of the personality. In short, there is basic damage to object relationships of the person or to the structures of the self. (St. Clair, 2000, p. 3)

The move away from instincts and toward objects is also a move toward intersubjectivity and away from biology, reductionism, and Freud's original bioenergetic model. The alternative idea of psychological "structure" waiting to unfold implies a level of organization beyond that of a mechanical, reducible universe. This can be equated with a move from a causal psychology to a teleological one. Chessick (1980) emphasized the potential difficulties inherent in this philosophical move:

> Kohut's psychology of the self rests on difficult philosophical assumptions about the nature of the self—a hotly disputed issue in philosophy—and in its later form requires new philosophical postulates about forces in the mind in order to account for the resumption of development and the formation of psychic structure in psychotherapy. (p. 508)

Kohut's concept of a cohesive self implies a philosophical teleology in that it is a primary organizing principle not built on the mechanistic model. Such an implication denies materialistic reduction yet uses vocabulary such as *force*, which rests on bioenergetic concepts. This is another example of the continued use of Freud's theoretical terms within a new paradigm implicating entirely new meanings—especially in regard to the physical world and the body. This tension is widely recognized in the literature:

> Adherents of classical drive theory often criticize relational model theories on the grounds that they constitute an extreme and naïve environmentalism, viewing mental life as a simple registering of external events. In this view, relational model theories, by abandoning the drive concept, omit the central role of the body in human development and the importance of innate factors in general. Physical sensations are the basis for all experience. The infant's life is dominated by physiological needs; bodily images and preoccupations pervade much of later psychopathology. The difference between the approach to the body in relational model and drive model theories is not in terms of whether the body is important, but in what way. (Greenberg & Mitchell, 1983, p. 226)

As noted in Chapter 2 of this volume, the role in which the body is cast is tied to a theory's metaphysical underpinnings. Increasing reliance on the centrality of self-structure and abandoning a biological bedrock of motivation are moves toward teleological implications. Such moves alter the dominance of the spirit–matter split, inasmuch as a teleological universe is not a mechanistic one. This chapter goes on to explore the ways in which this paradigm shift has altered conceptions of the body in the contemporary psychoanalytic theories of self-psychology and in the relational and intersubjective schools.

Psychic Energy

The changing use of the concept of energy is worthy of exploration because it was Freud's original tie between soma and psyche. Somatic energy, in Freud's model, was transformed into psychical energy and constructed the motivational force of all psychical life. As mentioned previously, psychic energy is incorporated into relational theories with entirely new meanings:

> Sullivan's concept of energy differs from Freud's as contemporary physics differs from Newtonian physics. For Newton, whose weltanschauung informed the vision of Freud and all other nineteenth-century scientists, the world is constituted by matter and force; energy acts upon matter, moving preexisting structures. Thus, for Freud the psychic apparatus is distinguishable from the energy (the drives) which propels it into motion. Within contemporary physics, on the other hand, matter and force are interchangeable; matter is energy. For Sullivan, as for Whitehead, the mind is a temporal phenomenon, energy transforming itself through time. The only meaningful referent for the term "structure" is a pattern of activity; the only meaningful referent for the concept of a psychic "energy" is the entire stuff of mental life, not separable quantities that propel mental life. (Greenberg & Mitchell, 1983, p. 91)

In relational models, the concept of psychic energy is used as a metaphor for innate relational tendencies. Psychoanalysts have struggled with the problem of the use of energy as metaphor rather than a literal biological force (L. Corbett, personal communication, December 9, 2004; Wallerstein & Applegarth, 1976). Although energetic terminology is useful for theoretical models, Corbett pointed out that metaphors are inappropriately used as explanatory formulations.

This quandary reveals a certain struggle for coherence in the new, evolving psychoanalytic metapsychological myth. Specifically, the retreat from Freud's biological bedrock invites a revisitation of the question of motivation. Meissner (2009) recently took up this question in an attempt to provide a theory of motivation that does not rely on drives but rather incorporates an interrelated theory of needs, motives, and actions and is consistent with current neuroscientific findings. This idea is explored further in Chapter 6. However, the field of self-psychology has historically struggled over the ambiguity of this concept.

Again, I am reminded of the Aristotelian–Platonian duality. Psychoanalysis has increasingly rejected dualist and materialist organizing principles; consequently, idealist notions inferring an abstract order imposing itself upon the psyche and secondarily becoming manifest in physical reality emerge as the alternative solution. Yet, psychoanalysis does not appear comfortable abandoning the more scientific foundation implied in dualist, materialist, or emergent materialist foundations. This is a conflict that has not been resolved but that complicates the meaning of biological and energetic terms still widely used in the literature. The schools of thought explored in this chapter increasingly search for a new language that does not carry the reductionistic implications of Newtonian energetics; one must keep in mind the difficult teleological questions that arise in this undertaking. Most notably, it would seem that the biological body has a secondary role in a teleological universe, and this is a reversal of Freud's model of motivation.

HEINZ KOHUT AND SELF-PSYCHOLOGY

Self-psychology is classified by some authors as an object relations theory in light of the fact that the internalization of objects shapes theory of development and psychopathology (Summers, 1994) and because of the emphasis on relationship and retreat from drive theory (St. Clair, 2000). However, Kohut viewed self-psychology as an intrapsychic theory not properly categorized as consisting of whole object relations (Kernberg, 1995a; Summers, 1994), and it can be said that the centralization of the structure and experience of the self places Kohutian psychoanalysis in an entirely new category from object relations. In fact, Kohut claimed not to be familiar with object relations theory (Strozier, 2001), and self-psychology is not an evolution of object relations theory but rather its own line of thinking.

In this view, Kohut is another key transitional figure in the historical development of psychoanalytic theories. Kohut both maintained a certain loyalty to classical drive theory and moved beyond it in his theories of the self (St. Clair, 2000). Kohut, who was most directly influenced by American ego psychology, is seen as having similarities with object relations ideas, but by 1977, in *The Restoration of the Self*, he had completely abandoned libido as an element of his theory and had significantly moved away from Freud's structural model.

For example, in 1971, Kohut spoke of "instinctual investments" (p. 4) or the "instinctual fuel" (p. 27) supplied by the archaic imagoes of self and other. However, he had already clearly stated that his "use of the terms object-instinctual and narcissistic libido does not refer to the target of the instinctual investment; they are *abstractions referring to the psychological meaning of the essential experience*" (Kohut, 1971, p. 39). Kohut maintained the use of Freudian metapsychological, drive-theory terms but completely altered their implication by stating that the forces of instincts were in no way biological, economic forces but rather abstractions that described the experience of relatedness.

This departure from the classical Freudian paradigm was completed in 1977: "I came to the decision that I would have to reformulate the old theories and that I required a terminology that was in harmony with the new interpretations of the clinical data that I had presented" (Kohut, 1977, pp. 114–115). This reformulation included the concept of the self and self-structure at the heart of the psychic model and the replacement of insight with empathy as the primary psychoanalytic aim (Detrick & Detrick, 1989).

As St. Clair (2000) pointed out, Kohut's theory raises the difficult dilemma of a definition of the *self*. Kohut's self is characterized as essentially related to one's sense of being a distinct entity separate from the individuals and world with which a self can relate. As intersubjectivity theorists would later state, this notion of a self is based on the "myth of an individual mind" (Atwood, Orange, & Stolorow, 2002). However, Kohut's role as a philosophically transitional figure is evident in the fact that it was the subjectivity of the self with which Kohut's method and theory were most concerned. Kohut felt strongly that he was speaking of a specific kind of self that was related to method of observation: empathic immersion. Kohut's notion of empathic immersion as the defining quality of psychoanalytic investigation emphasizes the subjectivity and intersubjectivity of the self.

The notion of self-objects highlights the evolving notion of a relational or interpersonal nature of the self; *self-objects* are "those persons or objects that are experienced as part of the self or that are used in the service of the self to provide a function for the self. The rudimentary self merges with the self-objects" (St. Clair, 2000, p. 142). The developmental role of self-objects in structure formation of the individual psyche highlights the ways in which Kohut's theories begin to transcend modern Cartesian notions of the isolated mind. This is a major difference between self-psychology and theories of the object relations school that consider the development toward a separate individual identity to be an implicit component of psychological health. For instance, Winnicott (1992) stated that "to study the concept of mind one must always be studying an individual" (p. 243).

As discussed in the Chapter 4, the object relations school tends to hold that the somatic pole of existence is where individuals are least differentiated and therefore least developed and that the psychological pole is, by definition, where an individual identity and thinking capacity become separate from the other. Self-psychology, as a precursor to the more fully developed two-person psychologies, begins to challenge this basic theoretical organization. This research then asks in what way this reorientation of mind as essentially relational alters the role of the body for self-psychological theories.

In 1959, Kohut mused:

> The inner world cannot be observed with the aid of our sensory organs. Our thoughts, wishes, feelings, and fantasies cannot be seen, smelled, heard, or touched. They have no existence in physical space, and yet they are real, and we can observe them as they occur in time. . . . But is the preceding differentiation correct? Do thoughts, wishes, feelings, and fantasies really have no physical existence? . . . The problem is an old and familiar one and it cannot be solved as long as it is posed in the form of the alternative of mindbody duality or unity. (pp. 458–459)

This example of Kohut's early thoughts introduces the way in which his later theories challenged the dualities of inner–outer and mind–body to eventually arrive at the concepts of introspection and empathy. This kind of thinking characterizes increasingly postmodern philosophical approaches to theories of self and other, mind and body. The implicit message appears to be that Kohut saw his metapsychology as surpassing both dualistic or idealistic and materialistic solutions to the mind–body problem.

However, Kohut did not himself directly address a new role for the body in his theory, besides rejecting the literal use of Freud's somatic energetic motivational system. However, with the discussion of somatization and self-fragmentation, he initiated a way to think about somatic states within a theory of the self. *Fragmentation* was defined as

> the feeling, in particular, that various body parts are beginning not to be held together anymore by a strong, healthy awareness of the totality of the body-self, leads to apprehensive brooding concerning the fragments of the body, often expressed by the patient in the form of hypochondriacal worry concerning his health. (Kohut & Wolf, 1978, p. 419)

Kohut (1979) emphasized the role of self-fragmentation rather than Freud's resistance. I now turn to the work of a self-psychological writer who has most directly taken on the issue of the implications of the emphasis on body, self, and fragmentation on the role of somatic states for self-psychology.

DAVID KRUEGER

David Krueger (1989) drew on a broad range of theorists, including Kohut, Winnicott, Mahler, Piaget, Stern, and Spitz in his discussion of a *body self* that underlies and contains the psychological self. Krueger emphasized

Freud's original notion that the ego is "first and foremost a bodily ego" and criticized psychoanalysis for not paying sufficient regard to the bodily self in developmental and clinical models: "The body and its evolving mental representation have been largely omitted from developmental and psychoanalytic theory" (Krueger, 1989, p. ix).

The body self is presumed to precede the capacity for a psychological self and is composed first of the kinesthetic awareness of the body boundary as definition between self and other.

> The development of a body self can be conceptualized as a continuum of three stages, the first of which is the early psychic experience of the body. The second stage is the early awareness of a body image, with an integration of inner and outer experience. This process forms body surface boundaries and internal state definition. The final stage is the integration of the body self as a container of the psychological self, the point at which the two merge to form a cohesive sense of identity. (Krueger, 1989, p. 5)

This passage speaks to the development of the body image, the process through which the self becomes embodied. Krueger (1989) continually emphasized the role of the body self in distinctness and separation; it is this primary ability to distinguish between me and not-me that composes the rudimentary identity:

> Bodily experiences and sensations, internal and surface, form the core around which the ego develops. As the kinesthetic body boundaries are being determined, an important parallel process occurs with psychic boundary formation and functioning. The subjective reality testing of what is inside and outside the body has its psychological counterpart in the distinction between self and nonself. Accurate, consistent perceptions of body self, psychological self, and their integration, are necessary to a cohesive sense of self. (p. 4)

This statement echoes Winnicott's (1992) notion of the psyche/soma collaboration required for healthy development and identity formation.

Krueger discussed Winnicott's notion of the holding environment in light of Kohut's concept of mirroring in such a way that discloses the somatic dimension of self-object functions for self-psychology. Drawing on the work of Stern and Lichtenberg, Krueger (1989) quoted Winnicott to point out the neuropsychological component of the developing mind in relation to self-object functioning.

> The conceptual language of most early developmental studies is biological and the hypotheses encompass an interactional model; neither language nor conceptualization address the role of internal experience.

What is "reality" for the infant? How does the infant experience the mother? The answer appears to be, at first, by sensorimotor perception of the mother's physical ministrations and responses to the infant's body. (p. 4)

Krueger collaborated the findings of neuropsychology and Kohut's theory of self-object function to elaborate the somatic dimension of early self-object experiences. This construction appears compatible with developmental models outlined in the object relations school and can also be used to elaborate the meaning of self-fragmentation and somatization of Kohut's ideas. Somatization is understood as evidence of self-fragmentation and therefore reinforces the idea that the earliest forms of self-cohesion are built on the body–mind-self and a basic continuity of the somatic experience. Kohut (1977, 1979) elaborated a clinical understanding of somatization in light of the emergence of archaic parts of the personality that destabilize this body–mind cohesion.

However, it is worthwhile to note a subtle paradox regarding the continuum among individuality, intersubjectivity, and merger in regard to the body. I have previously noted the ways in which object relations theorists speak of soma as a primitive dimension of experience that is identified with merger or complete lack of individuation. Krueger elaborated the ways in which soma is the dimension of experience in which an infant first discovers and makes clear his or her individuality and boundedness as a discreet entity. Further, the field of phenomenology emphasizes that the body and the physical world are the places in which individuals meet. As Robert Romanyshyn put it, "what links us to the rest of creation is the common field of the body, which, in all of its variations and permutations, is the locus or the site where we appeal to and address each other" (in Johnson & Grand, 1998, p. 56). Phenomenology, and its orientation toward the lived experience of psyche, inevitably led to the primary field of experience in the physical world. It appears to me that David Krueger's work speaks to the intersection of phenomenology and psychoanalytic self-psychology.

Self-psychology continues to struggle with the self–object inner–outer dilemma inherent in the psychoanalytic endeavor. Kohut intuited in 1959 that a theory must move beyond either–or solutions of duality or unity, and his defining notions of intersubjectivity and empathic immersion begin to lay down a path toward such a goal. Through the lens of intersubjectivity one begins to develop a language to express the ways that the body is both the definition of individuality and the medium of interrelationship with the world. Krueger's work, which utilizes and parallels the work of attachment theorists, further articulates the conceptualization of somatic states for self-psychology.

INTERSUBJECTIVE SYSTEMS THEORY

Intersubjectivity theory, or *intersubjective systems theory*, refers primarily to a school of theory first advanced by Robert Stolorow. It is a more radical departure from the Freudian drive model and ego psychological formulations that developed from self-psychology. Stolorow viewed this model as more fully embracing a postmodern paradigm. Intersubjectivity moves beyond the individual, isolated self toward "the fully contextual interaction of subjectivities with reciprocal, mutual influence" (Mitchell & Black, 1995, p. 167). Likewise, the analytic process is a field of interaction between two subjectivities. These ideas may be understood as a theoretical extension of Kohut's emphasis on empathic immersion and self-object function; however, intersubjectivity theorists feel that theirs is a new paradigm of reciprocal mutual influence, in which the analyst's character and beliefs constitute an unavoidable role in the therapeutic relationship (Stolorow, Brandchaft, & Atwood, 1987).

The term *intersubjectivity* is used in different ways and does not imply a clearly defined scope of theory. Rather, the term conveys a wide range of theories that radically depart from Freud's metapsychology and is sometimes used synonymously with *relational theory*, discussed later. Although both theories are based on a revisionist view of psychoanalytic theory for an increased emphasis on the subjective dyadic system of the therapeutic pair, this research examines separately the work of Stolorow and his colleagues, who have specifically addressed the role of the body in their own writings.

Stolorow and his colleagues challenged many of the embedded assumptions of classical theory. The authors primarily challenged the myth of the individual or isolated mind (Stolorow & Atwood, 1992; Stolorow et al., 1987, 1999; Stolorow, Orange, & Atwood, 2001b, 2001c). Intersubjectivity theory claims that classical analysis as well as object relations and self-psychology are based on the myth of the isolated mind and that this myth serves the primary psychological purpose of avoiding the anxieties contained in the fluidity and uncertainty of subjectivities (Stolorow & Atwood, 1992). This myth is said to pervade psychoanalytic theory as well as Western culture as an unconscious organizing principle and that freedom from this myth serves the psychoanalytic goal of greater reflexive awareness. Among the qualities of this stance of the isolated mind is alienation from others, the physical world, and nature, and from subjectivity itself. There is some conceptual overlap here between the intersubjective stance and Bion's conception of the protomental discussed in Chapter 4 in that both theories include a transpersonal dimension of the psyche. However, the two theorists are using different language to describe this dimension of the psyche. The concept of the interpersonal field conveys a sense that this dimension is perhaps an emergent property of the dyad; the protomental dimension of the psyche conveys the sense that there is a layer of the psyche that is primary, that is, comes before the individual or the dyad. The intersubjective concept lends itself less to theological implications.

In 1992, Stolorow and Atwood published *Contexts of Being,* which specifically addresses the role of the body for intersubjective theory. This text specifically addresses many of the themes of this research: the psychoanalytic distinction between self and other, mind and body as an essentially Cartesian problem, and the role of the isolated mind in forming a distinction between the somatic and the psychic. Stolorow and Atwood articulated the notion that these separations are an attempt to transcend the temporal realm—that is, to transcend mortality and the physical realities that threaten a narcissistic need for control and certainty.

Stolorow and Atwood (1992) contended that the doctrine of the isolated mind contains wide-ranging consequences for the experience and interpretation of being human. The consequences elaborated are of direct relevance to the role of the body in psychoanalytic models of the human psyche. The isolated mind serves a sense of alienation from the physical world and nature:

> Positing the existence of mind as an entity introduces a distinction within man's constitution between bodily and mental forms of being. This distinction diminishes the experience of the inescapable physical embodiment of the human self and thereby attenuates a sense of being wholly subject to the conditions and cycles of biological existence. These conditions include absolute dependence on the physical environment, kinship to other animals, subjection to biological rhythms and needs, and, perhaps most important, man's vulnerability and ultimate mortality . . . Insofar as the being of man is defined and located in mind, existing as an entity apart from the embeddedness of the body in the biological world, an illusion can be maintained that there is a sphere of inner freedom from the constraints of animal existence and mortality. This reassuring differentiation from physical nature may pass over into frank reifications of the self as an immortal essence that literally transcends the cycle of life and death. (Stolorow & Atwood, 1992, p. 8)[1]

An alienation from the temporal limitations of biology and its psychological function as defense is paralleled by "man's estrangement from the features of subjectivity itself" (Stolorow & Atwood, 1992, p. 11). Subjectivity is disavowed via metapsychological and ideological reifications such as the structures of the psyche; "these reifications confer upon experience one or another of the properties ordinarily attributed to things on the plane of material reality, for

---

[1]From *Contexts of Being: The Intersubjective Foundation of Psychological Life,* by R. Stolorow and G. Atwood, 1992, Hillsdale, NJ: Analytic Press. Copyright 1992 by R. Stolorow and G. Atwood. Selected quotes reprinted with permission.

example, spatial localization, extension, enduring substantiality, and the like" (Stolorow & Atwood, 1992, p. 11). As mentioned earlier, psychoanalytic reifications of psychic structure are criticized along these lines. The postmodern paradigm and the phenomenological view both attempt to deconstruct the defensive nature of such reifications of the abstract in the context of the anxieties of the modern world (Tarnas, 1991).

This contemporary predilection begins to shift the role and meaning conferred on the corporeal dimension of experience in psychoanalytic theories. As I have pointed out elsewhere, the role of the somatic in psychoanalytic metapsychology is directly related to a theory's sense of motivation. Intersubjectivity theory, in its criticism of what has been called the "developmental tilt" (Mitchell, 1988) embedded in isolated mind theories, works toward a centralization of affectual experience in motivation. It is said that a theory built on the idea of an isolated mind creates developmental models in which an artificial autonomy is overvalued and can be conceptualized as contained within the spatial metaphor of the individual, structural mind. Whereas Kohut emphasized the relational dimension via self-object theory, Stolorow and Atwood (1992) criticized the idea that transmuting internalization relies on this fundamentally— or ideally—isolated idea of the mature mind. In contrast, intersubjectivity theorists feel that the essentially psychoanalytic dilemma explored in this research as to the relationship between inner and outer, self and other, is rendered obsolete with a full embracing of new organizing principles for metatheory:

> Clearly, it is no longer satisfactory to view motivation in terms of the workings of a mental apparatus processing instinctual drive energies . . . Most important, in our view, has been the shift from drive to affect as the central motivational construct for psychoanalysis . . . Affectivity, we now know, is not a product of isolated intrapsychic mechanisms; it is the property of the child-caregiver system of mutual regulation (Sander, 1985; Rogawski, 1987; Demos, 1988). (Stolorow & Atwood, 1992, p. 26)

Atwood and Stolorow pointed to the work of Daniel Stern (1985) to show that the regulation of affect via affect attunement and intersubjective relating in the infant–caregiver dyad is being affirmed by contemporary neuropsychological research. The positing of affectivity as central to motivation reconfigures both the dynamic unconscious and reality principle: The dynamic unconscious becomes unmediated affective experience not integrated into the intersubjective experience, and reality becomes a sense of the self as real:

> "Reality," as we use the term, refers to something subjective, something felt or sensed, rather than to an external realm of being existing independently of the human subject. In classical Freudian theory, reality is pictured in the latter way, and psychological development is conceptualized as a gradual coming into contact with the constraints and conditions of this independent, external world. (Stolorow & Atwood, 1992, p. 27)

In the absence of the isolated mind looking out on an objective reality, reality itself becomes a subjective property of the experiencing self. The soma, in turn, is fundamental to the qualitative sense of the subjective self as real and alive. Stern (1977, 1985) and Stolorow (Stolorow & Atwood, 1992) expanded on the role of the somatic in the early affective-regulatory system of the mother–infant dyad. It is through the actual somatic interaction and attunement of this dyad that the infant begins to feel real, alive, effective, and cohesive. The dynamic unconscious is, within this model, conceived of as including the somatic dimension of the emotional exchange proper to the interpersonal field.

This reconceptualization of the dynamic unconscious and the nature of defense is contained in the centralization of affect and in a sense completes the object relations thrust to devise a theory of motivation that rests in the relational field rather than on the somatically based energetic model of drive theory. A corresponding criticism may be that this evolving view speaks more toward the psychological experience of the body, or body image, and less toward the actual body. However, the experience of the body is understood to be continually grounded in the actual body and, especially as an infant, its interaction with another actual body. Although contact with the actual body via drives is not retained, the actual body is very much alive in these theories.

As discussed throughout this book, it has been assumed that a primary gain in the separation of psyche and soma, self and other is presumed to be the ability for reflective consciousness. Here, Stolorow and Atwood (1992) claimed that freedom from the myths that allowed these distinctions does not collapse but rather leads to greater reflexive awareness. The authors distinguished between "the unalienated experience of the physical embodiment of the self just discussed and a class of defensive states entailing wholesale identifications of the self with the physical body" (Stolorow & Atwood, 1992, p. 9). Stolorow and Atwood were distinguishing between an unconscious and defensive identification with the physical dimension of reality to avoid psychological suffering and a conscious state of embodiment. Such a state may be said to share properties of identification; however, the identification is a conscious one that contains psychological space for reflection and capacity for emotional experience.

The intersubjectivity model does not discard the previous work of Winnicott (1962), for instance, who elaborated the development of symbolic and reflexive capacities via the emergence and distinction of a sense of self from early states of somatically dominated experience. However, Stolorow and Atwood (1992) stated that it is not the somatically driven drives and the resulting conflicts with the outer world about which one seeks to gain consciousness. Rather, it is the affective material of the intersubjective experience of being human—and being human in a physical body and world—of which healthy development requires reflexive awareness. As in Winnicott's model, the developmental move from sensorimotor experience to symbolic experience is maintained:

> The self-delineating selfobject function may be pictured along a developmental continuum, from early sensorimotor forms of validation occurring in the preverbal transactions between infant and caregiver, to later processes of validation that take place increasingly through symbolic communication and involve the child's awareness of others as separate centers of subjectivity. (Stolorow & Atwood, 1992, p. 27)

This conceptualization of development is echoed in theories of pathology. For instance, *concretization* is defined as a defense against chaos and fragmentation that may result from the failure to organize a center of subjective awareness: Concretization is "the encapsulation of configurations of subjective experience by concrete, sensorimotor symbols" (Stolorow & Atwood, 1992, p. 44). Psychosomatic symptoms are distinguished from conversion in that psychosomatization refers to presymbolic pathways of expression, whereas conversion is a symbolic process utilizing the body as a concrete symbol.

> In sexual and other physical enactments, the body is used in the service of mind, substantializing a needed experience but not substituting for it. In conversion symptoms, by contrast, concrete symbolization creates a bodily substitute for some conflictual experience and thereby modifies the boundary between mind and body in a manner similar to what occurs in psychosomatic states. The conversion . . . enlarges the experience of body at the expense of the mind. . . . Unlike psychosomatic states, however, which follow presymbolic pathways of affect expression, conversion symptoms are mediated by symbolic processes. (Stolorow & Atwood, 1992, p. 45)

This model shares with classical Freudian theory an assumption that the unconscious and the somatic are roughly correlated:

> Our thesis here is that the boundaries between the subjectively experienced mind and body are products of specific, formative intersubjective contexts. One domain in which this can be clearly demonstrated is the experience of affect. In the realm of affective experience, the boundary separating mind and body originates in intersubjective situations closely similar to those in which the division between conscious and unconscious takes form. (Stolorow & Atwood, 1992, p. 42)

In Winnicott's model, an essential duality that was present in Freud's theories is maintained between psyche and soma. In the intersubjectivity framework, however, affect is what mediates between the two, as opposed to Freud's instinctual drive. Affect holds the place that instinctual drive did for Freud and object relations theorists in that they are experienced both somatically and psychically; notably, the somatic is considered the first and *primitive* form of experience. Affects, like instinctual drives, are the frontier between the somatic and the psychic. Stolorow and Atwood (1992) went on to cite the

> evolution of affects from their early form, in which they are experienced as bodily sensations, into subjective states that can gradually be verbally articulated . . . Empathically attuned *verbal* [emphasis added] responsiveness fosters the gradual integration of bodily affective experiences into symbolically encoded meanings. (p. 42)

This developmental model follows the reasoning of McDougall (1989), in which the boundary between psyche and soma is marked by the ability of consciousness to mediate affect. Affects that have "fail[ed] to evolve from bodily states to feelings . . . are never able to become symbolically articulated" (Stolorow & Atwood, 1992, p. 43).

Intersubjectivity theory has shifted the understanding of psychosomatic disorders from that of classical theory, not in the course of action but in the explanation and understanding of symptoms. For intersubjectivity theorists, the emphasis is on the affective content and the intersubjective context (i.e., the field of the relationship), which either succeeds or fails to allow the symbolic mediation of sensorimotor and early affect experience. For instance, does a particular mother–infant relationship succeed in mediating affective and sensorimotor experiences of frustration or pleasure? However, intersubjectivity theory does not override the classical notion that there is a developmental hierarchy between the soma–unconscious and the mental–conscious. It is my interpretation that intersubjectivity theory has moved beyond the determinism inherent in all models derived from classical drive theory but that an essential duality and the power of an underlying ascension myth maintain a grip on these contemporary moves toward understanding the subjective meaning of somatic experience.

Put in terms of the philosophical framework of Chapter 2, intersubjectivity theory utilizes a language reminiscent of an essentially reductionistic or monistic stance to the mind–body problem: It appears that the psychological or symbolic dimension emerges "out of" the somatic dimension. I should note that I wonder whether the authors do not mean to imply this stance but that the conceptualizations of pathology noted earlier do imply such a stance. The alternative stance would be to assume that both psychic and somatic qualities are inherent in the infant and that both become articulated, defined, and consciously known as development progresses. This would represent a dual-aspect approach.

I find that the language of intersubjectivity subtly implies an experiential divide between psyche and soma. Although the subjective experience of embodiment is found to be central to selfhood, statements such as "the psyche is felt to reside within the soma" (Stolorow & Atwood, 1992, p. 46) imply a persistent duality between the two, wherein one contains the other. The developmental idea that "early affective experiences are, for the most part, a matter of physical sensations rather than psychologically elaborated feelings" (Stolorow & Atwood, 1992, p. 46) implies materialistic underpinnings with developmental goals that imply an emergent materialism. It is the intersubjective context that facilitates the emergence of psyche out of early somatic experience. Such a model is a philosophical reference to emergent materialism.

Stolorow and Atwood (1992) argued that mind–body problem solutions are a response to particular pathological states:

> The philosophical doctrine of materialism, for example, resembles the mind–body relationship found in psychosomatic states and conversion symptoms, in that the primacy of the body is affirmed and its domain of influence is greatly enlarged in comparison to that of the mind. Idealist doctrine, in contrast, is similar to unembodied or disembodied states, in that the eternal forms of the mind reign supreme, with the realm of the body being reduced to a mere shadow. Parallelism may corresponds to intermediate forms of mind–body disunity wherein mind and body are felt to exist on different planes or in separate locations, whereas interactionism may speak to a greater degree of mind–body integration. (pp. 49–50)

The authors were advocating for the idea that intersubjectivity is an interactionist model. I would suggest that the language of pathology and development utilized does not reflect this stance but rather draws on the historical assumptions built into theoretical notions.

The intersubjective critique of the isolated mind has begun to challenge the concept of reflexivity, as built solely on the distinction between soma and psyche, and named the defensive quality of transcendent notions underlying this paradigm. However, I would argue that the dualism of interactionism and the hierarchical implications of emergent materialism ultimately present in the metapsychological principles fail to foster a new creative theoretical language to meet the lived experience of mature embodiment. The centralization of affect has replaced drive as the mediating concept between psyche and soma and shifted motivation from determinism to a relational unfolding but maintained Freud's "accidental invitation" (Hughes, 1994) that associates the soma with that which is unconscious and therefore primitive or old.

Stolorow and Atwood (1999) took issue with the use of the term *two-person psychology* because it implies an atomistic, isolated mind philosophy limited by Cartesian dualism. I would argue that intersubjectivity has not overcome this very criticism in regard to the duality of psyche and soma. As long as one speaks of and experiences psyche as dwelling "in" the soma, one is speaking "as if there are two separated entities, bumping into each other" (Stolorow, Atwood, & Orange, 1999, p. 27).

RELATIONAL PSYCHOANALYSIS

The term *relational psychoanalysis* was first used by Jay Greenberg and Stephen Mitchell (1983) to elaborate a set of commonalities between strands of object relations, self-psychology, feminist psychoanalysis, and interpersonal psychoanalysis. Mitchell attempted to create an integrated model based fundamentally on the notion that human relations rather than drives structure metatheory. As in intersubjective theory, the motivational force of drives is completely omitted from the relational model. In fact, there is an overlap between the two schools of thought, described by Stolorow and Atwood (1992):

> Contemporary interpersonal psychoanalysis is well represented by Mitchell's (1988) effort to develop an integrated "relational model," drawing on the work of Sullivan and British object relations theorists, most notably, Fairbairn (1952). Mitchell's general description of relational-model theorizing in psychoanalysis is highly compatible with our own viewpoint .... Despite the harmony that exists between his overall vision and an intersubjective perspective, remnants of the isolated mind appear in Mitchell's work. (p. 21)

Intersubjective thought is also a relational theory, but Stolorow and Atwood felt that their own model was a more radical departure from the Cartesian underpinnings of classical theory. A primary criticism of the relational model by the intersubjectivists is that the clinical model of transference relationship is still an essentially unidirectional one (Stolorow & Atwood, 1992). As discussed earlier, the issue of the isolated mind and remnants of duality bear direct inference on the role of the body in a theory.

Mitchell's model is by and large an elaboration of the relational viewpoints discussed earlier—particularly the relational emphasis contained in the British object relations school—and, therefore, shares with them a basic shift in regard to the body from classical theory. Whereas each of the theorists discussed have thus far existed somewhere on a spectrum between drives and relational motivations, Mitchell, like Stolorow, represents an attempt to design metapsychological principles completely free of drive theory and terminology.

A common criticism (Greenberg & Mitchell, 1983; Mitchell, 1996) of these relational theories is that in the movement away from drives and the accompanying direct reference to the somatic dimension, there exists a danger of a disembodied psychology with no acknowledged place for the soma. In this light, this research examines the collection of essays edited by Lewis Aron and Frances Sommer Anderson (1998) in *Relational Perspectives on the Body*, which is a direct response to this criticism: "Our book is a response to Stephen Mitchell's (1996) call for relational theorists to attend to the place of the body and somatic experience in their models" (L. Aron & Anderson, 1998, p. xv). In 2008, a natural continuation of this work, titled *Bodies in Treatment: The*

Unspoken Dimension (Anderson, 2008) was published, edited by Frances Sommer Anderson. That book focused less on theoretical constructs and more directly on clinical accounts of body and somatic experiences and the ways they are attended to and understood from a relational perspective.

In that first book, the authors relayed that the body is of utmost importance to relational theory precisely because it is the medium of the primary sense of the self and of all relational experience:

> Whether or not we subscribe to Freud's bodily based drive theory, we are still left with the psychological experience of the body as fundamental to psychoanalysis. For the sake of clarity, I should also specify that no one, not even the most radical of relational theorists, denies that bodily urges matter in human life. (L. Aron & Anderson, 1998, p. xxii)

Aron, citing Gill (1994), noted that a theory must distinguish between the "body as such" and the "body in terms of its meanings" and felt that "the classical bias is to reduce the metaphoric to the concrete bodily part or function and to miss the opportunity to interpret conceptions about the body as metaphors as well" (L. Aron & Anderson, 1998, p. xxiii). In the clinical application of theory, this issue becomes a question of surface versus depth. At the level of theory, the soma itself is secondary to the metaphorical meanings it holds for the psyche. This is in fact a reversal of Freud's notion.

Aron differentiated between Freud's conceptualization of the body in the formulation of a cohesive ego and the body in terms of the instincts:

> Very often in psychoanalytic writing these two conceptualizations about the body and the place of instinct are not sufficiently differentiated. This very blurring of the meaning of instinctual drive and of bodily life and experience may be traced back to Freud's writings. (L. Aron & Anderson, 1998, p. xx)

Aron essentially believed that although instinctual drive theory is not useful for the relational school, the body as fundamental to the construction of selfhood is a commonality between the schools.

Lewis Aron, Adrienne Harris, and Muriel Dimen (L. Aron & Anderson, 1998) each proposed a path toward psyche/soma integration in the diverse field of relational psychoanalysis. The authors drew on a range of influences from attachment theorists, feminist psychoanalysis, French psychoanalytic and psychosomatic theory, and feminist philosophies. These credits included Bach (1985, 1994), Auerbach and Blatt (Auerbach, 1993; Auerbach & Blatt, 1996), Fonagy and Target (Fonagy, 2001, 2002; Fonagy & Target, 2007), Winnicott (1958a, 1992; Winnicott, Winnicott, Shepherd, & Davis, 1989), P. Ogden and T. H. Ogden (P. Ogden, Minton, & Payne, 2006; T. H. Ogden, 1986, 1989), Davies (1996), Krystal (Krystal & Krystal, 1988), McDougall (1985, 1989, 1995), Anzieu (1989), van der Kolk (1996), Taylor (Barron,

Eagle, & Wolitzky, 1992; Taylor, 1992), and Young-Eisendrath (1996). As such, it is inevitable that an integrationist model may draw on theories with divergent and even contradictory philosophical and metapsychological underpinnings. This research then asks whether or to what extent these still evolving relational models are creating roles for the body that are not limited by the constraints discussed in the more traditional schools. I therefore arrange this section of the research directly around what I have thus far proposed to be the implicit or unconscious assumptions governing psychoanalytic thought regarding the body.

The attainment of reflexive consciousness as well as the value of symbolism and language are driving principles in what is valued in psychological health or striven toward in developmental models. The history of philosophy as well as explicit psychoanalytic principles agree that duality and differentiation are precursors to reflexive thought and symbolic capacity. The inherent danger appears to be that duality taken to an extreme is dissociative for psyche and soma as well as isolationary for self and other. Winnicott (1992) spoke directly to this dissociation in his construction of psyche/soma, and the intersubjectivists (Stolorow & Atwood, 1992) discuss the alienation of self from the social world, nature, and subjective experience itself. Bion (1961) and T. H. Ogden (1989) also addressed the need for interplay and relationship between psychic and somatic poles of human experience in health and development.

I have also made the assertion that a primary implicit assumption guiding psychoanalytic theorizing is contained in the power of an unconscious ascension myth and that this mythological organizing principle reinforces a dissociative duality. As well, the philosophical tenets of Platonism—exemplified in modern idealism—at work in the modern world lend themselves to ascension-based developmental models that implicitly endorse dissociative and unembodied states. I have argued that both philosophy and psychoanalysis agree that the advantages of discrimination, separation, and duality include an increased capacity for symbolization and reflexive thought. This tenet appears to apply to discrimination between self and other as well as between mind and body. However, I have proposed that the unconscious power of an ascension myth has resulted in this idea not being counterbalanced by notions of recombination, integration, and embodiment in psychoanalytic metapsychologies. Ascension and differentiation have perhaps been taken to be one and the same, and it may be useful to extract and examine the usefulness of each on their own.

Intersubjectivity and phenomenology, on the other hand, attempt to challenge the essential dualities of the modern Cartesian paradigm. Psychoanalytic intersubjectivity has primarily investigated and challenged the assumed dualities of self and other, inner and outer. This project is explored below in light of the question of how this new paradigm may or may not also challenge the unconscious organizing principles contained in an ascension myth and the Cartesian duality of mind and body.

REFLEXIVE CONSCIOUSNESS, MENTALIZATION, AND SYMBOLIZATION

Lewis Aron (L. Aron & Anderson, 1998) directly addressed the issue of self-reflexivity, symbolization, and the body. Drawing on the works of both Winnicott and Freud, Aron proposed that relational and classical theories share the idea that somatic experience is fundamental to both identity and cohesion. He also claimed that all psychoanalytic theories aim for increased capacity for self reflection:

> Much of the psychopathology that we deal with seems to be mediated by this same inability for self-reflection. All dissociation is rooted in the primal dissociation of body from mind, of subjective awareness from objective awareness, of "I" from "me." Psychoanalysis is the only treatment that operates directly to improve the capacity for self-reflexivity. . . . Analysis is essentially a two-person joint exercise in self-reflexive functioning. (L. Aron, 1998, p. 27)

Aron recognized that "potential space" is needed for these reflexive capacities but that dissociation also defeats this ability.

Aron proposed that the development of reflexivity via the potential space of the intersubjective field enables the construction of a bodily self: "The construction of a bodily self requires self-reflexivity, and self-reflexivity emerges through intersubjectivity. On the other hand, under normal conditions, intersubjectivity (and for that matter any subjectivity) is always embodied" (L. Aron, 1998, p. 4). Further, he stated that

> self-reflection, from this point of view, is based on the capacity for internal division and dialogue, healthy dissociation, standing in the spaces between realities, the transcendent, oscillating, or dialectical function. Self-reflection is based on the ability to link up experiences, whereas trauma leads to dissociation as a result of "attacks on linking" (Bion, 1967). (L. Aron, 1998, p. 18)

Aron was acknowledging—as did Bion—that both linking and division are healthy components of mature psychological functioning, leading to self-reflective capacities. In this sense, Aron was also extracting a linear causality to say that reflexivity, potential space, and the bodily self are mutually dependent on each other for development. One does not necessarily precede the other, and trauma disrupts all three ongoing processes.

This model appears to differ from that of McDougall (1989) or T. H. Ogden (1989), for instance, in that self-reflexivity is not seen to be proportional to the differentiation between mind and soma. However, Aron cited both McDougall and T. H. Ogden as substantiating his own viewpoint. It is my assertion that Aron elaborated an element in his own theory that was not explicit in the previous works. In emphasizing the "embodiment of inter-subjectivity," Aron had spoken for a reflexive consciousness that, while it may recognize the potential space between self and other or psyche and soma, can operationalize an embodied intersubjectivity, precisely because the reflexive space does not exist solely between psyche and soma. In my opinion, this subtle move begins to undermine the implicit Cartesian duality between mentalization or symbolization and somatic experience present to some degree in Freud, T. H. Ogden, and McDougall's work.

Aron specifically defined the concept of self-reflexivity in a relational context, and this new context has resulted in radical implications in regard to both the Cartesian dualities and ascension principles previously imposed upon the body. Aron drew on conceptions of Auerbach and Bach (Auerbach, 1993; Auerbach & Blatt, 1996), Fonagy (2001, 2002), and Anzieu (1989) to define self-reflexivity in the context of the relational paradigm.

Aron drew on Auerbach's (Auerbach & Blatt, 1996) conception that reflexivity is the ability to maintain appropriate tension between the experience of self-as-object and the self-as-subject. This definition has profound consequences in light of the body. Self-as-subject is emphasized as the experience of self-hood, agency, and affectivity that is gained through the relational context, which is primarily mediated through somatic experience in early infancy. It allows the qualities of enlivenedness and the subjective reality of the self. "It is precisely our bodies, and in particular our skin sensations, that are constituted by the two poles in the dialectic with which we began our study of self-reflexivity, self-as-subject and self-as-object" (Auerbach & Blatt, 1996, p. 22). I believe that the implicit assumption in previous ideas about self-reflexivity instead assumed a dialectic tension between psyche and soma (Bion, 1961; McDougall, 1989; T. H. Ogden, 1989). Such a placement of the dialectic was built on and made room for dualistic notions of body and mind. Relational models based on philosophical paradigms of fluidity and multiplicity allow for new kinds of spaces in which reflexivity and the associated psychoanalytic value of symbolization can exist. A conscious acknowledgement of this possibility may lessen the association between body–unconscious–primitive. I would assert that such a development might allow for the discovery of "somatic intelligence" (Johnson & Grand, 1998) within psychoanalytic theories.

HIERARCHY AND THE ASCENSION MYTH

It is my view that the unconscious power of an ascension myth has been intertwined with psychological differentiation and mentalization, discussed earlier. I suggest that unconscious allegiance with an ascension psychology impedes the necessary linking that precedes differentiation in mature psychological functioning, enlivenedness, and creativity. I therefore wish to analyze separately how the language of ascension and an associated hierarchical valuation of transcendence over immanence may or may not remain present in relational theorists' creative explorations beyond the Cartesian paradigms that have contained this myth in psychoanalytic history.

It appears that because relational theorists do not adhere to a coherent or unitary theoretical structure but draw on multiple disciplines and psychoanalytic strands of thought, the language of the previous theories is often used but expanded on in new contexts. For instance, in speaking about the role of the body in reflective and symbolic capacities, Aron cited the work of William James as originally speaking to the ability to move between the experience of the self as subject and self as object:

> James believed that the body and the "bodily me" lie at the *bottom of the hierarchy* [emphasis added] formed by these constituents of the "me" and provide the structural basis to the "me." In this respect, James's ideas about the self anticipated those of Freud. (L. Aron, 1998, p. 5)

It strikes me that this pervasive use of a hierarchical language structure between psyche and soma implicitly endorses a primitivization of the body and discourages a mature embodiment of somatic awareness that the relational writers emphasized as the key to utilizing the somatic dimension in analytic treatment. I have pointed out the use of this hierarchical language in the work of Bion, McDougall, Krueger, and others.

For example, Aron noted his influence by McDougall in the subject of trauma and "psychosomatosis":

> In a breathtaking monograph, Krystal (1988) suggests that affects are initially experienced as bodily sensations and only gradually evolve into subjective states that are verbally articulated. Affects undergo developmental transformation as they become increasingly differentiated, articulated, and desomatized." (L. Aron, p. 12)

This general schema is employed by all of the modern psychoanalysts included in this research, including Winnicott, Stolorow, Atwood, Aron, and Harris.

Although Harris (in A. Harris, 1998) noted that "a *relational* body may be a rather different creature from the body of classical theory, more inevitably interpersonal and fluid, less reified and static, but no less sexual" (pp. 39–40), she also drew on the ideas of Ferenczi, Winnicott, and Bion, and again utilized a language that makes primitive all that is somatic: "we can now see that these *primitive* [emphasis added] mental states will inevitably involve body and somatic experiences" (p. 40). Harris was speaking to Bion's idea of the prepsychological matrix through which somatic states of awareness are shared in maternal reverie. Harris, like Aron, noted that these ideas are compatible with the neuropsychological theories of Stern; in these models affects are first experienced as somatic states in the absence of reflexive awareness. It is this absence of reflexivity that earns the name *primitive*. I wonder whether we may distinguish between prereflexive somatic states and "mature" somatic experience that might be returned to with the endowment of symbolic spaces.

Although Harris employed these familiar terms that I have criticized as placing hierarchical importance of language and psyche over soma, Harris also attempted to deconstruct this very hierarchy. For instance, Harris mentioned the work of Wilma Bucci on multiple coding, which attempts to address the multiple and fluid levels of meaning that can exist for somatic experience:

> Her *subsymbolic system is not simply identified with the body* [emphasis added], although it has some parallel to procedural memory, an organization of experience that is outside conscious awareness and distinct from a narrated, episodic memory formation. Bucci's multiple coding system clearly is intended to bridge the conscious-unconscious distinction. (A. Harris, 1998, p. 44)

I hear this as an attempt to dislodge the static correlation between the unconscious and the soma and a parallel correlation between consciousness and psyche to elaborate a more complex image of interplay that suits the postmodern relational paradigm. Harris acknowledged that while the body can be employed as a psychological defense against meaning—as in the work of McDougall—a relational paradigm does not embrace a static or unidirectional model of evolution of affect from the somatic to the psychic. Harris appeared rather to be discussing a dynamic interplay between the subsymbolic and symbolic levels of somatic experience.

> The second idea moves us in the opposite direction, toward an escape from meaning. Bodily life and experience also escape registration and symbolization. The body is more than language; it exceeds not only symbolization but also subsymbolic registration . . . there is material life—some ongoing stream of living activity that is inevitably lost to representation, whether analog or digital. This materiality, which exceeds registration, nonetheless impacts it, and this dialectical nonidentity of body and discourse/representation constitutes . . . the space within which the magic and power of psychoanalysis emanates. (A. Harris, 1998, p. 45)

Harris was speaking for the recognition of a multilayered or multiple-meaning body. Both Harris and Dimen (L. Aron & Anderson, 1998) challenged the identification of the body with the *real*, which in a deterministic paradigm is dualistically opposed with language and psyche. This dialogue challenges the supremacy of the "scientific body" (Romanyshyn, 1989) as the body of psychoanalytic theory and practice. It is the scientific body that lends itself to ascension precisely because it is opposed to an abstract or idealist notion of psyche. The *relational body*, of which one dimension is the scientific biological body, does not inherently invite this dichotomization and therefore does not contain an implicit allegiance to an ascension psychology.

Further, the construction of nonlinear developmental models undermines notions of ascension and dissociation in models of health. Harris addressed this issue in her elaboration of a relational body that is not correlated directly with the unconscious or the primitive. She began by challenging the very dichotomies of object relations: self and other, inner and outer.

> There is an advantage to abandoning the equation of deepness or innerness with authenticity or "realness" of identity. The usual metaphor of construction of body as "raw," mind as "cooked," maintains the very body-mind split Freud's theorizing of ego was designed to address and integrate. (A. Harris, 1998, p. 45)

She concluded with the idea that she had drawn on theorists who are

> dissatisfied with . . . the idealizing of cognition, and the simplification of the body as natural given, they search for metaphors, for theoretical apparatus and for evidence in neurological and clinical studies. One unifying framework is to see all this work under the rubric of a general systems theory; where complex processes of human skill and human interaction are the flexible, plastic, and multivariable outcome of interactions across persons and within body and mental life. (A. Harris, 1998, pp. 60–61)

This rubric of a general systems theory elucidates a more complex, multidimensional body with multidimensional meanings. This relational body lends itself less neatly to the linear developmental models of psychoanalysis. Although Harris had not outlined an alternative, she had eluded to a more circular model of development:

> In contemporary developmental theory, set on a strong tradition of empirical research, the principles of multiple pathways, emergent process, variation, and plasticity can help psychoanalysts live in less rigid and deterministic models . . . Perhaps because we are in this interesting, speculative phase of our understanding, we are proliferating a rich set of metaphors . . . I prefer to think of social and relational life as a "continuum of interacting embodied subjectivities" (Merleau-Ponty, 1962, p. 162), we are moving away from the body as machine and towards a more plastic and complex "body," where inside and outside fold around each other and distinctions like inside and outside are abstractions. (A. Harris, 1998, p. 61)

I would assert that Harris was speaking here to the very concerns that I have raised regarding linear developmental models with a language of "vertical assent" that is built around primitivization of the body and idealization of psyche. In these models, it is assumed that symbolization and reflection are gained as affect is "desomatized" (L. Aron, 1998, p. 12). I further assert that these relational theorists would be better served with a language not built on earlier theories that appear to take for granted the correlation between the primitive and the body.

CONCLUSION

The making of self-psychology by Heinz Kohut marks the initiation of a paradigm shift in psychoanalytic metapsychology. Kohut's centralization of the self and his development of self-object function, as well as his clear departure from a literalization of drives, foreshadow the contemporary centralization of affect as a substitute formulation for motivation. These shifts carry implicit philosophical problems and complications but open the psychoanalytic door to creative dialogue regarding new roles for the body. I am of the opinion that the implicit admittance of teleology into the philosophical underpinnings of contemporary psychoanalysis subtly undoes the spirit–matter split that has dominated the Western world during the lifetime of psychoanalysis. Although this is a hotly debated issue in philosophy and psychoanalysis, I believe that evidence of teleological as opposed to deterministic or mechanistic models reveals the timeliness of reconsidering the spirit–matter divide.

Intersubjective theory's centralization of affect makes it the new mediating border concept between psyche and soma. I have argued that this formulation freed psychoanalysis from the energetic principles of instinctual drive theory and elaborates the subjective meanings of the body but that it ultimately maintains a Cartesian duality between psyche and soma in which the somatic is equated with the unconscious and the primitive. Although intersubjective authors speak to a dynamic interplay between psyche and soma, they are still written about as if they are "two things bumping into one another." I have asserted that this duality is unconsciously informed by an underlying ascension myth and/or lends itself to unidirectional developmental models.

I have explored the works of Aron, Harris, and Dimen, who consider themselves relational theorists, and I have concluded that although these theories do not constitute a unified metapsychological framework, they begin to challenge the hierarchical valuation of psyche over soma by way of redefining self-reflexivity and, therefore, the developmental models for creating symbolic capacities. This line of thinking, although still in process, begins to breach the vertical assent that I have criticized as underlying the work of most previous theorists.

6

ATTACHMENT THEORY AND NEUROPSYCHOANALYSIS

This chapter looks specifically at the body of research on attachment theory and neurobiology as it has influenced psychoanalysis and may impact conceptualizations of the psyche/soma. Attachment theory and neuroscience differ from psychoanalysis in that they both draw primarily on empirical data about the actual body to make links with the psychological experience of the self and body. Psychoanalysis has primarily worked in the opposite direction: beginning with the experience of inner world and making inferences about the actual body. *Neuropsychoanalysis* refers to the trend within psychoanalysis to incorporate this body of knowledge with traditional conceptualizations of the mind. For instance, behavioral observations from attachment research and empirical observations from brain scans and the theories of cognitive neuroscience are utilized to enhance an analytic understanding of the workings of the mind and the impact of the analytic process (relationship) on the mind and brain.

Only in recent history have the works of neuroscience and attachment theory begun to make significant bridges between themselves, and these bridges have overlapped remarkably with the interests of psychoanalysis. In other words, there are today many links between the neurological workings of the brain, the psychological experience of the self and self as embodied, and the interpersonal context of relationships. These convergences are remarkably relevant to psychotherapy, because they have begun to show that not only is the brain not a static entity but also that it is built and then constantly rebuilt within the context experience, especially interpersonal experience (Cozolino, 2002; Schore, 1994, 2003). These advances have helped psychotherapists understand how the therapeutic relationship, understood through the lens of an attachment system, can best be utilized to effect change.

Bowlby's work on attachment relationships in the 1960s and 1970s was the starting point for this wave of thinking. Bowlby was ostracized from the mainstream of psychoanalysis in the 1960s; however, recent developments in attachment theory alongside increasingly relational developments in psycho-analysis have brought the fields into close and productive dialogue. Likewise, exploding research in neurobiology has been used to understand and refine both psychoanalytic theory and technique and to forge a link between the fields of attachment and psychoanalysis. These recent advances in empirical knowledge may highlight Freud's (Jones, 1961) conviction that the neurology of the future might provide clarity and fine tuning of metapsychological principles and clin-ical understandings of the psychosis and neurosis. The growing body of knowl-edge in the field of neurobiology and its applications to psychoanalysis deserve attention in this work.

This line of thinking was called neuropsychoanalysis and has been utilized in particular by authors such as Alan Schore (1994, 2003), Dan Siegel (Siegel, 1999a, 1999b; Siegel & Hartzell, 2003), and Regina Pally (Pally & Olds, 2000), who also drew on a renewed interest in Bowlby's (1988, 1999) writings on attachment theory. These authors introduced to psychoanalysis the formulation that experiences in relationships—especially early childhood relationships—pattern the neural circuitry of the brain. The neural circuitry of the brain in turn influences perception, memory, behavior, impulse control, and mood, all of which are fundamental to the clinical practice of the psychotherapist.

As Louis Cozolino (2002) outlined in his book *The Neuroscience of Psychotherapy*, technological advances in brain imaging have also shown that the neural circuitry of the brain is subject to development and change throughout the life span. This realm of research lends itself to new ways to explore the brain–mind relationship, which influences our understanding of how psychotherapy effects change. For instance, Pally (Pally & Olds, 2000) drew on the neurobiology of perception and the role of pattern matching and conscious attention to detail to conceptualize psychoanalysis "as a treatment method that encourages paying conscious attention to the specific details of the interpersonal transference situation in order to develop greater percep-tual accuracy and, when necessary, to be able to generate new categories of interpersonal experience" (p. 39).

The brain's ability to perceive on the basis of recognized past patterns, coupled with its ability to modulate past patterns on the basis of new experiences by directing consciousness to details not convergent with expected patterns, is a somatically based understanding of the role of consciously exploring the transference relationship in psychological terms. This model projects that the resulting change is both somatic and psychic and that each influences the other in mutually reciprocal ways.

Additionally, Pally used the neurological research in the mother–infant relationship and brain development (Hofer, 1996; Kalin, 1995) to point out that mammalian brains "develop in co-ordinated systems with other brains. Just as neurotransmitters carry the stimulus 'message' across the synapse to activate the adjacent neuron, non-verbal behaviors (and in human, probably words) cross the gap between one brain to activate another" (Pally & Olds, 2000, p. 13). The neuropsychosocial implications of this coordination of brains in the interpersonal field have become an orienting principle for theory and clinical practice. They both confirm in an empirical way the notions underlying relationally oriented psychotherapy and allow for expansion of the clinical interventions employed by clinicians.

This neurologically based research has been taken up in particular by attachment theorists such as Daniel Siegel, Mary Hartzell, Beatrice Beebe, Peter Fonagy, and Mary Target (Beebe & Lachmann, 2001; Fonagy, 2001, 2002; Siegel & Hartzell, 2003). These theorists articulated the role of attunement in early relationships in forming neurological systems that support adult mental capacities, affect regulation, and the capacity to engage in relationships. This area of psychoanalytic theory may be an area in which psyche/soma are spoken of in ways that defy the basic dualism of mind and body, due to the fact that psyche and soma are shown mutually and reciprocally to inform one another's development. What I attempt to begin in this chapter is to tie this emerging area of interest to the metapsychological systems of earlier systems of thought to question the coherence of this new way of thinking about somatic reality within an analytic paradigm.

My intent in writing about this body of work in light of the question of this book was to reflect on how this current wave of thinking may have altered or might alter primary assumptions about the body in prior psychoanalytic thought and provide pathways toward a metapsychology that fosters embodiment and a fully embodied capacity for relatedness. To think about this is indeed like aiming at a moving target because the literature is constantly expanding and forming new visions of how modern psychobiological research might expand or refine psychoanalysis. Further, neither attachment theory nor neuropsychoanalysis represents a coherent metapsychology to evaluate on the basis of other models presented in this book. However, this might be the most opportune moment in which to consciously reflect on meanings of and valuations of the somatic dimension of experience—as these new theoretical and technical advances are being synthesized. This chapter points toward avenues for an embodied metapsychology for psychoanalysis drawing on evolving trends, while outlining concepts or assumptions that I see as being at odds with such a metapsychology.

THE STORY OF JOHN BOWLBY AND ATTACHMENT THEORY

John Bowlby was a British psychiatrist and psychoanalyst who was effectively ostracized from the psychoanalytic community in the 1960s following the publication of his paper on the mother–infant relationship in the *Psychoanalytic Study of the Child* (Bowlby, 1960). Primarily, the importance that he gave to the actual mother and mother–infant relationship over the child's fantasies about the mother led to a disagreement with his supervisor, Melanie Klein, whose focus was on the child's unconscious fantasies about the mother. Also, as Bowlby expanded his theory of attachment relationships and their role in the health and development of children, psychoanalysts criticized his theory for being mechanistic and incompatible with a dynamic psychology. Bowlby, now working closely with Mary Ainsworth, published *Attachment and Loss* in 1969 and *A Secure Base* in 1988. These works largely departed from psychoanalytic models of the mind and drew on understanding from the fields of evolutionary biology, ethology, developmental psychology, and cognitive science to investigate the nature of the infant's tie to the primary caregiver in regard to human motivation and a developmental model of the mind. These works have been criticized in the analytic literature for neglecting unconscious fantasy, instincts, conflict, the oedipal complex, and the primacy of the inner world (A. Freud & Burlingham, 1967).

Bowlby's attachment theory was built around the idea of an "attachment figure" to whom the infant is primarily interested in the seeking of proximity, to ensure a sense of safety and the ability to calm distress or avoid danger. Patterns of attachment laid down with the parents were thought to repeat themselves in adulthood based on "internal working models" that guide perception and expectation in relationships. Mary Ainsworth developed a system of four attachment styles that describe the attachment pattern adopted by an individual in childhood and predicts attachment patterns in adult relationships. Bowlby's work developed in focus and understanding through his career and work with Ainsworth—first focusing on proximity seeking and moving toward more complex models of the mind used to structure and predict experiences in relationships and to regulate internal states. The later developments in attachment theory are clearly more conducive to an analytic model.

Attachment theory is an inherently relational theory: It supposes that infants enter the world not only predisposed to social interaction but also dependent on it for development of the mind and personality. Bowlby's theories outlined the ways in which absence or derailment of the mother–infant relationship results in the development of pathology. Pathologies of this kind range in severity from listlessness, depression, and guilt to more complete detachment, retardation of development, and lack of empathy and vitality. Thus, the attachment model looks at the early relationship as a major psychic determinant in the genesis of schizoid phenomenon, depression, false self presentations, antisocial tendencies, and detachment or dissociation.

Peter Fonagy's book *Attachment Theory and Psychoanalysis* (2001) outlines a detailed account of the relationship between attachment theory and psychoanalysis over the past century, including major points of convergence and divergence between the two. He clearly recognizes that attachment theory cannot be compared to psychoanalysis as a whole but that it converges or diverges quite differently with the different schools of analytic thought outlined earlier in this book. The trend is that, as psychoanalysis has become more relational, points of overlap between the two fields have become broader. For the purposes of this book, I narrow the discussion to the tenets of previous metapsychologies that have direct significance for the place of the somatic dimension of experience, to understand how these issues are affected by an attachment-based lens.

Attachment theory fits differently with different periods of Freud's work. The long-standing issue of motivation is the first to be wrestled with in any coherent theory. Attachment theory, by nature of its focus on a behavioral system, does not necessarily fit with the concept of libidinal and aggressive instincts as motivational bedrock:

> This is key to understanding the heated nature of the controversy between psychoanalysis and attachment theory. A behavioral system involves inherent motivation. It is not reducible to another drive. It explains why feeding is not causally linked to attachment and that attachment occurs to abusive caretakers. (Fonagy, 2001, p. 8)

Although Bowlby himself noted that Freud acknowledged the role of the mother as the original love object, whose loss was a primary source of anxiety and trauma and who laid down the prototype for future love relations, the two theories differ in regard to what motivates human behavior and development. Although Fonagy noted that Freud's early works and his later structural model overlap significantly with attachment theories, Freud did not allow for a primary need to be attached to another person. In other words, Freud's theory of motivation always refers back to the drive system, a physiological need for homeostasis and/or pleasure, and the need for the object is secondary. As discussed in Chapters 2 and 3, this motivational system, despite contradictions in other parts of Freud's theory, itself points toward a monistic or reductionistic approach to the mind–body problem.

Ego psychologists, developmental theories, and object relations theory have, to varying degrees, modified this arrangement; Fonagy (2001) cited Balint's "primary love," Winnicott's "ego relatedness," and Fairbairn's "object seeking" as examples. Balint and Winnicott went so far as to make the drive for the object primary over discharge, pleasure, or another biological reference. In short,

> modern psychoanalysis does not differ from attachment theory in the sense that it overlooks the child's need for a relationship. There are, however, too many competing formulations as to the nature and origin of this need. Thus, the relevance of a singular and coherent account drawn from attachment theory should be evident. (Fonagy, 2001, pp. 162–163)

Such a coherent account might come exactly from critical examinations such as this. My primary interest is a coherent account that actualizes and nourishes experiences of embodiment in the clinical encounter, as related to the therapeutic relationship, the generation of symbolization, thinking, and meaning making.

Because both attachment theory and the increasingly relational schools of analytic thought have included an interest not only in the inner world of the infant or patient but also in actual relationships, there is a significantly new encounter with the real world and therefore the actual body. For this reason I believe that this is fertile ground in which to reexamine several critical lines of this book: the temptation to equate the body with the unconscious and therefore prepsychological, a general distrust toward the somatic dimension as a regressive retreat from psychological maturation, and any notion that healthy development moves unilaterally in the direction of abstraction or desomatization. But first, a review of the new field of neuropsychoanalysis is in order.

NEUROSCIENCE MEETS HERMENEUTICS: NEUROPSYCHOANALYSIS

Over the past decade, the field of neuropsychoanalysis has evolved. In 1999, the journal *Neuropsychoanalysis* was founded, with the stated goal "to create an ongoing dialogue with the aim of reconciling psychoanalytic and neuroscientific perspectives on the mind" (Neressian & Solms, 1999, p. 3). Contributors to this field work at an attempt to integrate neurosciences with psychoanalysis because the two fields study the same thing: consciousness and processes of mind. Both are interested in naming and describing the underlying principles that govern the mind's behavior and functioning, a task underlying any coherent metapsychology. It is a well-known and often cited fact that Freud referred, throughout his career, to the belief in the eventual discovery of the "organic structure" underlying metapsychology (Freud, 1895/1966d; Freud, Masson, & Fliess, 1985). In 1920, Freud said, "We may expect [physiology and chemistry] to give the most surprising information and we cannot guess what answers it will return . . . of the questions we have put to it. They may be of a kind that will blow away the whole of our artificial structure of hypothesis" (S. Freud, 1920/1961a, p. 50). This statement implies that metapsychology in general is a structure of hypothesis, artificial in the sense that it is a working model for what we do not yet fully know.

Eric Kandel (1998, 1999) wrote two important articles outlining the historical and potential relationship between the two fields. As discussed earlier in this book, psychoanalysis and empirical science essentially divorced as Freud abandoned the *Project for a Scientific Psychology*, and psychoanalysis has turned increasingly toward a hermeneutic investigation of the psyche. Although the gain has been a rich experience in the subjectivity of human life, the loss has been a lack of intellectual sophistication and the ability to test and verify ideas that are often gleaned from a single case. This division was historically driven by the fact that cognitive neuroscience had means of studying phenomena associated with conscious processes. Because psychoanalysis and its metapsychology are driven by an interest in unconscious forces, there was realistically little chance for a reconciliation between the fields. However, cognitive neuroscience has increasingly made a case for examining and developing models of unconscious mental processes as well (Levin, 1998; Pally & Olds, 2000; Shapiro & Emde, 1995; Shevrin, 1998).

Kandel argued for the rapprochement of the two fields for their mutual enrichment, noting that current empirical science verifies that mind and brain are a bidirectional system, that genes and brain—and therefore mind—also form a bidirectional system. Therefore, it is learning and social experience, including psychotherapy, that impact the process of mind, the development of the brain, and the evolutionary coding of genes. In other words, the outcome of psychotherapy and the validity of the organizing principles could theoretically be measured in brain-imaging studies. Such a marriage of the two fields could not only show the somatic basis of the transference relationship process and its power to induce change but could also refine the understanding of how this change best occurs. Likewise, Louis Cozolino's (2002) book *The Neuroscience of Psychotherapy* draws on contemporary advances in brain imaging studies to call attention to the evidence that psychotherapeutic relationships are effective inasmuch as they are able to effect change in neural circuits in the brain. Cozolino believed that neuroscientific evidence is supporting psychotherapeutic and psychoanalytic models developed during the separation of the two fields and that the empirical perspective has practical applications as the two fields increasingly collaborate. This appears to be an increasingly widely held view.

There is, of course, a long history of debate as to the relationship between or superiority of an empirical basis for a psychoanalytic metapsychology. Some analysts have argued that biology is irrelevant to psychoanalysis (Kandel, 1999, p. 507) and that although there may be a "functional unity" between mind and brain, the two fields are not essentially unifiable, or attempts to do so might deplete one or both. Reiser (1975), for example, believed that "for all practical purposes . . . we deal with mind and body as separable realms" (p. 479). Although Reiser was speaking more to methodology than a final conceptualization, the statement implies an unbridgeable experiential and scientific gap between the actual body and the psychological experience of the body. Edelson (1984) elaborated that such a division between mind and body is not merely a lack of scientific knowledge, as Freud anticipated, but "something that is logically or conceptually necessary, something that no practical or conceptual developments will ever be able to mitigate" (p. 14). These voices claim that the subjective and objective realms speak in language so inherently different that they cannot be correlated or combined in any meaningful way.

It is arguable that, as analysts and psychotherapists, we are in the end most interested in the subjective experience of lived life. It is in this domain that we wish to be helped by or to help our patients. One fear seems to be that if we look to the objective sciences, we will lose our footing in the hermeneutics of subjective experience. Although this may have been more likely several decades ago, it is hard to argue in light of current neuroscience. In the past, neuroscience could not account for or speak to subjective, symbolic, or meaning-making experiences of interest to psychoanalysis. However, the view of the body from the outside (empirical studies) and the view of the self from the inside (psychoanalysis) are increasingly compatible and understood to be looking at the same process from different points of view. Each enriches and refines the other.

Another argument is that if psychotherapeutic models developed in ways now simply being verified by empirical sciences, why does psychoanalysis need neurobiology? I believe that the rapprochement is valuable in several ways. Kandel's (1998, 1999) point that psychoanalysis needs to evolve and collaborate with the sciences because of its unique contribution to the sciences as well as to the intellectual sophistication and relevance of psychoanalysis is a good one. Also, it seems likely that neurobiology can aid us, as analysts and psychotherapists, in refining our metapsychological principles and perhaps bring together some of the largely disparate versions of theoretical orientations. There is and has been so much debate and disagreement about a model of the mind or a model of what is helpful within the treatment relationship that the field is in many ways at odds with itself. Understandably, if a psychoanalytic treatment requires, as it does, an enormous investment of time, energy, trust, and finances, it seems reasonable that a student, patient, insurance company, doctor, or loved one would require some convincing and coherent foundation of knowledge on which to make such an investment. Might neuroscience be one means of revealing shared territory within disparate schools of analytic thought and force an evaluation of attractive beliefs not supported by ongoing reflection? I also see evidence, discussed later, that neuroscience may also be evolving as a basis for an embodied psychoanalysis and a more coherent metapsychology for an embodied clinical practice from which to draw.

Pally (Pally & Olds, 2000) and Kandel (1999) provided some practical links between a neurobiological and psychodynamic understanding, which do serve to clarify the psychotherapeutic process of change. Both authors have integrated the exploding body of neuroscientific research and consolidated trends relevant to neuropsychoanalysis or psychoanalysis. One of the most interesting to me is the growing research in both infant development (D. N. Stern, 1977, 1985, 2004) and cognitive neuroscience, which elaborate the ways in which capacities for emotional processing, regulation, memory, perception, and expectation are mapped and formed through the process of relating. The first chapter of Pally and Olds (2000), like Allan Schore's (1994, 2003) works, elaborated the now accepted view that the circuitry of the brain develops in a manner that reflects the early environmental influences. Thus, neural networks of the brain, the basis of cognitive processes both conscious and unconscious, are experience-dependent circuits. Just as the brain, and therefore mind and personality, are built from early experiences, each can be modified through new experiences in psychotherapy. But exactly how can we as psychotherapists best facilitate such change? Cozolino (2002) posited that a change-effective therapy works at the level of a safe, affectively attuned relationship, guided integration of cognition and affect at optimal levels of emotional arousal, and reality testing, all of which together contribute to the establishment of neural networks. Cozolino emphasized the need for simultaneous collaboration of these aspects of psychotherapy, because the mind and personality are not the result of one piece of the brain but of a complex integration of multiple systems.

Louis Sanders, Daniel Stern, and the Boston Process of Change Study Group were likewise interested in understanding what it is about the psychotherapeutic process that helps people, and how (Boston Change Process Study Group, 1998; D. Stern, 1998). These works, drawing on neurobiological discoveries about the brain, investigate memory on the shaping of expectations and perceptions relevant to pathological personality organization and affect regulation. A key finding is that much of the beneficial change occurring in psychotherapy is not, as previous metapsychological models have implied, a result of making unconscious content conscious by means of insight. Rather, key components of change occur in areas of procedural and implicit memory that may never be the direct subject of the verbal exchange in the therapeutic interaction. It appears to me that if the analytic process is not focused solely on making unconscious mentation conscious, it is no longer necessarily assisting a linear developmental process from somatic toward psychic. This may be a loosening of previous assumptions.

Yet it remains to clarify a new model based on the insights of neuroscience. To begin, neuroscientific evidence suggests that there is a constant dynamic bidirectional flux between conscious and unconscious and between psychic and somatic (or mind and brain). The goal is to free this dynamic system from rigid patterns embedded in previous, often traumatic, experience toward more fluid and flexible capacities. For instance, consider a traumatized patient for whom interpersonal conflict triggers physiological hyperarousal followed by physiological down-regulation. If the implicit assumption is that conflict will lead to damage to the attachment relationship or the sense of self, the patient may engage in recurrent withdrawal from social interactions, increasing depression, isolation, and poor sense of self. The goal is to use reflective insight on the nature of the process with reference to the implicit interpersonal expectations in the context of the therapeutic relationship, which simultaneously activates new experiential possibilities. These new experiential possibilities are stored as internal models on a neurological and imagistic level. Future interpersonal conflict may be accompanied by increased physiological calmness and implicit expectations that the situation can be managed. As explored later, I believe that this model is both supported and explained by a dual-aspect approach to the mind–body problem.

These understandings also speak to very literal decisions or assumptions in the analytic encounter: What is the impact of the use of the couch (removing facial and nonverbal cues) or telephone therapy? Neuroscience appears to emphasize the importance of not only nonverbal interactions in general but also of facial cues and eye contact, specifically. Neuropsychoanalysis is the field that can meaningfully take up this question, from both an objective and subjective point of view.

The field of neuropsychoanalysis has taken up a multitude of subjects: a neurobiological model of projective identification (Schore, 2003); a neurological basis for affect theory (Solms & Neressian, 1999); the modification of genes through learning and social experience; the neurological systems of perception, motivation, and processes of memory and learning (Pally & Olds, 2000); to name a few. Again, although this field does not at the present time represent a metapsychological stance, it provides new lenses through which a critical analysis of existing metapsychologies may yield further clarities and, potentially, unification among competing models of the mind:

> Notwithstanding the fact that psychoanalysis and neuroscience have approached this important scientific task from radically different perspectives, the underlying unity of purpose has become increasingly evident in recent years as neuroscientists have begun to investigate those "complications of mental functioning" that were traditionally the preserve of psychoanalysts. This has produced an explosion of new insights into problems of vital interest to psychoanalysis, but these insights have not been reconciled with existing psychoanalytic theories and models. Likewise, neuroscientists tackling these complex problems of human subjectivity for the first time have much to learn from a century of psychoanalytic inquiry. (Neressian & Solms, 1999, p. 3)

The best possible outcome might be a culture of depth psychology in which there is room for pluralism, yet increased coherence and testing of hypothesis might replace personalized, belief-driven debates. Although the task has just begun, I believe that the argument that neuropsychoanalysis can potentially bring psychoanalysis into the future and back into intellectual and clinical prestige, for the benefit of both psychoanalysis and the neurosciences, is a good one. I also think that the present is a fine time to reflect on the way in which a future metapsychology might reflect an evolved stance regarding the psyche/soma relationship, taking into account the philosophical and scientific advances of the past century. A few of these issues are explored later.

THEMATIC CONSIDERATIONS

Although a comprehensive review of the neuropsychoanalytic literature is beyond the scope of this chapter, I present here some thematic considerations about the somatic dimension that I believe are worth evaluating in the context of the likely increasing rapprochement between the two fields. Each are themes elaborated earlier in this work, including Freud's early belief that language and words served as the link between the somatic and psychic, the implicit or explicit equation of somatic and unconscious, the use of the somatic in reflexive consciousness, and the mind–body hierarchy. This process uses the framework established in Chapter 2 to engage a philosophical backdrop for evolving metapsychology. As well, the idea of *somatic intelligence*—a term employed by somatic psychologists—is explored in a neuropsychoanalytic sense in light of evolving research. Finally, I consider the bodily issue of sexuality—if as psychotherapists we move forward from some of the limitations of drive theory, where is the theory of sexuality in the development of the mind and personality?

Words and Affect as the Link Between Conscious and Unconscious

As noted in Chapter 3, Freud's initial attempt to understand the mysterious leap from psyche to soma depended on the use of words. Freud wrote about the "kinesthetic elements" of words that made them both somatic sensations and symbolic, psychological events. This is a view both supported and refined in cognitive neuroscience. Fonagy and Target (2007) pointed to the work of linguist George Lakoff (Lakoff & Johnson, 1999; Lakoff & Turner, 1989), a proponent of the embodied mind hypothesis, to develop an argument close to that of David Abram noted in Chapters 1 and 2—that language both historically and developmentally draws its full, experiential meaning from its embeddedness in the physical and somatic world.

Fonagy and Target (2007) called this dimension a second coding system within language, which communicates the affective content and gives language its depth of experience: the felt sense of words. It is this dimension that underlies the power of metaphor as well as the deepest meaning of language. It must be emphasized that this second coded system, separate from the dictionary definition meaning, itself draws on the sensory basis of the words and the word's origin in development. Meissner (2008) elaborated the same point: Patterns of meaningful interaction with caregivers begin with motoric and behavioral forms and proceed to verbal forms in the development of language, and this process constructs the sense of agency, self, and object representation. Fonagy and Target (2007) provided an illustration using the word *mother*—in which although the dictionary definition is relatively objective, the sense of the word "depends entirely on the person's actual and fantasied, probably mainly physical, experiences with a mother or motherlike figure, a combination of affects and sensations parts of which may be conscious while others remain outside awareness" (p. 433). The authors argued that metaphors draw on the embodied, experience-based coding system and gesture rather than dictionary meanings of language. The origin of symbolization, then, is movement, and is learned in order to anticipate the response of the other to his or her gesture. Vocalization of the gesture, the anticipation, the action, and the intent is a later development but always carries with it the preverbal dimension of experience.

In this way contemporary philosophy, as well as cognitive and neuroscience, articulates how language is in fact an experience that is both somatic and psychological, conscious and unconscious, a domain in which the two are never extricated from one another but always in constant dynamism. This way of thinking about the experience of language sheds light on the way in which clinicians sense rather than know the patient's inner world, conscious and unconscious, via the mood, emotional tone, and atmosphere of the interaction, condensed and carried by words. Conceptualizing this matrix of psyche and soma helps describe how speech can convey the depth of experience, relative to the early infant and unconscious mental experience, without equating the somatic with the unconscious.

Chapter 3 explored the evolution of Freud's model: the use of words in transforming the quantitative, somatic, or drive, into conceptualized psychical content in the topographic and structural model. I showed how, in both phases of Freud's metapsychology, words had an important place in providing the experienced continuity and relationship between somatic and psychic, while implicitly assuming that the somatic dimension was unconscious. The neuropsychoanalytic model appears to alter this equation with somatic and unconscious, precisely by noting that words carry both conscious and unconscious dimensions of meaning and that the gestural or somatic dimension of words are both conscious and unconscious. The new model does not drastically differ from Freud's but refines it by way of undoing an implicit assumption that appears to have been nestled in the old model. The new model is more fluid; there are not two sides of the equation across which content must pass. Rather, there is a constantly fluxing web of interaction among all that is somatic, represented, symbolized, verbal, preverbal, conscious, and unconscious. The unconscious does not reside in the somatic, nor does the conscious always reside in the psychical. A related implication is that words are not the only medium between the somatic and representational; the intersubjective or relational notion that affect also holds such a transitional and transformational role is not at odds with this model.

The Body and the Unconscious

The above section about the place of words as mediating unconscious–conscious and psychic–somatic dimensions has already shifted the equation of the body with the unconscious. Here I explore how attachment theory and a neuropsychoanalytic theory based on an embodied mind philosophy take this one step further. The embodiment of mind theory expands attachment theory into the domain of unconscious mental experience, and out of this evolution comes a further reformulation of the implicit equation between the somatic and the unconscious. Fonagy and Target's (2007) article "The Rooting of the Mind in the Body" begins the task of articulating a stance for a psychoanalytic metapsychology that does not equate somatic with unconscious. The authors begin with a historical account—the ways in which developments in cognitive science and the philosophical underpinnings of cognitive science over the past 20 years have made way for significant links between attachment theory and psychoanalytic thought. The cognitive science of Bowlby's day was an information-processing model in which the brain was assumed to be separable from the mind, that is, built on a dualistic notion of the psyche/soma. However, modern cognitive science is more of a neuro-science firmly grounded in the brain and therefore body: *embodied cognition* or *enactive mind*. These models, based on Damasio's (1994) notion of the mind–body problem, assume that "cognition depends upon the experiences that come from having a body with various sensorimotor capacities" (Varela, Thompson, & Rosch, 1991, p. 173) and draw on neurobiology for a psychology of development and cognition. Such a perspective on the mind–body dilemma is opposed to a dualistic notion, outlined in Damasio's Descartes' Error—Descartes failed to notice that there was no evidence of the process of mind independent or separable from physical body. The evolving model outlined by Fonagy and Target (2007) depends on the body for meaning, cognition, thinking, and language:

> Any separation between cognition and physical manifestations at the level of brain, bodily sensations, or actions is an artifact of the cognitivists' computer metaphor, which implies that cognitive processes can be independent of the body, just as software exists more or less independent of hardware. In general, it is the link of brain and body that generates mind and consciousness. . . . Meaning is acquired because cognition is embodied in action . . . this emphasis on "core consciousness" as the foundation of our basic sense of self, which is seen as emerging at the interface between bodily signals and signals from the outside world, brings cognitive science and psychoanalysis into close alignment. (p. 426)

This cognitive science recognizes that the brain cannot be separated from the body, in life or in research. This is a substantive change in models of the developing mind and provides a basis from which to reevaluate the notion of drives as a potentially useful notion.

Drive theory is, on the one hand, psychoanalysis's direct reference point to the physical body. Nowhere else in metapsychology is there such a link to the processes and experience of the body—that is, until the advent of neuro-science and attachment theory. Here the actual body is the locus of the relationship to the object, the basis for the process of mind, and the foundation of symbol formation. However, the framework of drive theory rests on notions that may be incompatible with the notions of attachment theory. Inasmuch as drive theory refers back to a motivational bedrock of physiological pleasure in service of survival, it is philosophically and perhaps clinically incompatible with attachment-based or embodied cognition-based models. These new models appear to prove, empirically speaking, that human beings are primarily motivated, and biologically predisposed, to relate for survival. Bodily pleasure is a secondary function, a barometer designed to motivate in service of relatedness. The body is also a meter of and literal container for the sense of self, without which no cognition, symbolization, or object relatedness is possible. In other words, conscious or reflective psychological actions are so dependent on the somatic dimension that it becomes impossible to assign unconscious material to the domain of the physical body.

However, there are arguments for reading drive theory in a manner consistent with the attachment-based understanding of motivation. In the opening issue of the journal *Neuropsychoanalysis*, Solms and Nersessian (1999) took up this issue via Freud's theory of affect and claimed that in fact Freud's pleasure principle reads like an attachment-based model: that pleasure is not the primary drive but the guiding principle toward object relatedness. Likewise, affect is understood to be the mediator between the somatic and the psychical: an understanding identical to that of contemporary relational schools. As has always been the case, everyone has their own Freud. I make no claim to know what Freud himself intended on the issue or how he actually practiced. However, as psychotherapists, we can become more conscious of how useful drive theory is in light of what we now know and/or reflect more consciously on our own interpretations and uses of drive theory. For myself, the neurobiological framework empirically underscores my sense that development cannot and should not be thought of as unidirectional "out of" the somatic and "into" the psychical. Rather, we aim for a cohesive and dynamic collaboration, as Winnicott (1958b) articulated.

The Mind–Body Hierarchy

In previous chapters, I have made explicit the assumption within most of psychoanalysis that the mind and its capacity for consciousness is the preferred goal of both developmental maturation and psychological treatment. I have argued that as psychotherapists we fail to explicitly acknowledge and attend to the need to reintegrate our developments in the somatic dimension and have named this failure an *ascension myth*. Analytically, we have historically assumed that our primary goal is to make unconscious material conscious via insight and reflection, that is, to make it a psychological and therefore desomatized process or content. We learned, earlier in this book, that the mind, properly speaking, never separates from the body and also that consciousness never lives separately from its somatic dimension. This evidence forces us to reexamine these sometimes subtle assumptions, including the equation of the body with the unconscious, discussed previously. The equation of the body with the unconscious is interwoven with the preference for language and mentation, or what I have called a *mind–body hierarchy*.

The neurobiological and attachment research has spoken to the way in which the very nature of thought influenced by characterizations of primary object relations—not only at the level of image or belief but also at the level of gesture and action known and remembered most potently at the somatic dimension. Fonagy and Target (2007) pointed to Susan Isaac's work to talk about the way mental representations are described as "proxies for actions that generated them and for which they stand" (p. 428). Thus, implicitly, the use of symbolic representation is embedded within the history of bodily and social experience of *actions* related to the symbol (Fonagy & Target, 2007). Fonagy and Target made explicit the physical origins of thought and the inherent relationship between thought and action, or behavior. They argued that these actions, beginning with the infant's first experience of initiated mobility, lie at origin of attachment representations and that these symbolic representations contain vestiges of sensations and predispositions that make the unconscious emergence of attachment experience a reality. To make explicit in our knowledge the immediacy of the presence of the early experience of object representations, as known primarily through the somatic dimension, as psychotherapists we recognize that "the experience of analytic intimacy would not have meaning without the backdrop of physical sensation evoked by the action language of metaphor" (Fonagy & Target, 2007, p. 530).

This point is related to issues with which psychoanalysis as a whole and relational theorists in particular have wrestled. One cannot isolate the inner world from the outer world; likewise, one cannot isolate mind from body or psyche from soma. As this becomes more explicit and obvious to us as psychotherapists, through neighboring disciplines, we more fully recognize that the idea of a hierarchy between mind and body is obsolete, which leads to new ways of attending to the somatic dimension in the analytic relationship. As such, we need new ways of conceptualizing the somatic dimension in our metapsychologies. At the very least, we need to actively challenge dimensions of our metapsychologies that implicitly hold a mind–body hierarchy.

The somatic is not merely prepsychological but rather the foundation of all things psychological, without which psyche is an impossibility. This impacts in a subtle way how as psychotherapists we think about things like alexithymia or somatization. Winnicott best understood this and had a language for speaking about it that prioritized the psyche/soma dialectic rather than a supposed evolution or one-way development. The necessity to strongly anchor a metapsychology in this kind of language is heightened by current neurobiological accounts of language, affect, thinking, symbolization, or any process of mind, and it appears to me that Fonagy and Target's (2007) evolving integration of attachment theory with neurobiological models within an analytic model provides this opportunity.

Somatic Intelligence

Somatic intelligence is a term used by somatic psychologists, bodyworkers, and at times, phenomenologists. I believe that it incorporates a sensibility necessary in evolving analytic metapsychologies. Current neurobiological research alongside philosophical underpinnings of contemporary analytic thought deny the possibility of an intelligence that is not embodied. It appears to me that, based on Cartesian beliefs—not just about mind and body but also about spirit and matter—underlying classical analytic models, it was implicitly supposed that the somatic dimension was devoid of intelligence. This was supposed in part due to the correlation between intelligence and consciousness, both properties dependent on a supposed mind–body chiasm. It is my personal viewpoint, based on both clinical and personal experience, one validated by current research, that the somatic dimension often portrays and guides with its own intelligence. This is an intelligence that the conscious mentation of the individual or, neurologically speaking, frontal cortex capacities, can and in fact must draw on to survive and thrive.

The above sections have shown how any remaining vestiges of a mind–body division are hypothetical at best and more probably missing the point of the complexity of the psyche. If as psychotherapists we unwittingly assume that the mind can ever separate from the body, or that it must to gain reflexive capacity, we might be missing the nature of thought, subjective experience, and what helps in psychotherapy. Increasing evidence has accumulated to show that many mutative aspects of psychotherapy are not in the act of making unconscious conscious via insight but are in modifications at the level of unconscious memory, expectations, and representations (Boston Change Process Study Group, 1998; D. Stern, 1998). Such modifications may or may not be accessed or articulated by conscious processing.

Here I would like to explore further what is implied by the term somatic intelligence, in light of the earlier neuropsychoanalytic findings, to elucidate a clinical sensibility and practical use of these metapsychological reflections. To begin, I draw on the highly illustrative writings compiled in Frances Sommer Anderson's (2008) book *Bodies in Treatment: The Unspoken Dimension*. The book begins with a personal disclosure about the author's own use of body-centered modalities in conjunction with psychoanalysis:

> Despite many years of formal education and evidence of mastery in some areas, I still feel at a loss when I confront dense, highly conceptual verbal and quantitative material. In contrast, when I meet someone for the first time or consult with a new patient, I "know" a lot immediately, even though I cannot always articulate what I "Know" in my body. I rely heavily on subsymbolic and nonverbal symbolic modes of processing as an analyst and often find it difficult to articulate the complexity of my awareness in discussions with colleagues and when writing. (Anderson, 2008, p. 2)

Anderson (2008) described her personal traverses between talk therapy and body therapy, providing pathways into affect states, self-representations, and true self-experiences not directly reached through analysis but which could subsequently be integrated in talk therapy.

What is it about working with the physical body more directly that facilitates this contact, and how can analysis maximize this capacity? Personally, as well as paying attention to the verbal content of the session, I tune one of my analytic receptors to my patient's body and one to my own body. I often verbalize information drawn from these realms and have found, like several authors in Anderson's (2008) book, that this information can lead through impasses or into affect states that might have gone unnoticed otherwise. For instance, an analytic patient had one day decided to lie on the couch in the opposite direction so that I could see his face. After an interpretation about a desire I sensed was in the room, the patient replied with a disaffected "Yeah, I guess," which I verbally would have taken as a rejection of the interpretation. However, the patient simultaneously looked me in the eye with a distinct look of surprise, pleasure, and embarrassment at this desire being named. I pointed to the contradiction between the verbal response and the look in his eyes, which led to an elaboration of previously hidden material.

There are many instances in which I do not believe I could adequately assess how a patient is taking in my interpretations without visual access to subtle changes in facial expression, eye contact, skin color, or gesture. It is often a somatic gesture or response in opposition to the verbalized content that signals the presence of highly meaningful or charged material. Anderson (2008), as well as William Cornell, Wilma Bucci, and other relational analysts, like many body-oriented psychotherapists mentioned in Chapter 1, related the true self to sensory, motoric, and visceral domain. Winnicott as well placed the source of spontaneous gesture and creativity in a healthy collaboration of the somatic dimension. A great deal of clinical work has used these notions in the treatment of trauma, essentially to recapture parts of the true self dissociated in order to survive a trauma, which appear to be most effectively reintegrated through a somatically oriented technique (e.g., P. Ogden, Minton, & Pain, 2006).

Bucci and Cornell made the case that the affective core of the self-object configuration is somatically experienced and that, therefore, the somatic dimension is the most direct route to the heart of the analytic matter:

> The affective core is dominated by sensory, motoric, and visceral elements, and in normal emotional development, these must be integrated into the emotion schemas. Bodywork, combined with traditional analysis, helped me discover developmental trauma at a visceral and affective level. (Anderson, 2008, p. 23)

As such, it becomes imperative that as psychotherapists we have eyes and ears with which to perceive at this dimension of experience. In other words, it is important that we have access to our own somatic selves: a capacity for *interoception*, the ability to access and utilize subsymbolic or subverbal dimensions of our own inner experience. I believe that Wilfred Bion spoke to this capacity, as discussed in Chapter 4 of this volume.

An important essay by Adrienne Harris (Anderson, 2008) addresses the issue of caretaking the analyst's visceral ear, so to speak. She

> had begun to wonder how it was going to be possible to metabolize the vast quantity of emotional and fantasy experiences I was involved with . . . self care often seems to involve the body. Analysis is often viewed, from the perspective of the analyst, as a primarily mental activity, rather than a fully embodied experience. (Anderson, 2008, p. 257)

To recognize that analysis is an embodied art on the part of the analyst also means that, as analysts, we must care take our own bodies because they are constantly working to receive, metabolize, attune to, and express the analytic material. An element of somatic intelligence is the capacity for somatic resonance with the other and somatic interoception into the process of this resonance.

William Cornell (Anderson, 2008) made an important contribution about the somatic organization of the self as it applies to the psychotherapeutic process. He saw the somatic dimension and attenuation to this as the primary door to understanding and modifying self-organization, precisely because self-organization is a somatic organization: a direct map of the shape of oneself in the world or against the world. This is not the case in defense or pathology but a common denominator in human experience. Attention to the somatic organization of the other and one's own somatic organization in response to the other is then a powerful psychotherapeutic tool to potentiate organizational change in the personality. I refer the reader to Cornell's (Anderson, 2008) illustrative clinical vignettes, which leave no doubt that an open eye and ear toward bodily awareness and movement can be utilized within traditional psychoanalysis. Other authors in this compilation (Anderson, 2008) addressed using bodywork as an adjunct to talk therapy, while recognizing a dilemma that powerful transference components arise in relation to the bodyworker and that that relationship does not provide a framework in which to address them.

All of the authors in *Bodies in Treatment* address the benefits and challenges of utilizing awareness of somatic intelligence in the analytic endeavor. As psychotherapists, we are at a point, with the advent of attachment theory and neuropsychoanalysis, of developing coherent organizing principles in which this somatic intelligence belongs and can be used. Neuroscience has shown that the mind does not reside localized within the brain; the mind is a process intensely involved in the body. Literally speaking, neurotransmitters, such as serotonin, which are thought of as transmitting brain information, are present in the intestines as well as in the brain. There is information and communication going on not just in the literal brain but also in the brain system of the body. As such, intelligence is not localized and not merely a property of the brain, although the brain is a locus of neural activity that reflects mind activities. In this light, as psychotherapists we might ask ourselves, clinically less "what comes to mind," and more "what comes to body." For the body is a dynamic sum total of conscious and unconscious psychic activity, including all that we hope to learn and at times modify in the course of psychotherapy. This is a fact that is well known and worked with by bodyworkers and somatic-focused psychotherapies, most of which are within the lineage of the Reichian model, discussed in Chapter 1. Neuroscience, along with the attachment-based understanding of the effects of relationships on the mind, provides a bridge between these two worlds that were essentially separated when Reich separated from the psychoanalytic movement in the 1930s.

A Place for Sexuality

Historically, one of the strongest arguments against attachment theory within the field of psychoanalysis has been to point out the lack of a theory of infantile sexuality and/or attention to the role of sexuality in character formation. As well, the question has been raised that if instinct theory is repudiated or has simply lost our attention, how exactly do we conceptualize the bodily experience of sexuality? A recent study (Shalev & Yemshalmi, 2009) of psychotherapists' focus on sexuality identified that the extent to which a therapist's conceptual model centralized sexuality as a motivation of human behavior directly influenced the attention to the issue in the therapeutic process and the clinician's formulations.

Historically, sexuality motivated not only development but also repression, and this made sense culturally. Perhaps, as the cultural attitudes toward sexual selves in general have evolved, sexuality holds less power as a primary organizing principle in the dynamic unconscious. However, sexuality is a lynchpin, in that it, like the body, is both biological and psychological, literal and symbolic. Attachment theory and neuropsychoanalysis have brought the physical dimension more fully back into a realm of relational psychoanalysis, but it is true that references to psychosexuality have decreased in the literature (Kandel, 1999). It seems to me that one factor has been modified simply by changing cultural norms over the preceding century: Within the theory of psychosexuality and the dynamic unconscious, the role of shame and disgust in regard to sexual or bodily feelings played a major role in psychic determinism, and as the culture has evolved, there is somewhat less overarching fear, shame, and disgust in relationship to sexuality in general. Consequently, the power of repression in regard to sexuality per se might hold less explanatory power in the formation of pathology and defense. I might speculate that increased repression has evolved—rather than on sexuality per se—but in regard to mortality, loss of control, or emotional vulnerability. Stolorow and Atwood (1992) made the convincing case that each of these issues is most present and visible in light of our physicality and therefore confronted primarily via the body.

It seems to me that a remaining area of interest for evolving theories is a more coherent and articulate role of sexuality. Can Freud's unique perspective on psychosexuality be integrated with evolving neuroanalytic and attachment-style paradigms? If so, as psychotherapists we might begin to tackle what I believe remain as areas of mystery in our body of knowledge: gender identity, sexual orientation, gender roles, and sexual perversions (Kandel, 1999).

CONCLUSION

Attachment theory and neuroscience attend to the behavioral and empirical body. Neuropsychoanalysis is the evolving dialogue that incorporates these fields of study into the classical analytic notions of the mind traditionally built on a study of the mind from the subjective point of view. Neuropsychoanalysis speaks to the brain and, increasingly, to the brain system of the somatic body that can be measured empirically, and, increasingly, it is tied to subjective experiences of the self and self–object–world relationships. The intersection between attachment theory, cognitive neuroscience, and psychoanalysis places particular evidence on the way the brain–body–mind system is built and influenced by the interpersonal context, including the psychotherapeutic one. This time in history provides exciting new pathways between classical psychoanalytic paradigms and neighboring disciplines of cognitive science, linguistics, neurobiology, and evolutionary biology. It offers the hope of refining and clarifying the metapsychological beliefs of psychoanalysis, as Freud had so strongly hoped and for which he himself tried.

Perhaps the challenge is to find the empirical body and simultaneously attend to the lived, subjective body with respect to the observable phenomena that can refine our ways of seeing and conceptualizing the body in intellectually sophisticated and new ways. The question arises as to the relationship between the biological body and the phenomenological body; as psychotherapists, we have long been searching for a model to explain this mysterious relationship. Neuroscience shows us increasingly how the two make sense together; our experience of ourselves, our memories, predictions, expectations, and representations are correlated with actual happenings in the physical brain and body. However, biology, like metapsychology, is only a set of ideas until utilized within the art of psychoanalysis and the subjective and intersubjective experiences of living. Psychoanalysis provides just this playing field and research tool and needs the benefit of this knowledge. The most exciting development is that neurobiology is increasingly able to explore the realm most interesting to psychoanalysis—the unconscious.

Several important points have been clarified already from the dynamism of these fields, and each of these bears significance to the topic of this book. The unconscious cannot be correlated with the body or consciousness with the mind; and the processes of mind not only rely on but also draw their richness and power from their immediate resonance and embeddedness in the somatic dimension of the mind, which is also the affective and representational core of the self-definition and self-object representation. Those processes or representations that we seek to modify in psychoanalytic treatment are largely outside of conscious awareness and may even remain so while undergoing important modifications. If as psychotherapists we fully understand the implications of this knowledge, we must respect and listen to the somatic dimension of experience in our consulting rooms. For it is in this dimension, sometimes consciously perceived and sometimes consciously but subverbally felt, that our careful attention can impact systems of pathology and foster more gratifying and enlivened existences for ourselves and our patients. I have focused here on the works of Peter Fonagy and Mary Target, who, with other analytic colleagues, seem to be most active in fostering forward-thinking developments in the field of psychoanalysis, which can be propelled by neurological and attachment-based perspectives. The philosophical and cognitive neuroscience concept of *embodied mind* is a lucrative one for psychoanalysis, supplying the intellectual momentum to integrate new ways of understanding the somatic dimension in analytic models of the mind, development, pathology, and health.

7

CONCLUSIONS

A lasting impression was made on me on the first day of my high school physics course. The instructor began with the lesson of the "black box." He presented the students with a black box to which we could do anything we wanted, except open. Our task was to design a model of what was inside the box that could explain the phenomena we observed as we moved it around. We made many attempts, but each new experiment with the box forced us to revise our theory. His point was that theories are just that—attempts to describe a phenomenon that in itself we can never fully know. Metapsychology is psychology's theory about the phenomena of the workings of the mind–brain–body–self matrix. The theories are constantly under revision, and as psychotherapists we must acknowledge that they are not the territory, but the map.

This book has examined the map of metapsychology to reveal unconscious or implicit assumptions about the body, which do not correspond to the territory experienced as a clinician and human being. This book has been a sojourn through much territory, hopefully for the sake of disclosing something barely known but not quite articulated, so that it can be utilized for further growth and evolution of our collective thinking. I would like here to summarize what has consolidated in my mind through this journey and to make some statements as to how this work has impacted and clarified my own clinical use of theory in the consulting room.

A consideration of Freudian, Kleinian, object relations, self-psychological, intersubjective, and relational schools of thought, as well as recent attachment and neurobiological contributions, has led me to several conclusions regarding unconscious assumptions embedded in theoretical principles. Because I am loyal to the hermeneutic method of investigation, my goal is not to state an absolute truth but to disclose that which may be hidden or unspoken in an effort to deepen awareness of the ways in which theory can speak to lived human experience.

This study has employed the methodology of textual hermeneutics, meaning that the work is in essence an interpretation of the texts that embody the theory through which depth psychologists make meaning of human experience—particularly human bodily experience. It is assumed that although there may be some gap between theory and clinical practice, the unspoken or implicit assumptions in theoretical language and structure imply the implicit assumptions that clinicians bring to the consulting room. Or, stated another way, it is likely that many theorists practiced in such a manner that was deeply embodied but that the language of theory has fallen short in representing or teaching an embodied method of practice. I suspect this to be particularly true of Freud and Bion, but I have little means of proving this to be the case.

The process consisted of an ongoing hermeneutic dialogue among several actions: a reading of theoretical text; immersion in clinical practice, written notes, and journaling; verbal dialogues including my own analysis and psychotherapy; and the ever-present backdrop of my own physical life. Such a method acknowledges the inevitability of the interpretation of text as a "re-creation of the text" (Gadamer, 1989, p. 386) in the researcher's own mind. I have therefore acknowledged my own biases, which are a part of the dialogue.

The process itself has further elucidated my own transference to the topic and has allowed me to clarify the importance of the topic in my own life, as well as my passion for the subject matter. The work was in part inspired by my need to reconcile the text of psychoanalytic theorizing with my own experience of being here in the world. My own resonance with the psychoanalytic attitude was felt to be slightly at odds with my interpretation of the portrayal of the body in psychoanalytic models. To this end, my personal experience is necessarily inseparable from the inquiry at hand. On the one hand, my experiences and the potential disparities between this experience and my reading of the texts ideally create a fresh dialogue and reflective space within which to examine the theories. On the other hand, by contextualizing my own, subjective context I have also been able to broaden the scope of thought inherent to the research beyond that of my own biases. The work was felt to be a source of constant discovery and often shifted my own biases or preconceived notions about what I thought I might find. However, a hermeneutic investigation such as this does not claim ever to be entirely free of the subjective context of the observer, and therefore the conclusions I have reached are necessarily the conclusions born out of a personal interpretation that is open to further dialogue.

I have concluded that the complexity of the mind–body problem bears a specific relationship to psychoanalytic theories of mind, development, and pathology. That is, the mind–body problem is interwoven with the essential psychoanalytic problem of the relationship between self and other, inner and outer, spirit and matter. As shown in Chapters 4 and 5, the result is that the body appears to bear the burden of existing in the paradoxical position of containing both self and other, inner and outer, and spirit and matter. I have asserted that psychoanalytic theory has historically been overly tempted to place the soma in an association with the unconscious or the primitive and has therefore limited the potential clinical elucidation of conscious somatic enlivenedness.

I have investigated the history of psychoanalytic theory in four chapters marked by four essential paradigm shifts, to conclude that each reconstruction of metatheory carries slightly different implications for the body. A reiteration of the nuances of the evolving and shifting role of the body ensues. My most general conclusion, however, is that each mind–body solution implies a theory of basic motivation. In other words, each mind–body solution implies something about the source of the animating, generative, or motivating energy of life. Therefore, the mind–body problem is inextricably interwoven with the spirit–matter divide and corresponding theological questions. I suggest that much of the ambivalence in metapsychology about a mind–body position relates to the hesitancy of psychoanalysis (and all sciences) to engage these essentially theological concerns.

I have concluded that the psychological development of differential and symbolic capacities has been inadvertently overlaid on a spirit–matter split, leading to developmental models governed by an *ascension myth,* the idea that human growth and fulfillment is movement ascending from the flesh toward the heavens. I suggest that the unconscious power of this myth subtly encourages a primitivization of the somatic and dissociation from the full enlivenedness of embodied experience, and I point toward possibilities within contemporary research and theory to consciously evolve a metapsychology that facilitates embodiment.

I advocate for a metapsychology built on a dual-aspect approach to the mind–body issue, which appears most consistent with current empirical research about the brain, subjective experience, and the importance of relationships on both. Metapsychological principles built on a dual-aspect approach are compatible with a language that supports embodiment rather than a linear developmental model that colludes with states of disembodiment and abstraction. I acknowledge that such a position does lead to teleological implications and related theological questions and suggest that psychoanalysis acknowledge that its field of study reaches the borders of this mystery. In other words, a dual-aspect approach supposes a third thing out of which the psyche and soma emerge. This third thing is the dimension of the unknown or, as Bion (1983) termed it, O. Carl Jung referred to this dimension as the *soul* (Jung & Franz, 1951; Samuels, Shorter, & Plaut, 1986).

A SUMMARY OF FINDINGS

The essential findings are succinctly reviewed here to elucidate the central themes and integrate implications suggested above.

The Mind–Body Problem, Western Philosophy, and Reflexive Consciousness

Chapter 2 began with a contextualization of the mind–body problem within the historical development of the modern Western mind and a contextualization of the history of psychoanalysis alongside the philosophical disposition of the 20th and 21st centuries. The development of the Western mind in this light is understood to be primarily characterized by a replacement of divinity and mythological explanations of the cosmos with the power of human reason. It is understood that the pursuit of knowledge and reflexive consciousness—a hallmark of the Western mind—is made possible by the novel creation of a *chiasm*.

A chiasm is the necessary space in which reflexivity can occur. This is also understood as a fundamental principle in psychoanalytic principles, whereby reflexive space between self and other or psyche and soma is a necessary precursor to language, symbolic capacities, reality testing, thinking, and self-identity. The very nature of this chiasm is continually investigated throughout the research—particularly the chiasm between psyche and soma as it is relates to psychological capacities.

A defining chiasm in the history of the Western world is that between matter and spirit, and this essential separation is understood to underlie the notion that psyche is "imprisoned in the soma as in a tomb" (Tarnas, 1991, p. 157) and that ultimate human potential is realized as the psyche or mind *ascends* toward the divine. I have spoken of this as an *ascension myth*—a fundamental unconscious organizing principle in the philosophical mythology of the Western mind (Abram, 1996; Berman, 1998; Tarnas, 1991).

I have outlined the role of Plato and Aristotle in the structuralization of this myth within the doctrines of the immortality of the soul and empiricism.

There is a sum qualitative shift from what Abram (1996) characterized as a pre-Socratic "embedded-in-the-world consciousness" toward a dissociation of the divine from the material world and the intellect from the senses. A sense of direct participation with and within the world is superseded by a sense of objective observation of the world. In this way I have understood the spirit–matter split as underlying the body–mind split and assisting the rise of a self-reflective quality valued in the modern Western world, and I have demonstrated that the myth of ascension has been intertwined with this novel sense of dualities in a way that foreshadows a hierarchical valuation of the immaterial over the material or corporeal.

The four major modern solutions to the mind–body problem are outlined: Descartes' dualism, Hobbes's reductive materialism, Berkeley's idealism, and Spinoza's double-aspect theory. A brief review of the principles inherent in each solution is provided as a context within which to critically analyze the mind–body solutions inherent in later psychoanalytic models. As well, the basic conflict between determinism and teleology as the causal foundations of metapsychology is discussed in relation to mind–body solutions. It is concluded that although many psychoanalytic authors may not directly state a position regarding the body, one can be inferred most directly from a theory's notion of motivation or causality. Teleological implications are inherent in idealist and dual-aspect theories, whereas determinism is implied in materialist and most dualist solutions. Teleological solutions subtly challenge the spirit–matter split and are therefore difficult to incorporate into the psychoanalytic models with a Western sensibility in any coherent way. This issue becomes relevant in the contemporary models of Heinz Kohut, Robert Stolorow, and others who have begun to assert metapsychological principles alternative to that of classical Freudian drive theory, which tend to rest on determinism or causality.

I point to the need for a theory of motivation, which reflects an approach to the mind–body problem that is consistent with other metapsychological principles. The problem with the concept of drives is that they initially referred to a monistic, reductionistic language and philosophical background. Such a concept implies a mind–body hierarchy and consequently a linear developmental model. Although psychosexuality expanded the concept of drives to entertain the possibility of a dualist, interactionist approach, this was not fully integrated or reconciled with the language and system of metapsychology. I argue for the recognition of the animating third thing out of which both mind and body become manifest as in a dual-aspect approach. Although as humans we cannot know what this third thing is, we can acknowledge the mystery. Such a conception neither prioritizes mind nor body but emphasizes collaboration.

A dual-aspect approach is consistent with neuroscientific evidence correlated with behavior research in the attachment field and provides a model of psychotherapy to understand how people change, both in brain and mind, which alters our experience of our body as well as our physiological responses to stress, intimacy, work, challenges, and affect. A dual-aspect approach is supported philosophically by phenomenology and the work of Damasio discussed in Chapter 2. These works do acknowledge a teleological dimension of life, but do not claim theological answers. This approach encourages and supports the embodiment so necessary to mental health and is an antidote to elements of many maladies of the modern world, including depression, schizoid phenomena, self-harm propensities, and dissociative phenomena.

History of the Unconscious

A history of the medical and spiritual professions reveals that the separation between priest and doctor as one who cares for the soul and the body, respectively, assisted a rationalist approach to the world in which the physical senses were separated from spiritual truth accessible only through the church. I have asserted that this division sets the stage for "doctors of the psyche" to distrust the physical body. I have also raised the issue that the depth of the psychological unconscious displaces the centrality of reason and rationality that underlies this situation, and I concluded that for this reason the history of depth psychology reveals an unconscious conflict regarding its philosophical allegiances.

A review of the origins of the concept of the unconscious serves to name the philosophical assumptions contained in this defining principle of psychoanalysis. I have raised the issue of the relationship between the unconscious and the corporeal world in particular and concluded that the origins of the unconscious in Mesmer's magnetism, de Puysegur's psychologizing of magnetic fluid, and James Braid's 1843 coining of the term *hypnotism* reveal the romantic origins of a concept ultimately made accessible to Freud in his milieu of empirical science.

The competing influences of romanticism and empiricism are explored in relationship to Freud by way of his mentors, to conclude that Freud was indeed influenced by two very different worldviews and that he appears to have felt a certain affinity for both. These mixed influences are evident in the fact that the concepts of the id, drives, and the transference relationship are rooted in early hypnotic concepts governed by an actual substance bearing remarkable similarities to *Qi*. Like de Puysegur's magnetic fluid, Qi is a borderline substance that is both physical and psychic and composes both the manifest world and the intangible worlds of psyche. I have found this to be the most remarkably romantic notion to underlie Freud's psychoanalytic endeavor; the way in which this romantic notion was subsequently transformed into the positivistic drive model reveals the repression of the living body in favor of what

Romanyshyn (in Sheets-Johnstone, 1992) called the *abandoned body* or the *anatomical body*, which is known empirically in the scientific paradigm.

Although Freud was influenced by a dualistic worldview in which both materialism and idealism were heavily employed to explain the relationship between the newly divorced *psyche* and *soma*, I have concluded that it is an oversimplification to view Freud as a pure determinist. However, I have found that most psychoanalytic authors, when contrasting themselves with Freud, see Freud as a "hard determinist" (Symington & Symington, 1996). A careful reading of the progression of Freud's thought appears to reveal that Freud's approach was in fact an evolution betraying conflicted allegiances between materialism, determinism, and a clinical theory of more complexity and strands of dualism. This evolution is particularly evident in the movement from the topographic to the structural model. When viewed through the lens of the body, classical psychoanalysis is almost always referred to as pertaining to the "real body" via the drives, a somatic force of energy impinging on the mind and thereby explaining the mind–body connection for psychoanalytic metapsychology.

Freud's Fundamental Assumptions

The evolution of Freud's work is considered in light of the body in an effort to comprehend the role of the body in the founding ideas of psychoanalysis. A review of the literature leads to the conclusion that there is no consensus as to Freud's position on the mind–body problem. The most common trends in the literature are either to see Freud as a positivistic reductionist loyal to his training at the Helmholtz School or to see him as having evolved from a neurobiologist to a hermeneutic scientist concerned primarily with the meaning of the body. Freud himself was said to have stated that if he "had to choose among the views of the philosophers, he could characterize himself as a dualist" (in Nunberg & Federn, 1975, p. 136).

The development of Freud's instinctual drive theory is investigated as a central organizing principle in Freud's metapsychology, which contains a very specific role for the somatic dimension of experience and its ties to the mental. Freud's encounter with Charcot and the psychosomatic symptoms of hysterics initiated his interest in the neurosis and brought him into a direct encounter with the mind–body problem. I argue that this encounter was a profound challenge to Freud's training in positivistic science and that Freud was ultimately loyal to the scientific model of observation, leading to the proposal of laws that might explain observed phenomena. However, psychosomatic symptoms did not obey the laws of the positivistic anatomical science that Freud knew. Rather, it was apparent to Freud that symptoms were influenced by ideas as well as by anatomy and neurology.

I also argue that the Helmholtz school had a lasting effect on Freud, primarily in the quest to remove any form of vitalism from scientific theories. I suggest that this insistence is built upon the spirit–matter split, which the Enlightenment quest for new knowledge held as an absolute. It appears that Freud struggled to devise a metatheoretical model that might account for his observations without descending into mysticism.

Classical Freudian thought is primarily characterized by instinctual-drive theory, an energetics model that employs the language of Newtonian physics. Based on the idea that anxiety is first a somatic factor, Freud developed a system in which somatic stimuli produce a demand on the mind for work—that is, somatic energy becomes psychical and available to consciousness. This basic framework was retained through Freud's lifetime. In particular, it is solidified in his theory of sexuality and the topographic model of the mind. The concept of the erotogenic in particular provides a vehicle for the drives of the soma to correspond to the meanings of the soma in the psyche. Nonetheless, the problem of describing the mechanism by which somatic drives *become* psychological images and ideas eluded Freud, and in 1926 he admitted that it was a leap he could not explain. Psychoanalytic literature tends to resolve this dilemma with the notion that this process is a metaphorical one rather than the literal one that Freud sought to explain in the *Project for a Scientific Psychology*.

I suggest that this model contains the landmark assumptions regarding the body in psychoanalytic thought and that although there have been many theoretical advances beyond drive theory, these assumptions have become largely embedded in future models. The primary assumption I have named is that *the psychological is a developmental advance from the somatic*. I find that this organizing principle implies a hierarchical valuation of psyche over soma and that it may encourage a developmental notion of disembodiment accompanying notions of maturity. I have pointed out the similarities between this developmental model and a myth of ascension, which is fostered by the spirit–matter split characterizing the history of Western thought.

With this model comes a direct association between the somatic and the unconscious; I argue that this is a correlation that has not been overcome in psychoanalytic theory, in that the somatic is equated with that which is primitive—that is, without reflexive consciousness. I have pointed out that differentiation between psyche and soma does appear to be a healthy capacity involved in symbolic capacities but that psychoanalysis might more consistently consider a dimension of circularity in a developmental model that might speak toward integration and embodiment of these very capacities.

I have also discussed the relationship between the association of the body with the unconscious and the particularly Western notion of abstract space utilized in the concepts of displacement and projection. I argue that the uninhabited, disembodied soma might appear in psychological theory as *abstract space—space without a place*. I argue that this abstraction of space is inherent to Freud's model of displacement and projection underlying somatic symptomatology.

Object Relations: Recasting of the Body

Several transitional figures are invested as initiating the metapsychological principles moving from classical Freudian theory toward object relations. Drives as a somatic basis for motivation began to be gradually replaced with the idea that human beings are essentially driven by the innate capacity for relatedness. I have pointed out that the classical view can be seen as dualist or materialist, whereas the relational views begin to take on an idealist stance. The body is seen not as the originator of somatic motivation but as the vehicle for the expression of that which is more primary: relatedness. Most Kleinians and object relations writers exist somewhere along this continuum.

Wilfred Bion's Protomental Layer

Bion's protomental layer and later formulation of beta-elements in the grid are explored to elaborate conceptualizations of the role of the body for this contemporary Kleinian. Bion rejected the determinism and mechanistic mind of Freudian theory and has sometimes been referred to as either a mystic or psychotic. Bion asserted that the protomental layer of the psyche is both composed of undifferentiated somatic elements and also transpersonal, in that the individual is here undifferentiated from the collective. Bion's grid is a conceptual organization for the development of thinking based on differentiation from the protomental.

Contained in this model is the implicit assumption that differentiation from the somatic and simultaneously from unconscious merger with the other is the definition of psychological development. I have asserted that Bion's conception of the protomental subtly undermines the spirit–matter split by placing a transpersonal unity in the somatic dimension of experience. To the extent that the protomental is undifferentiated psychic and somatic elements, it rests on a dual-aspect foundation. However, I have pointed out the correlation between Bion's notion of development via the grid as informed by an ascension myth, emergent materialism, or both, to the extent that development is seen as moving toward the abstract. Bion's notion of development reads as if it implicitly values autonomy and abstraction and correlates the two with a desomatization of mind. It is as if human development should proceed from a "primitive" transpersonal somatic unity toward a disembodied and idealist sense of autonomy and truth. Alternatively, if the concept of the protomental is grounded firmly within a dual-aspect framework, the protomental becomes the dimension of undifferentiated somatic and psychic energy, which ideally becomes manifest as differentiated but dynamically interrelated as in threads in a tapestry.

If one acknowledges explicitly that the protomental level is inherently psychical as well as somatic, it does not remain open to this bias. Development is then a constant differentiation–reunion and dynamism. Perhaps making this explicit challenges the priest–doctor divide discussed in Chapter 2: If one acknowledges a psychic dimension of the protomental, there are subtle theological implications. I argue that one can acknowledge this dimension without claiming religious knowledge.

Thomas Ogden's Autistic–Contiguous Mode

Ogden's notion of an autistic–contiguous position is posited as an addition to Klein's paranoid–schizoid and depressive positions. This model shares the association between the somatic dimension of experience with that which is "most primitive" in the human psyche. In other words, the autistic–contiguous position is a place of undifferentiated, raw somatic elements. This mode of experience is characterized by a lack of differentiation, subjectivity, and reflexivity but provides the qualities of immediacy and enlivenedness when integrated with the other modes of experience. I argue that while Ogden's model continues the association between the somatic and that which is most unconscious, most primitive, and inherently lacking in reflexive or symbolic capacities, Ogden's model also recognizes a circularity of development in that models of maturity are imagined as an ongoing and increasingly flexible dialectic between all three modes of experience.

Donald Winnicott: Paradox and Psyche/Soma

Winnicott's contribution was unique in that he defined psyche as the "imaginative elaboration of somatic parts, feelings and functions" and specifically defined health as a state of coordination of the psyche/soma and disease as a dissociation of mind from the psyche/soma. I have found the language of Winnicott's writing as well as his style of embracing paradox to undermine developmental models implying ascension. The interpretation of somatization as dissociation of psyche/soma is a clear departure from the more common assumption that somatization is a failure to symbolize because of a developmentally impaired or regressive slide from a mature state of differentiation between psyche and soma. I have pointed out that although McDougall drew on the work of Winnicott in her own formulations, she had essentially reversed Winnicott's emphasis. I have attributed this to the unconscious organizing power of an ascension myth. Winnicott also addressed what I have criticized as the abstraction of space in classical theory, by challenging the notion of the mind as localized in the head.

Marion Milner: Challenging Symbolization and the Body

I have included the work of Milner because she specifically addressed the relationship between symbolization and the body. I have asserted that psychoanalytic models tend to polarize the two, in the idea that differentiation between mind and body is required for symbolic capacities. Milner, drawing on the work of Winnicott, claimed that words—the primary symbol—are a vehicle for making conscious the somatic dimension of experience. She claimed that psychoanalysis aims not only to uncover the repressed but also to recover a feeling of primary bodily awareness and an accompanying quality of spontaneity, creativity, and aliveness proper to Winnicott's idea of the true self. I believe that Milner has provided a psychoanalytic link in which sensory awareness may become more than presymbolic or prepsychological and that symbolization may not be equated with a desomatization of the mind.

Relational Trends

Kohut's theories began another major transition in the metatheoretical principles of contemporary psychoanalysis. Kohut's concepts of self-objects and empathic emersion foreshadowed the increasing emphasis on the subjective and intersubjective qualities of psychic life, as opposed to the objective notions of reality inherent to positivistic science. For this reason self-psychology and the later intersubjective and relational schools rest largely on the philosophical foundations of phenomenology and the science of hermeneutics. I have discussed the teleological implications of this move and the complications associated with this attempt to devise a new metapsychological framework that in no way rests on classical drive theory or the terminology inherited from it.

In this move away from the actual body (via instincts) and toward the body image (as body self), the question has been raised whether we subtly disembody our psychology. This would be the argument that relational theories lean toward an idealist mind–body stance—a monistic reduction toward the psychic or imagistic. I argue that this is not necessarily the case but that there are confusions related to language inherited from problems of earlier models. Around 1977, Kohut began in earnest to develop a new language free from the implications of drive theory, which would reflect this new framework of motivation and psychic structure. Kohut specifically stated that he was not concerned with a literal energetic force when he used the term *drive*, but that he was referring to the psychological experience and meaning of being driven.

This new theoretical framework is built on the philosophical principles of phenomenology. Notions of autonomy, objectivity, and the "isolated mind" are challenged. These ideas were taken up by Kohut's followers; I investigate the work of David Krueger, who specifically addressed the notion of a bodily self that underlies Kohut's psychological self. Krueger elaborated the somatic dimension of self-object functioning in a manner consistent with the work of Winnicott and Daniel Stern. Thinking about these relational trends led me to articulate an implicit question: Is the somatic dimension that of undifferentiated merger with the other or the medium of discovery of one's boundary of individuality, or both.

Stolorow and Atwood's work particularly challenged the myth of the individual or isolated mind in psychoanalytic models and claimed that such an idea was built on a Cartesian worldview and corresponding division between mind and body, self and other. Intersubjectivity authors claimed that these divisions serve a psychological defensive purpose of insulating the individual from the vulnerabilities of full relatedness, temporality, and the fluctuations of the physical body and world.

The centralization of affect is in essence a substitution of the concept of drives as the mediating factor between psyche and soma. Stolorow and Atwood claimed that affects are first experienced as somatic phenomena and that it is the mediating space of the intersubjective experience that allows the transformation of experience from somatic to psychological. These theories redefine the nature of reflexivity and therefore address a central concern of this endeavor. I assert that the bulk of psychoanalytic authors discussed assume that reflexivity and symbolization are built on a chiasm between psyche and soma. Aron redefined the chiasm proper to reflexivity as between the experiential poles of self-as-subject and self-as-object. Bodily experience is seen to inform the reality of the self-as-subject; however, it is no longer the soma or the drives of which psyche is assumed to gain reflexive awareness—rather, it is affective experience mediated in the interpersonal field that requires reflexivity. I assert that this reorientation of the structure of reflexive space allows for a recasting of the meaning of somatic experience because the hierarchical valuation of psyche over soma in the quest for symbolic capacities has been undermined. Although relational theory does not constitute a unified metapsychological framework, these works are useful dialogues that appear to leave room for movement beyond an ascension myth informing psychoanalytic models.

Attachment Theory and Neuropsychoanalysis: Gateway to New Models

Attachment theory and cognitive neuroscience both incorporate empirical observations into models of the mind and models of relationships impacting the mind. Neuropsychoanalysis is a field of psychoanalysis that uses these observations to modify or articulate its own models. Again, as this research is exponentially increasing, it is currently affecting psychoanalytic models in ways that are not coherently integrated but that are offering gateways to refine analytic models of the mind. Several important implications relevant to central themes of this book appear to be on the immediate horizon. In particular, neuropsychoanalytic models, providing a link between attachment theory and psychoanalysis, are empirically undoing the equation of the somatic to the unconscious, an implicit hierarchical valuation of psychic over somatic or even the possibility of disembodied psychical processes. Further, the research provides pivotal pathways for a psychoanalytic understanding of somatic intelligence, a concept denoted to the realm of somatic psychologists, since Reich split from psychoanalysis in the 1930s.

These researchers and writers largely drew on the philosophical works of Antonio Damasio, essentially a double-aspect approach to the mind–body system. It seems to me that this philosophical attitude best describes the values and sensibility of psychoanalytic practice. There are many open questions being wrestled with in the literature and in the minds of depth psychologists. For instance, if we fully acknowledge and embrace the implications of these ideas, will there be a place for drive theory and/or the language system of drive theory? Does neuroscience provide an alternative way of understanding and incorporating the actual body into a coherent metapsychology, or could it refine classical drive theory or the language of drive theory to make it more explicitly coherent with what we now know about the mind? Contemporary cognitive neuroscience increasingly is able to investigate these unconscious processes and reflect on how they are structured and modified over time, a contribution that seems sure to influence psychoanalysis significantly in the future. It is my wish that these understandings will aid psychoanalysis in developing a metapsychology that supports an embodied practice of depth psychology, and it appears that this wish is already being gratified.

DISCUSSION OF IMPLICATIONS FOR CLINICAL PSYCHOLOGY

The overarching aim of researching unconscious or implicit assumptions in theoretical works is to address clinicians' liability to perpetrate unconscious biases in clinical work. If a theory is unable to reflect on its own unconscious assumptions, clinicians working from that theory may collude with acts of disavowal or devaluation based on these assumptions. I have asserted that the mind–body and spirit–matter split is a powerful unconscious organizing principle in the Western mind and that this principle has become intertwined with a basic depth psychological principle of reflexive consciousness in particular. I have challenged the implicit notion that the chiasm necessary for reflexivity is one solely between psyche and soma or that a differentiation of psyche and soma is unidirectional.

I have asserted that the organizing principle of the spirit–matter and mind–body split aids the association of the body with the unconscious and may preclude what somatic psychologists speak about as the somatic intelligence. Further, I assert that the unconscious power of an ascension myth subtly encourages disembodiment and abstraction or at least fails to encourage embodiment.

The combination of these assumptions leads to several clinical implications. Primarily, distrust of the body and the senses, based on the inheritance of the Judeo-Christian ascension myth, appears to underlie the "body as beast" metaphor implied in Freud's instinctual drive theory. A body essentially at odds with humankind's social nature and the ideals of social functioning may be demonized in the individual psyche and in the psychologist's consulting room. I have asserted that although increasingly relational theories have moved beyond the body as beast metaphor, an implicit primitivization of the soma and hierarchical valuation of psyche over soma is by and large maintained.

I have also highlighted works of contemporary writers who are undermining this hierarchical valuation, particularly in the evolution of relational and neuropsychoanalytic ideas. What has yet to be done is to integrate a more cohesive metatheoretical system to hold these ideas. Neuropsychology potentially promises to either scaffold and/or refine metatheory—replacing or refining hypothetical ideas with increasing empirical evidence as to the nature of the mind, consciousness, perception, and development. It seems to me that these exciting developments have much to teach us regarding both the psychotherapeutic process in general and several clinical disorders in particular.

In regard to the psychotherapeutic process, I feel that depth psychology might benefit from further investigation into the usefulness of somatic awareness in relationship to the transference–countertransference relationship. For instance, Harris (in L. Aron & Anderson, 1998) advocated for the analyst's use of unconscious communication registered in body states:

> A kind of unconscious communication through shared, induced, and projected body states. Much of how this works seems, as I say, still a mystery, but I am convinced that among the important triggers in these shared body-mind states are certain crucial features of language and speech practices. Speech practices can alter the phenomenological experience of certain states of body-mind. Speech performs an action, and the hallowed split between word and deed, so fundamental to psychoanalysis, no longer always holds. (p. 41)

Conscious acknowledgement of unconscious fears or distrust of the body may leave room for increased utilization of somatic awareness in clinical work.

As well, it appears to me that a distrust of the body or image of psychological development as a unidirectional desomatization of mind may impede clinical work with symptomatology arranged around dissociation, psychosomatic symptoms, and eating disorders. To call on Winnicott's model of pathology as a discoordination between psyche and soma or a malfunctioning dissociation of mind from psyche–soma, we can see that an unconscious distrust or distancing from soma may impede psychological health. I can also speculate, via my own personal experience as a psychotherapist, that the lack of enlivenedness, immediacy of experience, spontaneity, and creativity present in depressive disorders may be aided by an eventual embodiment of reflexive consciousness and symbolic capacities.

CONCLUSION

One of my favorite definitions of depth psychological work states that "the analysis is the diagnosis of the inner truth" (Symington & Symington, 1996). As such, I have asked: "What is the truth of the experienced body," and "how do psychoanalytic theories either speak to this truth or prevent its disclosure due to hidden biases or assumptions?" As Symington and Symington (1996) stated, "a model or theory in the mind can obstruct learning" (p. 2). This research has led me to the conclusion that the cultural or historical models about the body have obstructed psychoanalytic learning about the lived experience of the body and its place in psychological health.

The four areas of concern I have raised are

1. the unconscious organizing principle of the spirit–matter split and the ensuing mind–body split;
2. the overlay of a Judeo-Christian ascension myth on the mind–body split and the consequent valuation of psyche over soma;
3. the association between the body and the unconscious; and
4. the assumption that the reflective capacities are built on the chiasm between mind and body.

These ideas are intertwined in varying ways across psychoanalytic theoretical development. The relevant founding idea of Freud's metapsychology is contained in the elusive transformation of somatic energy into psychological energy. This essential mystery lives on in relational ideas about transformation of affect from a somatic experience to a relational one.

It appears that Freud's ultimate myth about the soma has been retained in some form in the overwhelming majority of psychoanalytic thinking: Psychological development is a move from the somatic toward psychic abstraction, and with this move comes the capacity for reflexive thinking. In this model, psyche is seen to originate in the soma but to acquire the properties of the mental as it becomes desomatized or differentiated from the material plane. I have found this basic myth reflected in the original and mysterious neurological transformation explored in the *Project for a Scientific Psychology*, carried through in Bion's grid, McDougall's somatization theory, Ogden's autistic–contiguous position, and the contemporary thrust to integrate psychoneurological models of development. I suggest that this is a useful metaphor in many ways; I am not stating that it is false. However, if a goal of depth psychology is to speak toward the lived truths of human experience, then as psychotherapists we must ask if the language of this metapsychological myth has prevented us from learning about bodily experience. Particularly, is the metaphorical placement of soma as below circumventing or preventing a full-bodied awareness, allowing a real dynamism of lived experience fully alive in the soma?

As symbol and language are valued and seen as a remedy for somatization as defense, the somatic dimension may not be understood for its living dynamism in a mature psychology. This research grapples with the issues of the unconscious and the symbolic, in light of the physical body as a primary medium between conscious and unconscious processes. In this vein, it is useful to consider the root of the word *symbol*, which comes from the Greek *sumbállein*, which literally means "together" (*sum*) "thrown" (*bállein*; Ayto, 1991). The body then may be understood as the ultimate symbol, the throwing together of matter and spirit, psyche and soma. I suggest that soma is symbol and is both conscious and unconscious. This consciousness becomes imbibed with new possibilities when linked with the psychological reflective function. In this view perhaps the somatic is not merely polarized against the symbolic and relegated to a defensive or primitive position in formulations of development, character structure, and experience.

Metapsychology fully grounded in the dual-aspect philosophy, especially as elaborated by Damasio, as discussed in Chapter 2, allows for a stable configuration of metapsychology that does not collapse into a biological reductionism or linear development. Here pathology is a collapse into either pole of the somatic or the psychic, and health is the successful dynamic interplay between both manifestations. The teleological question is: Mind and body are manifestations of what? Bion's concept of the protomental begins to answer this question in an analytic manner, that is, without religious affiliation or authority. Bion is at times considered mystical for having leaned further toward such spiritual questions than any other theorist. I would argue that there is no way around acknowledging the mystery of this third thing from which both psychic and somatic emerge.

In a "psychoanalysis of psychoanalysis" such as this research, I suggest that the assumptions inherent in the psychoanalytic paradigm are not incorrect but incomplete and that the seemingly intractable nature of this limitation is related to a deep-seated fear of the body—partially because of the fact that unconscious material has found a comfortable home in the "body reviled." For instance, it is not difficult to directly link expressions of sexuality, violence, mortality, or deep ecstasy and existential fear to the physical body.

I believe that psychologists have lost a way to speak to the experience of embodiment. I further believe that the experience of personal conscious, unconscious, and collective consciousness through and within the body provide a psychological experience that cannot be omitted in our models of psychological health. The pure power of this reality corresponds directly to the power with which the body has been reviled through history and therefore relegated to the layers of the unconscious. I believe that people largely experience the body as the dumping ground for the unconscious material because of this history of fear and distrust of the body and senses. Only within this framework must the body carry the material of the unconscious.

In conclusion, I would ask that the reader consider T. S. Eliot's (1943) poem "Little Gidding" from *Four Quartets*:

> We shall not cease from exploration
> And in the end of all our exploring
> Will be to arrive where we started
> And know the place for the first time. (p. 39)[1]

The poet grasps my essential point that we cannot nor do we wish to return to a pre-Socratic experience of unconscious identification with the somatic or the corporeal but that we may use the knowledge gained from the chiasm of duality to return to or integrate the embodied matrix of being. Toward this aim, I envision a psychoanalytic theory for the unconscious that reflects this sensibility in order to remain vital in the scientific community and useful as a therapeutic guide that speaks to the heart of personal experience. True to psychoanalytic principles, it is by first recognizing unconscious biases or assumptions that we can begin to move beyond them.

---

[1]Excerpt from "Little Gilding" in *Four Quartets*, copyright 1942 T.S. Eliot and renewed 1970 by Esme Valerie Eliot, reprinted by permission of Houghton Mifflin Harcourt Publishing Company.

REFERENCES

Abram, D. (1996). *The spell of the sensuous: Perception and language in a more-than-human world.* New York, NY: Pantheon Books.

Alexander, F. M., & Maisel, E. (1986). *The resurrection of the body: The essential writings of F. Matthias Alexander.* New York, NY: Random House.

Amacher, P. (1965). *Freud's neurological education and its influence on psychoanalytic theory.* New York, NY: International Universities Press.

Anderson, D. (1962). *Studies in the prehistory of psychoanalysis.* Stockholm, Sweden: Svcnska Bokforlaget.

Anderson, F. S. (2008). *Bodies in treatment: The unspoken dimension.* New York, NY: Analytic Press.

Anzieu, D. (1989). *The skin ego.* New Haven, CT: Yale University Press.

Armstrong, D. M. (1999). *The mind–body problem: An opinionated introduction.* Boulder, CO: Westview Press.

Aron, L. (1998). The clinical body and the reflexive mind. In L. Aron & F. S. Anderson (Eds.), *Relational Perspectives on the Body* (pp. 3–38). Hilldale, NJ: The Analytic Press.

Aron, L., & Anderson, F. S. (1998). *Relational perspectives on the body.* Hillsdale, NJ: The Analytic Press.

Aron, W. (1964). Freud and Spinoza. [Harofe Haivri]. *Hebrew Medical Journal, 37,* 282–300.

Atwood, G., Orange, D., & Stolorow, R. (2002). Shattered worlds/psychotic states: A post-Cartesian view of the experience of personal annihilation. *Psychoanalytic Psychology, 19,* 281–306. doi:10.1037/0736-9735.19.2.281

Auerbach, J. (1993). The origins of narcissism and narcissistic personality disorder: A theoretical and empirical reformulation. In *Empirical Studies of Psychoanalytic Theories,* (Vol. 4, pp. 43–108).

Auerbach, J., & Blatt, S. (1996). Self-representation in severe psychopathology: The role of reflexive self-awareness. *Psychoanalytic Psychology, 13,* 297–341. doi:10.1037/h0079659

Ayto, J. (1991). *Dictionary of word origins.* New York, NY: Arcade.

Bach, S. (1985). *Narcissistic states and the therapeutic process.* New York, NY: Aronson.

Bach, S. (1994). *The language of perversion and the language of love.* Northvale, NJ: Aronson.

Barron, J. W., Eagle, M. N., & Wolitzky, D. L. (1992). *Interface of psychoanalysis and psychology.* Washington, DC: American Psychological Association. doi:10.1037/10118-000

Beebe, B., & Lachmann, F. M. (2001). *Infant research and adult treatment: A dyadic systems approach.* Hillsdale, NJ: Analytic Press.

Berman, M. (1998). *Coming to our senses: Body and spirit in the hidden history of the West*. Seattle, WA: Seattle Writers Guild.

Bion, W. R. (1961). *Experiences in groups, and other papers*. New York, NY: Basic Books. doi:10.4324/9780203359075

Bion, W. R. (1963). *Learning from experience*. New York, NY: Basic Books.

Bion, W. R. (1967). *Second thoughts: Selected papers on psycho-analysis*. London, England: Heinemann Medical.

Bion, W. R. (1983). *Transformations*. New York, NY: Aronson.

Bischler, W. (1939). Schopenhauer and Freud: A comparison. *The Psychoanalytic Quarterly, 8*, 88–97.

Boadella, D. (1973). *Wilhelm Reich: The evolution of his work*. London, England: Vision Press.

Boston Change Process Study Group. (1998). Report 2. Interventions that effect change in psychotherapy: A model based on infant research. *Infant Mental Health Journal, 19*, 277–353.

Bowlby, J. (1960). Grief and mourning in infancy and early childhood. *The Psychoanalytic Study of the Child, 15*, 3–39.

Bowlby, J. (1988). *A secure base: Parent–child attachment and healthy human development*. New York, NY: Basic Books.

Bowlby, J. (1999). *Attachment and loss* (2nd ed.). New York, NY: Basic Books.

Brooks, C. V. W. (1974). *Sensory awareness: The rediscovery of experiencing*. New York, NY: Viking Press.

Capra, F. (1975). *The Tao of physics: An exploration of the parallels between modern physics and Eastern mysticism*. London, England: Wildwood House.

Chessick, R. (1980). Some philosophical assumptions of intensive psychotherapy. *American Journal of Psychotherapy, 34*, 496–509.

Cozolino, L. J. (2002). *The neuroscience of psychotherapy: Building and rebuilding the human brain*. New York, NY: Norton.

Crane, T., & Patterson, S. (2000). *History of the mind–body problem*. London, England: Routledge.

Damasio, A. R. (1994). *Descartes' error: Emotion, reason, and the human brain*. New York, NY: Putnam.

Damasio, A. R. (1999). *The feeling of what happens: Body and emotion in the making of consciousness*. New York, NY: Harcourt Brace.

Damasio, A. R. (2003). *Looking for Spinoza: Joy, sorrow, and the feeling brain*. Orlando, FL: Harcourt.

Davies, J. M. (1996). Linking the "pre-analytic" with the postclassical: Integration, dissociation, and the multiplicity of unconscious process. *Contemporary Psychoanalysis, 32*, 553–576.

Detrick, D. W., & Detrick, S. P. (1989). *Self psychology: Comparisons and contrasts*. Hillsdale, NJ: Analytic Press.

Edelson, M. (1984). *Hypothesis and evidence in psychoanalysis*. Chicago, IL: University of Chicago Press.

Eigen, M. (1985). Toward Bion's starting point: Between catastrophe and faith. *International Journal of Psycho-Analysis*, 66, 321–330.

Eigen, M. (1998). *The psychoanalytic mystic*. London, New York, NY: Free Association Books.

Eliot, T. S. (1943). *Four quartets*. New York, NY: Harcourt.

Ellenberger, H. F. (1970). *The discovery of the unconscious: The history and evolution of dynamic psychiatry*. New York, NY: Basic Books.

Faber, M. (1988). Back to a crossroad: Nietzsche, Freud, and the East. *New Ideas in Psychology*, 6, 25–45. doi:10.1016/0732-118X(88)90021-9

Fadiman, J., & Frager, R. (2002). *Personality and personal growth* (5th ed.). Upper Saddle River, NJ: Prentice Hall.

Fairbairn, W. R. D. (1952). *Psychoanalytic studies of the personality*. London, England: Tavistock Publications.

Fairbairn, W. R. D. (1954). *An object–relations theory of the personality*. New York, NY: Basic Books.

Feldenkrais, M. (1977). *The case of Nora: Body awareness as healing therapy*. New York, NY: Harper & Row.

Feldenkrais, M. (1990). *Awareness through movement: Health exercises for personal growth*. San Francisco, CA: HarperSanFrancisco.

Fonagy, P. (2001). *Attachment theory and psychoanalysis*. New York, NY: Other Press.

Fonagy, P. (2002). *Affect regulation, mentalization, and the development of the self*. New York, NY: Other Press.

Fonagy, P., & Target, M. (2007). The rooting of the mind in the body: New links between attachment theory and psychoanalytic thought. *Journal of the American Psychoanalytic Association*, 55, 411–456.

Freud, A., & Burlingham, D. T. (1967). *The writings of Anna Freud*. New York, NY: International Universities Press.

Freud, S. (1953). *On aphasia: A critical study*. New York, NY: International Universities Press. (Original work published 1891)

Freud, S. (1961a). Beyond the pleasure principle. In J. Strachey (Trans.), *The collected works of Sigmund Freud* (Vol. 18, pp. 3–66). London, England: Hogarth Press. (Original work published 1920)

Freud, S. (1961b). Instincts and their vicissitudes. In J. Strachey (Ed., and Trans.) *The standard edition of the complete psychological works of Sigmund Freud* (Vol. 14, pp. 117–140). London, England: Hogarth Press. (Original work published 1915)

Freud, S. (1961c). Psychical (or mental) treatment. In J. Strachey (Trans.) *The collected works of Sigmund Freud* (Vol. VII). London, England: Hogarth Press. (Original work published 1900)

Freud, S. (1961d). The ego and the id. In J. Strachey (Ed. and Trans.), *The standard edition of the complete psychological works of Sigmund Freud* (Vol. 19, pp. 3–66). London, England: Hogarth Press. (Original work published 1923)

Freud, S. (1961e). The interpretation of dreams. In J. Strachey (Trans.), *The collected works of Sigmund Freud* (Vol. IV). (Original work published 1900)

Freud, S. (1961f). Three essays on the theory of sexuality. In J. Strachey (Trans.) *The collected works of Sigmund Freud* (Vol. VII). London, England: Hogarth Press (Original work published 1905)

Freud, S. (1962). Appendix: The emergence of Freud's fundamental hypotheses. In J. Strachey (Ed. and Trans.), *The standard edition of the complete psychological works of Sigmund Freud* (Vol. 3, pp. 62–70). London, England: Hogarth Press. (Original work published 1894)

Freud, S. (1966a). Beyond the pleasure principle. In J. Strachey (Ed. And Trans.), *The standard edition of the complete psychological works of Sigmund Freud* (Vol. 18, pp. 3–66). London, England: Hogarth Press. (Original work published 1920)

Freud, S. (1966b). Hypnosis. In J. Strachey (Ed. and Trans.), *The standard edition of the complete psychological works of Sigmund Freud* (Vol. 1, pp. 103–114). London, England: Hogarth Press. (Original work published 1891)

Freud, S. (1966c). Hysteria. In J. Strachey (Ed. and Trans.), *The standard edition of the complete psychological works of Sigmund Freud* (Vol. 1, pp. 39–62). London, England: Hogarth Press. (Original work published 1888)

Freud, S. (1966d). Project for a scientific psychology. In J. Strachey (Ed. and Trans.), *The standard edition of the complete psychological works of Sigmund Freud* (Vol. 1, pp. 283–398). London, England: Hogarth Press. (Original work published 1895)

Freud, S. (1966e). Some points for a comparative study of organic and hysterical motor paralyses. In J. Strachey (Ed. and Trans.), *The standard edition of the complete psychological works of Sigmund Freud* (Vol. 1, pp. 160–174). London, England: Hogarth Press. (Original work published 1893)

Freud, S., Masson, M., & Fliess, W. (1985). *The complete letters of Sigmund Freud to Wilhelm Fliess, 1887–1904*. Cambridge, MA: Belknap Press of Harvard University Press.

Gabbard, G. O. (2000). *Psychodynamic psychiatry in clinical practice* (3rd ed.). Washington, DC: American Psychiatric Press.

Gadamer, H. G. (1989). *Truth and method*. New York, NY: Crossroad.

Gendlin, E. T. (1978). *Focusing*. New York, NY: Everest House.

Giegerich, W. (1985). *The nuclear bomb and the fate of God*. Evanston, IL: C. G. Jung Institute of Chicago.

Gill, M. M. (1994). *Psychoanalysis in transition: A personal view*. Hillsdale, NJ: Analytic Press.

Goldenberg, N. R. (1990). *Returning words to flesh: Feminism, psychoanalysis, and the resurrection of the body*. Boston, MA: Beacon Press.

Goldenberg, N. R. (1993). *Resurrecting the body: Feminism, religion, and psychotherapy*. New York, NY: Crossroad.

Greenberg, J. R., & Mitchell, S. A. (1983). *Object relations in psychoanalytic theory*. Cambridge, MA: Harvard University Press.

Grigsby, J., & Stevens, D. (2000). *Neurodynamics of personality*. New York, NY: Guilford Press.

Grosskurth, P. (1991). *The secret ring: Freud's inner circle and the politics of psychoanalysis*. London, England: J. Cape.

Grosskurth, P. (1995). *Melanie Klein: Her world and her work*. Northvale, NJ: J. Aronson.

Guralnik, D. B. (1970). *Webster's new world dictionary of the American language* (2nd. College ed.). New York: World.

Harris, A. (1998). Psychic envelopes and sonorous baths: Sitting the body in relational theory and clinical practice. In L. Aron & F. S. Anderson (Eds.), *Relational Perspectives on the Body* (pp. 39–64). Hilldale, NJ: The Analytic Press.

Harris, M., & Bick, E. (1987). *Collected papers of Martha Harris and Esther Bick*. Perthshire, Scotland: Clunie Press for Roland Harris Trust.

Hasker, W. (1999). *The emergent self*. Ithaca, NY: Cornell University Press.

Heidegger, M. (1962). *Being and time*. London, England: SCM Press.

Hofer, M. A. (1996). Multiple regulators of ultrasonic vocalization in the infant rat. *Psychoneuroendocrinology, 21*, 203–217. doi:10.1016/0306-4530(95)00042-9

Horne, M., Sowa, A., & Isenman, D. (2000). Philosophical assumptions in Freud, Jung and Bion: Questions of causality. *The Journal of Analytical Psychology, 45*, 109–121. doi:10.1111/1465-5922.00140

Hughes, J. M. (1989). *Reshaping the psychoanalytic domain: The work of Melanie Klein, W. R. D. Fairbairn, and D. W. Winnicott*. Berkeley, CA: University of California Press.

Hughes, J. M. (1994). *From Freud's consulting room: The unconscious in a scientific age*. Cambridge, MA: Harvard University Press.

Idhe, D. (Ed.) (1983). *Interpreting hermeneutics: Origins, developments, prospects. existential techniques*. Albany, NY, SUNY Press.

Johnson, D., & Grand, I. J. (1998). *The body in psychotherapy: Inquiries in somatic psychology*. Berkeley, CA: North Atlantic Books.

Jones, E. (1961). *The life and work of Sigmund Freud*. New York, NY: Basic Books.

Jung, C. G., & Franz, M. L. V. (1951). *Aion*. Zurich, Switzerland: Rascher.

Kalin, N. H. (1995). Opiate systems in mother and infant primates coordinate intimate contact during reunion. *Psychoneuroendocrinology, 20*, 735–742. doi:10.1016/0306-4530(95)00023-2

Kandel, E. R. (1998). A new intellectual framework for psychiatry. *The American Journal of Psychiatry, 155*, 457–469.

Kandel, E. R. (1999). Biology and the future of psychoanalysis: A new intellectual framework for psychiatry revisted. *The American Journal of Psychiatry, 156,* 505–524.

Kaptchuk, T. J. (2000). *The web that has no weaver: Understanding Chinese medicine* (Rev. ed.). Chicago, IL: Contemporary Books.

Keleman, S. (1975). *The human ground: Sexuality, self, and survival* (Rev. ed.). Palo Alto, CA: Science and Behavior Books.

Keleman, S. (1979). *Somatic reality.* Berkeley, CA: Center Press.

Kernberg, O. F. (1995a). *Love relations: Normality and pathology.* New Haven, CT: Yale University Press.

Kernberg, O. F. (1995b). Psychoanalytic object relations theories. In B. E. Moore & B. D. Fine (Eds.), *Psychoanalysis: The major concepts* (pp. 450–462). New Haven, CT: Yale University Press.

Kidner, D. W. (2001). *Nature and psyche: Radical environmentalism and the politics of subjectivity.* Albany, NY: State University of New York Press.

Kim, J. (1998). *Mind in a physical world: An essay on the mind–body problem and mental causation.* Cambridge, MA: MIT Press.

Klein, M. (1957). *Envy and gratitude, a study of unconscious sources.* New York, NY: Basic Books.

Klein, M. (1961). *Narrative of a child analysis; the conduct of the psychoanalysis of children as seen in the treatment of a ten year old boy.* New York, NY: Basic Books.

Klein, M., & Mitchell, J. (1987). *The selected Melanie Klein* (1st American ed.). New York, NY: Free Press.

Klein, M., & Riviere, J. (1937). *Love, hate and reparation.* London, England: Hogarth Press and The Institute of Psychoanalysis.

Kohut, H. (1959). Introspection, empathy, and psychoanalysis—an examination of the relationship beween mode of observation and theory (1). *Journal of the American Psychoanalyic Association, 7,* 459–483. doi:10.1177/000306515900700304

Kohut, H. (1971). *The analysis of the self; a systematic approach to the psychoanalytic treatment of narcissistic personality disorders.* New York, NY: International Universities Press.

Kohut, H. (1977). *The restoration of the self.* New York, NY: International Universities Press.

Kohut, H. (1979). The two analyses of Mr. Z. *The International Journal of Psycho-Analysis, 60,* 3–27.

Kohut, H., & Wolf, E. S. (1978). The disorders of the self and their treatment: An outline. *The International Journal of Psycho-Analysis, 59,* 413–425.

Kremerling, G. (2001). Philosophy pages. Retrieved from http://www.philosophy pages.com

Krueger, D. W. (1989). *Body self & psychological self: A developmental and clinical integration of disorders of the self.* New York, NY: Brunner-Mazel.

Krueger, D. W. (2002). *Integrating body self and psychological self: Creating a new story in psychoanalysis and psychotherapy*. New York, NY: Brunner-Routledge.

Krystal, H., & Krystal, J. H. (1988). *Integration and self healing: Affect, trauma, alexithymia*. Hillsdale, NJ: Analytic Press: Lawrence Erlbaum.

Lakoff, G., & Johnson, M. (1999). *Philosophy in the flesh: The embodied mind and its challenge to Western thought*. New York, NY: Basic Books.

Lakoff, G., & Turner, M. (1989). *More than cool reason: A field guide to poetic metaphor*. Chicago, IL: University of Chicago Press.

Lee, P. (1988). Hermeneutics and vitalism. *ReVision, 10*, 3–13.

Levin, F. (1998). A brief history of analysis and cognitive neuroscience. *American Psychoanalyst, 32*, 26–27..

Lowen, A. (1967). *The betrayal of the body*. New York, NY: Macmillan.

Lowen, A. (1990). *The spirituality of the body: Bioenergetics for grace and harmony*. New York, NY: Macmillan.

Lowen, A. (1994). *Bioenergetics*. New York, NY: Penguin/Arkana.

Lowen, A. (2003). *Spirituality of the body: Bioenergetics for grace and harmony*. Alachua, FL: Bioenergetics Press.

Macmillan, M. (1997). *Freud evaluated: The completed arc*. Cambridge, MA: The MIT Press.

Mahler, M. S., Pine, F., & Bergman, A. (1975). *The psychological birth of the human infant: Symbiosis and individuation*. New York, NY: Basic Books.

Mann, T. (1956). Freud and the future. *The International Journal of Psycho-Analysis, 37*, 106–115.

Mann, T., & Lowe-Porter, H. T. (1947). *Essays of three decades*. New York, NY: Knopf.

McDougall, J. (1985). *Theaters of the mind: Illusion and truth on the psychoanalytic stage*. New York, NY: Basic Books.

McDougall, J. (1989). *Theaters of the body: A psychoanalytic approach to psychosomatic illness*. New York, NY: Norton.

McDougall, J. (1995). *The many faces of eros: A psychoanalytic exploration of human sexuality*. New York, NY: Norton.

Meissner, W. W. (2000). *Freud & psychoanalysis*. Notre Dame, IN: University of Notre Dame Press.

Meissner, W. W. (2003a). Mind, brain, and self in psychoanalysis: I. Problems and attempted solutions. *Psychoanalysis and Contemporary Thought, 26*, 297–320.

Meissner, W. W. (2003b). Mind, brain, and self in psychoanalysis: II. Freud and the mind–body relation. *Psychoanalysis and Contemporary Thought, 26*, 321–344.

Meissner, W. W. (2008). The role of language in the developmetn of the self I: Language acquisition. *Psychoanalytic Psychology, 25*, 26–46. doi:10.1037/0736-9735.25.1.26

Meissner, W. W. (2009). The question of drive vs. motive in psychoanalysis: A modest proposal. *Journal of the American Psychoanalytic Association, 57*, 807–845.

Meltzer, D. (1967). *The psycho-analytical process*. London, England: Karnac Books.

Meltzer, D. (1973). *Sexual states of mind*. London, England: Karnac Books.

Merleau-Ponty, M. (1962). *Phenomenology of perception*. London, England: Routledge.

Merleau-Ponty, M., & Lefort, C. (1968). *The visible and the invisible; followed by working notes*. Evanston, IL: Northwestern University Press.

Milner, M. B. (1936). *A life of one's own*. London, England: Chatto & Windus.

Milner, M. B. (1950). *On not being able to paint*. London, England: Heinemann.

Milner, M. (1969). The hands of the living God: An account of a psycho-analytic treatment. *The International Psycho-Analytical Library, 76,* 1–426.

Milner, M. B. (1987). *The suppressed madness of sane men: Forty-four years of exploring psychoanalysis*. New York, NY: Tavistock.

Mitchell, S. (1996). Editorial statement. *Psychoanalytic Dialogues, 6,* 1–3.

Mitchell, S. A. (1988). *Relational concepts in psychoanalysis: An integration*. Cambridge, MA: Harvard University Press.

Mitchell, S. A., & Black, M. J. (1995). *Freud and beyond: A history of modern psychoanalytic thought*. New York, NY: Basic Books.

Moore, B. E., & Fine, B. D. (Eds.). (1990). *Psychoanalytic terms and concepts*. New Haven, CT: The American Psychoanalytic Association and Yale University Press.

Nersessian, E., Solms, M. (1999). Editors' introduction. *Neuropsychoanalysis, 1,* 3–4.

Nunberg, H., & Federn, E. (Eds.). (1975). *Minutes of the Vienna Psychoanalytic Society* (Vol. 4, 1912–1918). New York, NY: International Universities Press.

Ogden, P., Minton, K., & Pain, C. (2006). *Trauma and the body: A sensorimotor approach to psychotherapy*. New York, NY: Norton.

Ogden, T. H. (1982). *Projective identification and psychotherapeutic technique*. New York, NY: J. Aronson.

Ogden, T. H. (1986). *The matrix of the mind: Object relations and the psychoanalytic dialogue*. Northvale, NJ: Aronson.

Ogden, T. H. (1989). *The primitive edge of experience*. London, England: J. Aronson.

Ogden, T. H. (1994). *Subjects of analysis*. Northvale, NJ: J. Aronson.

Ogden, T. H. (2001). *Conversations at the frontier of dreaming*. Northvale, NJ: J. Aronson.

Packer, M. J., & Addison, R. B. (1989). *Entering the circle: Hermeneutic investigation in psychology*. Albany, NY: State University of New York Press.

Pally, R., & Olds, D. (2000). *The mind-brain relationship*. London, England: Karnac Books.

Palmer, R. E. (1969). *Hermeneutics; interpretation theory in Schleiermacher, Dilthey, Heidegger, and Gadamer*. Evanston, IL: Northwestern University Press.

Parisi, D., & Castelfranchi, C. (1987). *La macchina e il linguaggio*. Torino, Italy: Bollati Boringhieri.

Percy, W. (1983). *Lost in the cosmos: The last self-help book*. New York, NY: Farrar, Straus, & Giroux.

Pinkel, B. (1992). *Consciousness, matter, and energy: The emergence of mind in nature*. Santa Monica, CA: Turover Press.

Proctor-Gregg, N. (1956). Schopenhauer and Freud. *The Psychoanalytic Quarterly, 25,* 197–214.

Reich, W. (1960). *Selected writings; an introduction to orgonomy*. New York, NY: Farrar.

Reich, W. (1972). *Character analysis*. New York, NY: Farrar.

Reich, W. (1973a). *The function of the orgasm; sex-economic problems of biological energy*. New York, NY: Farrar.

Reich, W. (1973b). *Selected writings; an introduction to orgonomy*. New York, NY: Farrar.

Reiser, M. (1975). *Changing theoretical concepts in psychosomatic medicine* (2nd ed., Vol. IV). New York, NY: Basic Books.

Ricoeur, P. (1970). *Freud and philosophy; an essay on interpretation*. New Haven, CT: Yale University Press.

Roazen, P. (1992). *Freud and his followers*. New York, NY: Da Capo Press.

Rodman, F. R. (2003). *Winnicott: Life and work*. Cambridge, MA: Perseus.

Rolf, I. P. (1977). *Rolfing: The integration of human structures*. Santa Monica, CA: Dennis-Landman.

Romanyshyn, R. D. (1989). *Technology as symptom and dream*. London, England: Routledge.

Rycroft, C. (1995). *A critical dictionary of psychoanalysis* (2nd ed.). London, England: Penguin Books.

Samuels, A., Shorter, B., & Plaut, F. (1986). *A critical dictionary of Jungian analysis*. London, England: Routledge & Kegan Paul.

Schore, A. (1994). *Affect regulation and the origin of the self: The neurobiology of emotional development*. Hillsdale, NJ: L. Erlbaum Associates.

Schore, A. (2003). *Affect dysregulation & disorders of the self*. New York, NY: Norton.

Schutz, W., & Turner, E. (1976). *Evy: An odyssey into bodymind*. New York, NY: Harper & Row.

Shalev, O., & Yemshalmi, H. (2009). Status of sexuality in contemporary psychoanalytic psychotherapy as reported by therapists. *Psychoanalytic Psychology, 26,* 343–361. doi:10.1037/a0017719

Shapiro, T., & Emde, R. N. (1995). *Research in psychoanalysis: Process, development, outcome*. Madison, CT: International Universities Press.

Sheets-Johnstone, M. (1992). *Giving the body its due*. Albany, NY: State University of New York Press.

Shevrin, H. (1998). Psychoanalytic and neuroscience research. *American Psychoanalyst, 32.*

Siegel, D. J. (1999a). *The developing mind: How relationships and the brain interact to shape who we are*. New York, NY: Guilford Press.

Siegel, D. J. (1999b). *The developing mind: Toward a neurobiology of interpersonal experience*. New York, NY: Guilford Press.

Siegel, D. J., & Hartzell, M. (2003). *Parenting from the inside out: How a deeper self-understanding can help you raise children who thrive*. New York, NY: Tarcher/Putnam.

Silverstein, B. (1985). Freud's psychology and its organic foundation: Sexuality and mind-body interactionism. *The Psychoanalytic Review, 72*, 203–228.

Silverstein, B. (1989). Contributions to the history of psychology: LVIII. Freud's dualistic mind-body interactionism: Implications for the development of his psychology. *Psychological Reports, 64*, 1091–1097.

Silverstein, S. M., & Silverstein, B. (1990). Freud and hypnosis: The development of an interactionist perspective. *The Annual of Psychoanalysis, 18*, 175–194.

Siverstein, B. (1997). A follow-up note on Freud's mind-body dualism: What Ferenczi learned from Freud. *Psychological Reports, 80*, 369–370.

Solms, M., & Neressian, E. (1999). Freud's theory of affect: Questions for neuroscience. *Neuropsychoanalysis, 1*, 5–14.

Southard, E. (1919). Sigmund Freud, pessimist. *The Journal of Abnormal Psychology, 14*, 197–216. doi:10.1037/h0072095

Spinoza, B. D., Boyle, A., & Parkinson, G. H. R. (1989). *Ethics*. London Rutland, VT: J. M. Dent.

St. Clair, M. (1996). *Object relations and self psychology: An introduction* (2nd ed.). Pacific Grove, CA: Brooks/Cole.

St. Clair, M. (2000). *Object relations and self psychology: An introduction* (3rd ed.). Belmont, CA: Brooks/Cole.

Stern, D. (1998). The process of therepeutic change involving implicit knowledge: Some implications of developmetnal observations for adult psychotherapy. *Journal of Infant Mental Health, 19*, 300–308. doi:10.1002/(SICI)1097-0355(199823)19:3<300::AID-IMHJ5>3.0.CO;2-P

Stern, D. N. (1977). *The first relationship: Mother and infant*. Cambridge, MA: Harvard University Press.

Stern, D. N. (1985). *The interpersonal world of the infant: A view from psychoanalysis and developmental psychology*. New York, NY: Basic Books.

Stern, D. N. (2004). *The present moment in psychotherapy and everyday life*. New York, NY: Norton.

Stewart, W. A. (1967). Psychoanalysis: The first ten years, 1888–1898. New York, NY: Macmillan.

Stolorow, R., & Atwood, G. (1992). *Contexts of being: The intersubjective foundations of psychological life*. Hillsdale, NJ: Analytic Press.

Stolorow, R., Atwood, G., & Orange, D. (1999). Kohut and contextualism: Toward a post-Cartesian psychoanalytic theory. *Psychoanalytic Psychology, 16*, 380–388. doi:10.1037/0736-9735.16.3.380

Stolorow, R., Brandchaft, B., & Atwood, G. (1987). *Psychoanalytic treatment: An intersubjective approach*. Hillsdale, NJ: Analytic Press.

Stolorow, R., Orange, D., & Atwood, G. (2001a). Cartesian and post-Cartesian trends in relational psychoanalysis. *Psychoanalytic Psychology, 18*, 468–484. doi:10.1037/0736-9735.18.3.468

Stolorow, R., Orange, D., & Atwood, G. (2001b). Psychoanalysis—a contextual psychology: Essay in memory of Merton M. Gill. *Psychoanalytic Review, 88*, 15–28. doi:10.1521/prev.88.1.15.17545

Stolorow, R., Orange, D., & Atwood, G. (2001c). Cartesian and post-Cartesian trends in relational psychoanalysis. *Psychoanalytic Psychology, 18*, 468–484. doi:10.1037/0736-9735.18.3.468

Stromsted, T. (2005). Cellular resonance and the sacred feminine: Marion Woodman's story. *Spring, 72*, 1–30.

Strozier, C. B. (2001). *Heinz Kohut: The making of a psychoanalyst*. New York, NY: Farrar, Straus and Giroux.

Sulloway, F. J. (1979). *Freud, biologist of the mind: Beyond the psychoanalytic legend*. New York, NY: Basic Books.

Summers, F. (1994). *Object relations theories and psychopathology: A comprehensive text*. Hillsdale, NJ: Analytic Press.

Symington, J., & Symington, N. (1996). *The clinical thinking of Wilfred Bion*. London, England: Routledge.

Tarnas, R. (1991). *The passion of the western mind: Understanding the ideas that have shaped our world view*. New York, NY: Harmony Books.

Taylor, G. J. (1992). Psychoanalysis and psychosomatics: A new synthesis. *Journal of American Academic Psychoanalysis, 20*, 251–275.

Tustin, F. (1981). *Autistic states in children*. London, England: Routledge & Kegan Paul Ltd.

Van der Kolk, B. A. (1996). The body keeps the score: Approaches to the psychobiology of posttraumatic stress disorder. In V. A. van der Kolk, A. C. McFarlane, & L. Weisaeth (Eds.), *Traumatic stress: The effects of overwhelming experience on mind, body, and society* (pp. 214–241). New York, NY: Guilford Press.

Varela, F. J., Thompson, E., & Rosch, E. (1991). *The embodied mind: Cognitive science and human experience*. Cambridge, MA: MIT Press.

Wallace, E. R. (1992). Freud and the mind-body problem. In T. Gelfand & J. Kerr (Eds.), *Freud and the history of psychoanalysis*. Hillsdale, NJ: The Analytic Press. pp. 231–269.

Wallerstein, R. S., & Applegarth, A. (1976). Psychic energy reconsidered. *Journal of the American Psychoanalytic Association, 24*, 647–657.

Winnicott, D. W. (1953). Transitional objects and transitional phenomena—a study of the first not-me possession. *International Journal of Psycho-Analysis, 34*, 89–97.

Winnicott, D. W. (1958a). *Collected papers, through paediatrics to psycho-analysis*. London, England: Tavistock Publications.

Winnicott, D. W. (1958b). *Collected papers: Through paediatrics to psycho-analysis.* New York, NY: Basic Books.

Winnicott, D. W. (1962). Ego integration in child development. In *The maturational processes and the facilitating environment.* Madison, CT: International Universities Press, 1965, pp. 56–63.

Winnicott, D. W. (1965). *The maturational processes and the facilitating environment; studies in the theory of emotional development.* New York, NY: International Universities Press.

Winnicott, D. W. (1971). *Playing and reality.* New York, NY: Basic Books.

Winnicott, D. W. (1975). Through paediatrics to psycho-analysis. *The International Psycho-Analytical Library, 100,* 1–325.

Winnicott, D. W. (1992). *Through paediatrics to psycho-analysis: Collected papers.* New York, NY: Brunner/Mazel.

Winnicott, D. W., Winnicott, C., Shepherd, R., & Davis, M. (1989). *Psycho-analytic explorations.* Cambridge, MA: Harvard University Press.

Wright, J. P., & Potter, P. (2000). *Psyche and soma: Physicians and metaphysicians on the mind–body problem from antiquity to enlightenment.* New York, NY: Clarendon Press.

Wurtzel, E. (1995). *Prozac nation: Young and depressed in America.* New York, NY: Riverhead Books.

Young, C., & Brook, A. (1994). Schopenhauer and Freud. *The International Journal of Psycho-Analysis, 75,* 101–118.

Young-Eisendrath, P. (1996). *The gifts of suffering: Finding insight, compassion, and renewal.* Reading, MA: Addison-Wesley.

INDEX

Abram, David, 31–33, 36–37, 59–60, 92, 94, 95
Active intellect, 35
Actual space, 93–96
Acupuncture, 50
Affective core, 172
Affectivity, 141
Affects, 143–144
Affect theory, 164, 169
Aggression, 120–121
"Aggression in Relation to Emotional Development" (D. W. Winnicott), 120
Ainsworth, Mary, 158
Alexander technique, 14
Alienation, 140, 148
Alpha function, 109, 111
Amacher, P., 71
American Psychoanalytic Association, 87
Amnesia, 74
Analytic thought, 7
Ancient Greek thought, 30–36
Anderson, D., 66
Anderson, Frances Sommer, 146–147, 171, 173
Animism, 131
Anxiety, 77, 114
A priori knowledge, 40, 42
Archetypal forms/ideas, 34
Archetypes, 105
Aristotle, 34–36, 38–40, 44, 101, 134
Aron, Lewis, 146, 147, 149–151
Ascension myth, 55, 151–154, 179
    and the body, 100
    and differentiation, 148
    and mind–body hierarchy, 169
    and mind–body problem, 31
Ascension psychology, 116
Ascetism, 55
Atomism, 33
Attachment and Loss (John Bowlby & Mary Ainsworth), 158
Attachment theory, 155–160, 175–176
    the body and the unconscious, 167–169
    incompatibility of drive theory with, 168

integration of neurobiological models with, 170
    and mind–body hierarchy, 169–170
    models using, 188–189
    and philosophy, 62
    and psychoanalytic metapsychology, 7
    and sexuality, 174
Attachment Theory and Psychoanalysis (Peter Fonagy), 159
Attunement, 157
Atwood, George, 18, 140–146, 175
Autistic-contiguous position, 113–116, 186
Ayto, John, 19

Balint, 160
Beebe, Beatrice, 157
Behavioral systems, 159
Berkeley, George, 41
Berman, M., 30–31, 95
Beta elements, 106, 109, 111
Beyond the Pleasure Principle (Sigmund Freud), 89
Bioenergetics, 14
Biology
    as basis for psychology, 92
    influence on Sigmund Freud, 69
    and mysticism, 110–111
    neuro-. See Neurobiology
Bion, Wilfred, 17–18, 106–111, 192
    and Marion Milner, 124
    protomental layer, 185–186
    and somatic experience, 152
    and D. W. Winnicott, 121
Bischler, W., 74
Black, M. J., 99, 102, 117, 139
Bleuler, Eugen, 21
Bodies in Treatment (Frances Sommer Anderson), 146–147, 171, 173
The Body
    Wilfred Bion and, 106, 108
    defining, 18–20
    and depression, 11–12
    dissociation from, 31
    equating of the unconscious with, 88
    Sigmund Freud and, 70

The Body, *continued*
    in intersubjective systems theory, 142
    in intersubjective theory, 140
    Melanie Klein and, 103
    Heinz Kohut and, 136
    Marion Milner and, 123–125, 187
    phenomenological perspective of,
        59, 61
    in post-Freudian psychoanalysis,
        99, 100. *See also* Object
        relations
    as psychological defense against
        meaning, 152
    in relational models, 132
    and relational psychoanalysis,
        146–147
    scientific understandings of, 54–55
    scientific vs. relational, 153
    and the unconscious, 167–169
    unconscious assumptions about, 13
    D. W. Winnicott and, 120–122
"Body and Soul" (Stromsted), 12–13
Body awareness, 15, 123
Body image, 19, 137
The Body in Psychotherapy (D. Johnson
    & I. J. Grand), 15
Body-oriented psychotherapies, 14–16
Body self, 136–138
Body therapy, 171
Bodywork, 6, 172
Boston Process of Change Study
    Group, 163
Bowlby, John, 156, 158–160
Bradley, Andrew Cecil, 41
Braid, James, 51
Brain. *See also* Neuropsychology;
    Neuroscience
    abilities of, 156–157
    development of, 157
    Sigmund Freud and, 93
    physiology of, 67
Brain imaging, 156, 161
Brentano, Franz, 59, 60, 67
Breuer, Josef, 72
British Middle object relations school,
    116–125
    Marion Milner, 122–125
    and relational psychoanalysis, 146
    D. W. Winnicott, 117–122

Brook, A., 74
Brücke, Ernst, 71, 72
Bruhl, Carl, 70
Bucci, Wilma, 152, 172

Capra, F., 24
Castration complex, 104
Cathexis, 81
Catholic church, 48, 49
Causality, 44–45
Change-effective therapy, 163
Charcot, Jean-Martin, 73–75
Chessick, Richard, 29, 57, 64, 131
Chiasm, 37
Child development, 104
Chinese medicine, 50
Christianity, 48, 49
Classical psychoanalysis, 17, 101, 129,
    175, 183
Clinical psychology, 13, 16, 189–191
Clinical theory, 21
Cognitive neuroscience, 161, 163
Cognitive science, 62, 167–168
Communication, 190
*The Complete Letters of Sigmund Freud to
    Wilhelm Fliess,* 75
Concretization, 143
Conflict, 164
The Conscious
    in neuropsychoanalysis, 164
    words as link between unconscious
        and, 91–93, 166–167
Consciousness, 3
    abstraction of, 31–32
    dualist views on, 39–40
    embedded-in-the-world, 33, 36, 93
    isolation from physical world, 9
    and mind, 19
    phenomenological perspective on,
        60–61
    reflexive, 36–39, 148–150, 152,
        180–182
Constancy principle, 78, 109
Contexts of Being (R. Stolorow &
    G. Atwood), 140
Conversion theory, 87, 88
Cornell, William, 172, 173
Countertransference, 6, 52, 190
Cozolino, Louis, 156, 161, 163
Crane, T., 34

Damasio, Antonio, 62–63, 168
De Anima, 34
Deconstructionism, 59
Defense mechanisms, 5
Defensive identification, 142
Depression, 11–12
Depressive modes, 107, 116
Depth psychology, 13, 56
    coining of term, 21
    distinction between mind and
        psyche for, 118
    and neuropsychoanalysis, 165
    physical vs. psychological illness, 47
    and romanticism, 53
    somatic awareness in, 190
    and unconscious, 10
Descartes, René, 30, 39, 43, 168
Determinism, 42, 131
Detrick, D. W., 130
Detrick, S. P., 130
Development
    child, 104
    circular model of, 153
    infant, 118–121, 137–138, 163
    libidinal, 106
    and pathology, 143
Developmental deficit model, 132
Developmental theories, 160
Dictionary of Word Origins, 19
Differentiation, 37–38, 148
Dimen, Muriel, 147
Directive breathing techniques, 14
Disease, 47, 107
Disembodiment, 10–11, 31, 179
Dissociation, 9, 31
Disturbance, 132
Double-aspect theory, 43–46, 50, 62,
    67, 179
Dreams, 82
Drives, 101–103, 131, 146. *See also*
    Drive theory
Drive-structural models, 101–103
Drive theory, 16, 21, 52, 84–85
    and attachment theory, 159
    Wilfred Bion and, 108
    Heinz Kohut and, 129, 132, 134, 135
    and neuropsychoanalysis, 168, 169
    and soma, 92
Dual-aspect approach, 51, 61, 109,
    181–182, 192. *See also*
    Double-aspect theory

Dualism, 8, 36–40
    and causality, 44
    Sigmund Freud and, 65–66
    and idealism, 55
    of mind and body, 30. *See also*
        Mind–body problem
    and neuroscience, 62
    and phenomenology, 61
    of soul and body, 31
    two-person psychology, 145

Eating disorders, 12
Edelson, M., 162
Ego, 89, 115. *See also* Ego psychology
    building relationship between
        unconscious and, 123
    and infant development, 121
    observing, 118
    and philosophy, 55, 56
The Ego and the Id (Sigmund Freud), 89
Ego psychology, 89–90, 136
    and attachment theory, 160
    and drive theory, 85
Eigen, M., 108, 114
Einstein, Albert, 24
Eliot, T. S., 193
Ellenberger, H. F., 49, 52, 53, 69–74
Embedded-in-the-world consciousness,
    33, 36, 93
Embedded mind, 63
Embodied cognition, 63
Embodied mind, 63, 166, 167
Embodiment, 193
    in intersubjective systems
        theory, 144
    and metapsychology, 179–180
    and psychotherapy, 15
    of self, 137
Emergent materialism, 40–41, 145
Emergent property, 41
Empathic immersion, 135
Empathy, 131
Empiricism, 8, 9, 24, 52–57
    and Aristotle, 34
    and idealism, 41
    influence on Sigmund Freud,
        70, 71
    and materialism, 40, 41
    rationalism vs., 40
Enactive mind, 168

Energy
    orgone, 14
    psychic, 133–134
    somatic, 86, 133
The Enlightenment, 44
Epiphenomenalism, 39, 40
Erotogenicity, 87
Ethics, 35
Evolutionary reductionism, 68
Existentialism, 58
Exner, Sigmund, 71, 72
Experiences in Groups, and Others Papers
    (Wilfred Bion), 106

Fairbairn, W. R. D., 101, 117
False localization, of the mind, 119, 120
Fantasy, 87
Fechner, Gustav Theodor, 71
Feldenkrais method, 14
Felt experience, 15
Fichte, Johann Gottlieb, 41
Fine, B. D., 87, 89
Fliess, Wilhelm, 77
Fluid theory, 50, 51
Focusing, 16
Fonagy, P., 63, 157, 160, 166–170
Four Quartets (T. S. Eliot), 193
Fragmentation, 136
Freud, Sigmund, 65–97. *See also Project*
    for a Scientific Psychology
    1885–1894 period, 75–77
    and attachment theory, 159
    and Wilfred Bion, 106
    cultural context of work, 9, 22
    depth psychology, 53
    drive theory, 16, 21, 52, 84–85, 169
    early influences on, 69–75
    on the ego, 121
    ego psychology, 89–90, 136
    fundamental assumptions of,
        183–185
    hermeneutic vs. materialist view of,
        66–68
    hysteria, 4, 11
    and importance of words, 123
    instinct, 84–86
    The Interpretation of Dreams, 81–84, 91
    and Melanie Klein, 103
    and Heinz Kohut, 132, 135
    metaphorical vs. actual space, 93–96

    metapsychological points of view, 102
    models of the mind, 56
    and mysticism, 108, 110–111
    and neurology, 156
    and neuroscience, 160–161
    and Newtonian physics, 57
    philosophical influences on, 52, 55, 64
    and psyche/soma relationship, 11
    and psychoanalytic metapsychology,
        17
    psychosexuality, 86–88
    rationalist influence on, 51
    rejection of animism, 131
    somatic energy, 133
    stance on mind-body problem,
        65–67
    and D. W. Winnicott, 120, 122
    and words as link between
        unconscious and conscious,
        91–93, 166, 167
Freud and Beyond (S. A. Mitchell &
    M. J. Black), 99

Gabbard, G. O., 5
Geigerich, Wolfgang, 8
Gendlin, Eugene, 16
Genes, 164
Gill, M. M., 19, 21, 58
Giving the Body Its Due (Maxine
    Sheets-Johnstone), 15–16
Goethe, Johann Wolfgang von, 70
Grand, Ian, 5, 15, 16
Greenberg, J. R., 99–103, 106, 117, 132,
    133, 146
The Grid (Bion's grid), 106, 109–111
Grigsby, J., 40
Grossinger, Richard, 15
The Group, 106–108

Harris, A., 147, 151–154, 173
Hartzell, Mary, 157
Hegel, Georg Wilhelm Friedrich, 41,
    53, 54
Heidigger, Martin, 59
Heisenberg, Werner, 24
Herbart, Johann Friedrich, 71
Hermeneutic circle, 20, 23
Hermeneutics, 20–24, 178–179
    Sigmund Freud and, 66–68, 79
    and postmodernism, 59

Hierarchy
    and ascension myth, 151–154
    mind–body, 169–170
Historicity, 104–105
Hobbes, Thomas, 40
Holifield, Barbara, 15
Homeostasis, 78
Homer, 33, 35
Horne, M., 44
Horowitz, Milton, 93
Hughes, J. M., 67–68, 78, 86–88, 91, 94
Hume, David, 41, 42
Husserl, Edmund, 59, 60
Hypnosis (Sigmund Freud), 75
Hypnotism, 49–52, 73
Hysteria, 4, 11, 69, 73–76, 95
Hysteria (Sigmund Freud), 74, 75

Id, 55, 85, 89
Idealism, 41–43, 55–57
    and the body, 100
    movement in psychoanalysis
        toward, 105
    in relational-structural models,
        101, 102
    and romanticism, 53
Identification, 106, 112, 142, 164
Identity, 137
Illness, 47, 51, 54, 132. *See also* Pathology
Images, 19, 105, 137
Immaterialism, 41
The Individual, 106–108
Individualism, 111
Infants. *See also* Mother–infant dyad
    and attachment theory, 158
    development of, 118–121, 137–138,
        163
    minds of, 103–105, 107, 112, 115
Insight, 21
Instinct, 84–86, 147
    and attachment theory, 159
    as frontier between somatic and
        psychical, 109
Instinctual drives, 103, 143
Integration, 37–38
Intellect, active, 35
Intelligence, somatic, 165, 170–174
Intentionality, 67
Interactionism, 39, 68
Interoception, 172, 173

Interpersonal conflict, 164
Interpersonal experience, 156
Interpersonal field, 139
Interpretation, 21, 22, 178. *See also*
    Hermeneutics
The Interpretation of Dreams (Sigmund
    Freud), 81–84, 91
Intersubjective systems theory, 18, 135,
    139–145
Intersubjectivity, 18, 138, 139, 148–149
Isaac, Susan, 169–170
Isenman, D., 44
Isolated mind, 140–142, 146

James, William, 150
Johnson, D., 5, 15, 61
Jung, Carl, 53

Kandel, Eric, 161–163
Kant, Immanuel, 41–42, 63
Kaptchuk, Ted, 50
Keleman, Stanley, 14–15
Kidner, David, 10, 11, 38
Klein, Melanie, 17, 102–105. *See also*
    Object relations
    and John Bowlby, 158
    historicity, 104–105
    influence of, 102
    and Marion Milner, 123
    phylogenetic inheritance, 105
    and D. W. Winnicott, 117–118
Kleinian thought and theory, 107,
    113–115, 121
Knowledge, 34, 36
    a priori, 40, 42
    pursuit of, 106
    sensual, 110
Kohut, Heinz, 18
    and self-psychology, 134–136
    and shifts in contemporary meta-
        psychology, 129–130
    and teleology, 131, 132
Kremerling, Garth, 39, 40, 43, 61
Krueger, David, 18, 136–138

Language, 31–32, 91–93, 138, 166–167
Learning, 164
Leibniz, Gottfried, 40
Levin, F., 66
Libidinal development, 106

Libido, 134
Linear perspective, 8–9
Linear time, 94
Locke, John, 41
Logical positivism, 70

Magnetism, 49–54
Mahler, M. S., 112
Materialism, 40–41
    and causality, 44
    and drive-structural models, 101–103
    emergent, 40–41, 145
    Sigmund Freud and, 66–68
    and idealism, 55
    and intersubjective systems theory, 145
    movement in psychoanalysis away
        from, 105
Materialist–reductionism, 67
Matter, 8, 10, 111. *See also* Spirit–matter
    split
McDougall, Joyce, 18, 111–112, 144, 150
Mechanical reductionism, 68
Medicine, 47–48, 54
Meissner, W. W., 19, 66, 68, 77–79,
    81–85, 89, 100, 133–134
Memory, 164
Mentalization, 149–150
Merleau-Ponty, Maurice, 59–61, 63,
    130, 153
Mesmer, Franz, 49, 51
Metaphorical space, 93–96
Metaphors, 133, 166
Metaphysics, 17
Metapsychology, 179–180
    abstractions of, 10
    defined, 17, 131
    and dual-aspect approach, 192
    and mind–body problem, 67
    natural science framework in, 21
    and neurobiology, 170
    and neuropsychoanalysis, 161
    object relations concepts, 131
    philosophical shifts in, 129–134
    psychoanalytic. *See* Psychoanalytic
        metapsychology
    role of drives in, 102
Metatheory, 21, 190
Meynert, Theodor, 71, 72
Middle Ages, 34
Milner, Marion, 18, 122–125, 187

The Mind, 10
    defining, 18–20
    distinction between psyche and, 118
    embodied, 63, 166, 167
    enactive, 168
    isolated, 141–142, 146
    models of, 4, 56
"Mind and its Relation to the Psyche/
    Soma," 118
Mind–body problem, 3–6, 29–47,
    169–170
    in Ancient Greek thought, 30–36
    and causality, 44–45
    and cognitive science, 168
    complexity of, 179
    and double-aspect theory, 43–46
    and dualism, 36–40
    findings on, 180–182
    and Sigmund Freud, 65–67, 86–87
    and hermeneutics, 21
    history of, 7–9
    and idealism, 41–43
    and intersubjective systems theory,
        145
    materialistic view of, 40–41
    and neuropsychoanalysis, 162
    philosophical-historical context of, 23
    and psychoanalysis, 10
    and psychoanalytic metapsychology,
        17
    and reflexive consciousness, 36–39
    and somatic symptoms, 11
Mitchell, Juliet, 104, 105
Mitchell, S. A., 99–103, 106, 117, 132,
    133, 139, 146
Modernism, 9
Monism, 43
Moore, B. E., 87, 89
Morality, 34, 35
Mother–infant dyad, 112, 118
    in attachment theory, 158–159
    in intersubjective systems theory, 142
    and neuropsychoanalysis, 157
Motivation
    and attachment theory, 159, 169
    in intersubjective systems theory, 141
    neurological systems of, 164
    and object relations, 101–102
Multiple coding, 152
Muscle manipulation, 14
Mysticism, 108, 110–111

Natural world, 36
Nature, 32, 54, 140. *See also* Physical
    world
Nature and Psyche (David Kidner), 11
Neressian, E., 160, 165, 169
Neural circuitry, 156
Neurobiology, 168
    emergent materialist stance in, 40
    Sigmund Freud and, 66–68, 72
    metapsychological principles, 162
    research in, 156
    somatic intelligence, 170–171
Neurons, 78, 80, 81
Neuropsychoanalysis, 155–157, 160–165,
    175–176
    the body and the unconscious,
        167–169
    defined, 155
    evolution of field, 160–162
    increasing research in field, 188–189
Neuropsychoanalysis (journal), 160, 169
Neuropsychology. *See also* Neuropsycho-
        analysis
    and metatheory, 190
    and psychoanalytic metapsychology, 7
    and self-object experiences, 138
    and somatic states, 152
Neuroscience, 62–63, 160, 161, 163–165,
    173. *See also* Neurobiology
The Neuroscience of Psychotherapy
        (Louis Cozolino), 156, 161
Neurosis, 68, 74
Neurotransmitters, 157, 173
Neutral monism, 43
Newton, Isaac, 41, 42
The New World Dictionary, 19
Nietzsche, Friedrich, 58–59
"The Nuclear Bomb and the Fate of
        God" (Wolfgang Geigerich), 8

O (psychoanalytic object), 110, 111
Object relations, 17–18, 99–127, 185
    and attachment theory, 160
    British Middle school, 116–125
    D. W. Winnicott, 117–122
    dichotomies of, 153
    and historicity, 104–105
    Joyce McDougall, 111–112
    Marion Milner, 122–125
    Melanie Klein, 102–105

metapsychological concepts in, 131
    and motivation, 101–102
    and phylogenetic inheritance, 105
    role of drives in, 101–103
    and self-psychology, 134
    shift toward developmental deficit
        model, 132
    Thomas Ogden, 112–116
    Wilfred Bion, 106–111
Object Relations and Self Psychology
        (M. St. Claire), 99
*Object Relations in Psychoanalytic
        Theory* (J. R. Greenberg &
        S. A. Mitchell), 99
Observing ego, 118
Oedipal complex
    and evolutionary reductionism, 68
    Melanie Klein's reformulation of,
        103, 104
Ogden, Thomas, 112–116
    autistic-contiguous position, 186
    and self-reflexivity, 150
Omega system, 80
On Aphasia (Sigmund Freud), 67, 75, 76
Orange, Donna, 18
Orgone energy, 14
Other, distinction between self and,
    100, 140

Pally, Regina, 156, 157, 163
Palmer, R. E., 20
Panajian, A., 116
Paradox, 118, 121, 186–187
Parallelism, 39–40, 67, 145
Paranoid-schizoid mode, 104, 107,
    113, 114
Parmenides of Elea, 33
Pathology, 5, 143, 144, 159, 191.
        See also Illness
Pattern matching, 156–157
Patterson, S., 34
Perception, 156–157, 164
Percy, Walker, 61–62
Phenomenology, 58, 59–62, 130,
    138, 148
Philosophy, 180–182
    Ancient Greek thought, 30–36
    causality, 44–45
    double-aspect theory, 43–46
    dualism, 36–40

Philosophy, *continued*
   history of, 148
   idealism, 41–43
   and language, 166
   materialism, 40–41
   and neuroscience, 62–63
   phenomenology, 59–62
   postmodernism, 58–59
   and reflexive consciousness, 36–39
   teleology, 131
Phylogenetic inheritance, 105
Physical illness, 47
Physical world, 34, 35, 42
   alienation from, 140
   and the body, 138
   dissociation from, 31
   in intersubjective systems theory, 142
   relationship between unconscious
      and, 49
   as secondary by-product, 57
Physiological needs, 85
Plato, 31, 32, 35, 36, 38–40, 44, 101, 134
Pleasure principle, 108, 169
Positivism, 24
Postmodernism, 9, 58–59, 139
Potter, P., 18, 30
Pragmatism, 59
Prepsychological, 7
Primitive states of mind, 104–105,
      114, 152
Project for a Scientific Psychology
      (Sigmund Freud), 75, 77–82,
      89–91, 109, 161
   and drive theory, 84, 108
   Freud's abandonment of, 4, 11
   goal of, 68
   intellectual stance of, 71
   psychiatry in, 86
   studies published in, 74
Projection, 93
Projective identification, 106, 112, 164
Protomental layers, 107–108, 139,
      185–186, 192
Prozac Nation (Elizabeth Wurtzel), 11–12
Psyche
   defining, 18, 19–20, 118
   distinction between mind and, 118
   etymology of term, 48
   and group experiences, 107
   interpersonal field, 139–140
   as primary, 57
   and somatic experience, 105
   subjectivity of, 106
   use of term, 30
Psyche and Soma (J. P. Wright &
      P. Potter), 18, 30
Psyche/soma relationship, 9, 11, 13.
      See also Mind–body problem
   as animate phenomenon, 106
   in double-aspect theory, 46
   as dualistic dilemma, 111
   as a group state, 108
   and hermeneutics, 22
   hierarchical language structure
      between, 151
   and instinct, 86
   in intersubjective systems theory,
      143–145
   Marion Milner and, 124–125
   and modern consciousness, 37
   and psychosexuality, 87
   and relational psychoanalysis, 146–148
   role of ego in, 115
   and spirit–matter split, 109
   D. W. Winnicott and, 118, 119, 170,
      186–187
   and words, 91
Psychiatry, 53, 86
Psychical locations, 93
"Psychical (or Mental) Treatment"
      (Sigmund Freud), 67
Psychic energy, 133–134
Psychoanalysis, 47–57
   classical, 101, 129, 175, 183
   creation of term, 74
   and empiricism/romanticism, 52–57
   engagement of somatically linked
      consciousness with, 4
   and hermeneutics, 20
   hypnotism and the unconscious in,
      49–52
   neuro-. *See* Neuropsychoanalysis
   notions of reality in, 22
   and postmodernism, 58–59
   relational, 146–150, 187–188
   relationship between attachment
      theory and, 159
   and religion, 47–49
   role of the body in, 13, 16
   and science, 24

and self-knowledge, 37
self-reflexivity in, 149
tradition of, 10
Psychoanalytic metapsychology, 17–18
and attachment theory/
neuropsychology, 7
biases and limitations in, 9
and cognitive science, 167
empirical basis for, 162
and hermeneutics, 24
and model of the mind, 4
role of somatic experience in, 104
unconscious organizing principles
in, 13
Psychoanalytic object (O), 110, 111
Psychoanalytic Terms and Concepts
(B. E. Moore & B. D. Fine), 21
Psychoanalytic Terms and Concepts
(B. E. Moore & B. D. Fine), 87
Psychoanalytic theory
contemporary developments in,
99–102
Heinz Kohut and, 130
and neurological systems, 157
Psychogenesis, 51
Psychological illness, 47, 132
Psychology
ascension, 116
biology as basis for, 92
clinical, 13, 16, 189–191
depth. *See* Depth psychology
ego, 85, 89–90, 136, 160
history of, 52–53
meta-. *See* Metapsychology
neuro-, 7, 138, 152, 190. *See also*
Neuropsychoanalysis
pure, 70
scientific, 70
self-, 18, 130, 132, 134–136, 138
somatic, 14–16
two-person, 145
Psychopathology, 119
Psychosexuality, 86–88
Psychosis, 83
Psychosomatic symptoms, 4
Sigmund Freud and, 67, 69, 74, 76,
94, 95
in intersubjective systems theory,
143, 144
Joyce McDougall and, 111
D. W. Winnicott and, 122

Psychotherapy, 14–16. *See also*
Psychoanalysis
Pure psychology, 70
Puységar, Marquis de, 50–51

Q (neuron doctrine), 78
Qi, 50
Quantum physics, 9

Raphael, 36, 101
Rapport, 51, 52
Rationalism, 40, 48, 51
Rationality, 33, 38
Reality, 22, 53, 112, 141
Reason, 33, 46, 53, 55
Reductionism, 68
Reflection, 36, 154
Reflexive consciousness, 36–39, 148–150,
152, 180–182
Reflexivity, 145
Reich, Wilhelm, 14
Reiser, M., 162
Relational body, 153
Relational Perspectives on the Body
(Lewis Aron & Frances Sommer
Anderson), 146, 147
Relational psychoanalysis, 146–150,
187–188
Relational-structural models, 101, 132.
See also Object relations
Relational theory, 139, 158. *See also*
Intersubjectivity
Relationships
experiences in, 156
role of attunement in, 157
Relativism, 58
Relativity, theory of, 24
Religion
in Ancient Greek though, 33–36
and the birth of philosophy, 32
and causality, 44, 45
and idealism, 42
and psychoanalysis, 47–49
science vs., 54–55
soul vs. body, 31
Repression, 89, 112, 174–175
The Restoration of Self (Heinz Kohut),
129–130, 134
Reverie, 121

Ricoeur, Paul, 21
Rodman, F. R., 120–122
"The Role of Illusion in Symbol Forma-
    tion" (Marion Milner), 123
Rolfing, 14
Romanshyn, Robert, 60, 61, 94, 95, 138
Romanticism, 8, 9, 24, 51, 52–57, 70–71
Romanyshyn, Robert, 8
"The Roosting of the Mind in the Body"
    (P. Fonagy & M. Target), 167
Rosch, E., 168
Royce, Josiah, 41

Sachs, Heinrich, 71
St. Clair, M., 99, 101, 117, 132, 135
Sanders, Louis, 163
Schelling, Friedrich Wilhelm Joseph
    von, 54, 56, 57
The School of Athens (Raphael), 36, 101
Schopenhauer, Arthur, 55, 57, 74
Schore, Alan, 156
Schubert, Gotthilf Heinrich von, 54
Science, 24
    in 16th and 17th centuries, 52
    and Catholic church, 48
    Sigmund Freud and, 67–70
    neuro-. See Neuroscience
    religion vs., 54–55
Scientific body, 153
Scientific psychology, 70
A Secure Base (John Bowlby & Mary
    Ainsworth), 158
Seduction theory, 87
Self
    alienation of, 148
    distinction between other and, 100,
        140
    embodiment of, 137
    Heinz Kohut and, 131, 132
    as object, 151
    as subject, 151
Self-fragmentation, 136, 138
Self-knowledge, 21, 37
Self-objects, 135, 138, 172
Self-psychology, 18, 130, 132, 134–136,
    138
Self-reflection, 36, 149–150
Sense perceptions, 41
Sensory awareness exercises, 14

Sensory experience, 33, 82–83, 94,
    110, 113. See also Somatic
    experience
Sensual knowledge, 110
Separation–individuation, model of, 112
Sexuality, 174–175
    and assumptions about the mind, 67
    and evolutionary reductionism, 68
    and idealism, 55
    and mind–body problem, 81
    psycho-, 86–88
Sheets-Johnstone, Maxine, 15
Siegel, Dan, 156, 157
Silverstein, Barry, 65–67, 73, 76, 79–81
Skepticism, 42
Sleep, 82–83
Socrates, 32, 34
Solms, M., 160, 165, 169
Soma, 9, 11. See also Psyche/soma
    relationship
    defining, 18, 19
    and drive theory, 92
    Sigmund Freud and, 89, 90
    in Freud's early writings, 85
    in intersubjective systems theory, 142
    roots of aggression in, 120–121
    use of term, 30
Soma–psyche, 108. See also Psyche/
    soma relationship
Somatic (term), 19
Somatically linked consciousness
    defined, 6
    engagement with psychoanalysis, 4
    and psychoanalytic metapsychology,
        13
Somatic awareness, 190
Somatic energy, 86, 133
Somatic experience, 83–84, 137, 138
    in drive-structural theory, 101–102
    in intersubjective systems theory,
        142, 143
    as psychologically primitive, 104–105
    and reflexive consciousness, 152
    and relational psychoanalysis, 146–147
    in relational theory, 149
    symbolic levels of, 152
Somatic intelligence, 165, 170–174
Somatic mapping, 62
Somatic psychology, 14–16

Somatic Reality (Stanley Keleman), 14

Somatic resonance, 173

Somatic symptoms, 11, 112. *See also* Psychosomatic symptoms

Somatization, 5, 136, 138, 192

Somatoform disorders, 5

Some Points for a Comparative Study of Organic and Hysterical Motor Paralyses (Sigmund Freud), 75

Soul, 31, 34, 35, 180

Sowa, A., 44

Space, 93, 94

Speech, 166–167, 190

Spinoza, Baruch, 43, 62, 74

Spirit, 7–10, 54

Spirit–matter split, 8, 9, 109, 120, 125

Spoken word, 92

Steele, Robert, 22

Stern, Daniel, 141, 152, 163

Stevens, D., 40

Stewart, W. A., 66

Stolorow, Robert D., 18, 139–146, 175

Stone, M. W. F., 34

Stromsted, T., 12, 13

Structural integration, 14

Structural models, 87, 89, 91–92, 101–103

Subjectivity, 58–60
    and alienation, 140
    inter-. *See* Intersubjectivity
    and neuropsychoanalysis, 165
    of psyche, 106

Subsymbolic levels (somatic experience), 152

Sulloway, F. J., 66, 68–70, 76, 77, 79

Superego, 89

Symbol formation, 123, 192

Symbolic experience, 142, 143

Symbolic levels (somatic experience), 152

Symbolization, 187
    capacity for, 112
    gaining of, 154
    origin of, 166
    psychoanalytic value of, 150
    uses of, 123, 124

Symington, J., 106, 108–110, 191

Symington, N., 106, 108–110, 191

Symptomatology, 107

Symptoms
    emphasis on, in Freud's later work, 57
    psychosomatic. *See* Psychosomatic symptoms
    somatic, 11, 112

Synapses, 78

Talk therapy, 171

Target, M., 63, 157, 166–170

Tarnas, Richard, 30, 32, 36, 39, 42, 45–46, 51, 53, 58

Teleology, 44, 56, 131–133

Textual interpretation, 20, 178

Textual unconscious, 22

Thales of Miletus, 33, 36

Therapy
    body, 171
    change-effective, 163
    psycho-, 14–16
    talk, 171

Thompson, E., 168

Thought, 33, 170

"Three Essays on Sexuality" (Sigmund Freud), 86

Topographic model, 88, 89, 91–93, 95

Transcendence, 100

Transference, 6, 52, 100, 190

"Transitional Objects" (D. W. Winnicott), 118

Trauma, 172

True Self, 120, 123, 124

Truth, 33

Two-person psychology, 145

Uncertainty principle, 24

The Unconscious, 49–52, 74, 76
    association of somatic dimension with, 7
    and the body, 167–169
    building relationship between ego and, 123
    correlation of the somatic with, 143
    and depth psychology, 21
    in dreams, 83
    equating of the body with, 88
    history of, 182–183
    and mind–body problem, 67
    words as link between conscious and, 91–93, 166–167

The Unconscious (Sigmund Freud), 67
Unconscious communication, 190
Unenlivened body, 12

Varela, F. J., 168

Will, 67, 74
Winnicott, D. W., 17, 117–122
    and intersubjective systems theory,
        142, 143
    and David Krueger, 137
    and Marion Milner, 122, 124
    and mysticism, 108
    paradox and psyche/soma, 170,
        186–187

psyche/soma relationship, 148
    self-psychology, 135
Woodman, Marion, 12–13
Words
    and abstraction of consciousness,
        31–32
    as link between unconscious and
        conscious, 91–93, 166–167
    Marion Milner and, 123, 124
Wright, J. P., 18, 30
Written word, 31–32, 92
Wurtzel, Elizabeth, 11–12

Yoga, 6
Young, C., 74

ABOUT THE AUTHOR

Perrin Elisha, PhD, is a psychologist maintaining a private practice in Los Angeles, California, specializing in the treatment of health, body image, and eating concerns. She is currently on the organizing and planning committee and teaching faculty of the Los Angeles Eating Disorders Study Center and Training Program. She is also a former staff member of several inpatient and substance treatment centers, where she led groups related to mind–body integration and recovery from eating disorders. She is a psychoanalytic candidate at the New Center for Psychoanalysis as well as a graduate of the Wright Institute of Los Angeles postdoctoral program. She holds a master's degree in transpersonal psychology from the Institute of Transpersonal Psychology and a doctorate in clinical and depth psychology from Pacifica Graduate Institute. Before becoming a psychologist, Dr. Elisha completed certification in emotionally focused bodywork and a degree in psychobiology from the University of California, Santa Cruz.